THE **BIG** BOOK OF

David Norman
Consulting Editor

WELCOME
New York · San Francisco

First published in the U.S. in 2001 by

Welcome Enterprises, Inc.

588 Broadway, New York, NY 10012

(212) 343-9430; Fax (212) 343-9434

e-mail: info@wepub.com

Distributed by Andrews McMeel Distribution Service

Order Department and Customer Service

Toll-Free (800) 826-4216

Orders Only Fax (800) 437-8683

Sales and Marketing Department: (800) 851-8923

Library of Congress Control Number: 00-136012

Printed in Singapore

10 9 8 7 6 5 4 3 2 1

ARRHINOCERATOPS

In spite of its name, *Arrhinoceratops* (no nose-horned face), did have a small nose horn.

When William Parks described *Arrhinoceratops* in 1925, he claimed that it did not have a proper nose horn. But there was a sort of bump where a nose horn would normally be found. This was made by a lumpy thickening of the bones surrounding the dinosaur's nose.

SMALL AND STUMPY

As there was no evidence of a separate bone, Parks decided that the ceratopid had no horn at all. Now experts agree that *Arrhinoceratops*, like its relative *Triceratops*, did indeed have a small stumpy nose horn.

TWO-PRONGED ATTACK

There was no mistaking *Arrhinoceratops*' two long brow horns. These useful weapons pointed forwards above its eyes and looked very threatening. *Arrhinoceratops* probably defended itself against predators by charging at them with its head down so the sharp tips of the horns ripped into its enemy's unprotected flesh.

WINNER TAKES ALL

Arrhinoceratops also used its brow horns to fight with other males in tests of strength. The two sturdy dinosaurs locked horns and shoved their heads together until one of them was too weak to go on. The winner of this battle became the leader and was popular with females at mating time.

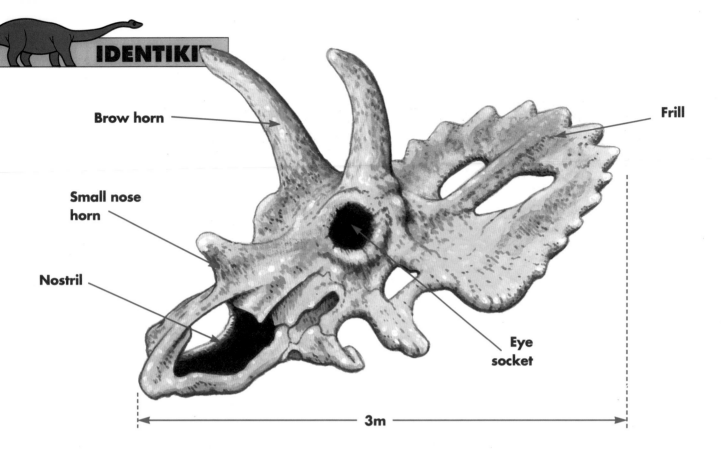

Brow horn

Small nose horn

Nostril

Frill

Eye socket

3m

WIDE AND WAVY

Like *Triceratops*, *Arrhinoceratops* had a broad neck frill. A row of rounded, bony bumps ran all along the outer edge and gave the frill a wavy outline.

SIZE WISE

9m

IMPRESSIVE SHOW

When its head was up, the frill lay back against the dinosaur's shoulders. But when *Arrhinoceratops* bent its head down the frill stood up and made quite a show.

COLOURFUL DISPLAY

Two small openings in the frill made it light and easy to move. Some experts have suggested that these frills were brightly coloured to help ceratopids attract a mate.

MONSTER FACTS

- **NAME:** *Arrhinoceratops* (a-rye-no-<u>serra</u>-tops) means 'no nose-horned face'
- **GROUP:** dinosaur
- **SIZE:** 9m long
- **FOOD:** plants
- **LIVED:** about 80 million years ago in the Late Cretaceous Period in Alberta, Canada

LONG IN THE JAW

As it lumbered through the meadows of Alberta, *Arrhinoceratops* munched low-growing plants with its parrot-like beak. At the back of its long, tapering jaws were rows of teeth which ground down the leaves and shoots to a pulp. As they were worn down, new ones grew to replace them. *Arrhinoceratops* probably spent most of its day browsing and nibbling. It needed plenty of food to sustain its large body.

BIG AND BULKY

Arrhinoceratops was almost as long as a bus and heavier than an elephant. Its bulky body and sharp horns probably put off all but the most hungry predators.

RING OF SAFETY

Baby dinosaurs were much more at risk and experts think that ceratopids had a special way of protecting their young. *Arrhinoceratops* may have lived in herds. When predators lurked, the adults may have formed a protective circle around their young to keep them safe.

IT'S A FACT

Fossils
Fossils of *Arrhinoceratops* are rare. This may be because there were very few of these dinosaurs or because *Arrhinoceratops* lived in dry upland places where fossils do not easily form.

SOLID FRAME

The frame of a dinosaur like *Arrhinoceratops* had to be immensely strong to support its great weight. Large bones in its neck and back were attached to powerful muscles which moved its heavy head and legs.

The outcome of this battle between two male *Arrhinoceratops* will decide which leads the herd.

BASILOSAURUS

With its snake-like body and tiny head, this sea mammal was mistakenly named 'king reptile'.

lthough it was as long as a modern whale, *Basilosaurus* did not have a bulky body and huge head. Fifty-four million years ago, it was the largest mammal and preyed on the fish and sea creatures with which it shared the ocean. A layer of blubber around its body probably ensured it did not lose too much heat.

MAKING WAVES

Experts think that *Basilosaurus* moved through water by curving its body in a series of wave-like movements. These wiggles helped it to propel itself along as it chased herring and other tempting prey.

TERROR TEETH

Basilosaurus had 44 teeth set in its small head. At the front of its jaw it had long fang-like teeth for spearing fish and behind a set of large saw-edged teeth to crunch through its victim's bones.

SMALL – BUT PERFECTLY FORMED!

There were two hind limbs on its long body. Although they were too small to be of use they were like tiny hind legs. This shows a link with its ancestors that lived on land.

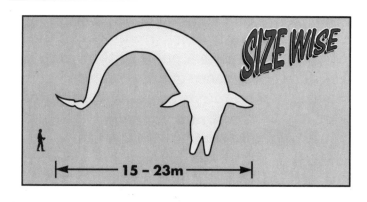

SIZE WISE

15 – 23m

MONSTER FACTS

- **NAME:** *Basilosaurus* (ba-zil-oh-<u>saw</u>-rus) means ' king reptile'
- **GROUP:** mammal
- **SIZE:** 15 – 23m long
- **FOOD:** fish
- **LIVED:** about 54 million years ago in the Eocene in African and North American seas

COLORADISAURUS

Coloradisaurus was a plant-eating South American dinosaur, as long as a car.

 oloradisaurus was named after the Los Colorados rock formation in Argentina where it was found. Scientists have had few clues to work from because only the skull and jaw have been found.

OUT OF REACH
Coloradisaurus was a prosauropod and probably walked on two or four legs like *Plateosaurus*. It tipped back on to its back legs when it wanted to reach leaves and shoots from branches above its head.

SIZE WISE

|← 4m →|

WELL BALANCED
Coloradisaurus probably had a long and slender neck which was balanced by a tapering tail as it walked.

SIMPLE TEETH
Like *Plateosaurus*, *Coloradisaurus* had a deep, narrow snout. But the back of its skull was much broader than its relative's. Inside its slender jaw, *Coloradisaurus* had coarse teeth with jagged edges which it used to shred leaves. *Coloradisaurus* probably used gastroliths to grind its food to a pulp so that it could digest more easily.

GROWN-UP PUZZLE
Some experts think that *Coloradisaurus* is, in fact, a full grown *Mussaurus,* the tiny hatchling that lived in southern Argentina at around the same time.

MONSTER FACTS

- **NAME:** *Coloradisaurus* (koll-or-rah-di-<u>saw</u>-rus) means 'Colorados reptile'
- **GROUP:** dinosaur
- **SIZE:** about 4m long
- **FOOD:** plants
- **LIVED:** about 200 million years ago in the Late Triassic Period in Los Colorados, Argentina

Creodonts and other meat-eaters

The first meat-eaters evolved in all shapes and sizes.

I f a food supply exists, then something will evolve to eat it. After the dinosaurs died out, there were plants with nothing eating them any more. The plant-eating mammals stepped in to fill the gap.

CREODONTS FOR COURSES

All the different meat-eating mammals which lived in Palaeocene, Eocene and Miocene times belonged to the group called the creodonts. The creodonts were one of nature's early attempts at producing meat-eating mammals.

Tritemnodon

Like these modern foxes, small creodonts hunted small meat-eaters.

Hyenodon

PLANT-EATERS HUNTED

Within a few million years, mammals evolved that ate low-growing plants, bushes and trees. These plant-eating mammals themselves were a food supply. As a result many different meat-eating mammals evolved to hunt them.

THE HUNTERS

Sinopa was one of the first of the fox-sized meat-eaters, and it probably fed on smaller mammals. *Tritemnodon*, a swift-footed creodont, with long legs and slim body similar to a greyhound, probably chased fast-moving prey through open woodland.

Sinopa

10

NIGHTMARE CREODONT

There was one creodont that was perhaps the largest land-living flesh-eating mammal that ever lived. Bigger than a modern grizzly bear, with a head like that of a modern tiger but twice the size, *Megistotherium* hunted down the huge elephants and rhinoceros-like creatures that abounded in Miocene North Africa. What a monster!

Today's cheetah can sprint at speeds of up to 100 kph – probably faster than any of the creodonts.

SCAVENGER

The big heavy teeth of the creodont *Hyenodon* may have been used for tearing up the bones and flesh of dead animals, just like today's hyenas.

Megistotherium

Like today's hyenas, *Hyenodon* was both a killer and a scavenger.

WHAT HAPPENED TO THE CREODONTS?

We don't know. They were the top of the food-chain until the Miocene and then they died out, and were replaced by the modern carnivore groups. Perhaps they were less intelligent than modern types. Or maybe they did not evolve as fast as the fleet-footed grassland-dwellers. Perhaps we will never know.

 **A CREODONT?**

The skeleton of a creodont is like that of a modern carnivore, with its killing and meat-shearing teeth. (The name means 'flesh-tooth'.) However the foot bones are shorter – giving the animal a flat-footed appearance – and there is a split in the claw bones. Creodonts were not related to carnivores.

TAKE OVER

So what replaced the creodonts? The modern carnivore groups did. These consist of the hyenas, the dogs, the cats, the bears, the raccoons and coatis, the weasels and otters, and the mongooses and civets. They all evolved to hunt different animals in different ways.

TAKING WHAT'S LEFT

Ictitherium was one of the first hyenas. It was a scavenger – eating the leftovers from another animal's kill – as well as a hunter.

One of the earliest hyenas *Ictitherium* looked more like today's civet.

Agriotherium (above), ate berries, insects and fish, much like today's Indian sloth bear pictured right.

TEAMWORK

The dogs, such as *Osteoborus*, opted for cooperative hunting and the later types worked in packs chasing down their prey until it collapsed exhausted.

Osteoborus from the Pliocene of North America was actually a dog, but it could crush up bones like a hyena.

IT'S A FACT

BEFORE THE CREODONTS

The first animals to prey on the early plant-eaters were crocodiles and giant flightless birds. Then came a group of meat-eating mammals related to today's hooved plant-eaters such as deer. Wolf-like *Mesonyx* was one of these. This group did not last long before the creodonts took over.

STEALTH

The cats became the stealthy ambushers – killing their prey swiftly with a surprise attack. The biggest mammals were hunted by the sabre-tooths of Pleistocene times.

I'LL EAT ANYTHING

The bears, such as *Agriotherium*, turned their backs on the purely meat-eating diet of their ancestors and became omnivores. Like modern bears, *Agriotherium* ate berries, insects and fish as well as meat.

TREE DWELLERS

Today's raccoons and coatis are basically tree-living hunting animals and so tend to be quite small in size. But *Chapalmalania* was a huge raccoon about the size of a modern giant panda. Raccoons are omnivores too.

Chapalmalania's modern descendant – a raccoon.

Looking a bit like a modern panda, *Chapalmalania* roamed South America in Pliocene times.

AFTER THE LOWLIFE

Today's weasels, stoats, mongooses and civets are small carnivores that hunt through the undergrowth.

HALF AND HALF

One group of modern-type carnivores is now completely extinct. These are the amphicyonids which were somewhere between the bears and the dogs. *Amphicyon* lived in Europe in the Miocene.

INTO THE WATER

The water-living meat-eaters and fish-eaters today are also related to the carnivore group. Seals and sealions, and the whales, are all descended from the same stock.

The bear-dog *Amphicyon* has no living relatives.

13

GIANTS OF THE PAST

Two vicious *Daspletosaurus*, with jaws wide open, prepare to rush at a peaceful herd of *Arrhinoceratops*. A large male defends the group against these marauding predators by lowering its head to display an enormous neck frill. Moving its head slowly from side to side the *Arrhinoceratops* threatens to counter attack using its formidable horns.

TROODON

In Late Cretaceous Canada, *Troodon* rest after a hard day's hunting. Several small mammals have breathed their last today thanks to the lightning attack and sharp teeth of the adult *Troodon*. One mother stays alert for danger.

Helping hands

Long and grasping or short and feeble, dinosaurs used their hands in many different ways.

Some dinosaurs were armed to the tops of their fingers with deadly claws. Others used their hands to help them hunt or hold down prey. Dinosaur hands came in a great variety of shapes and sizes, some with only two fingers and some with as many as five.

HANDS UP!

Psittacosaurus had four long fingers on each hand. It probably used them mainly for walking. But when it spied an inviting tree, it stopped and reared up on its hind legs. *Psittacosaurus* reached up and drew down the tempting branch to within biting distance of its parrot-like beak.

GRAPPLING IRONS

For its size, *Tarbosaurus* had the smallest hands in the dinosaur world. With only two fingers, such feeble hands were no good for fighting but experts think *Tarbosaurus* may have used its claws as hooks to hold on to the ground so it could push against them and heave its heavy body upright. It also used its fingers and claws to grip wriggling prey while it ripped at them with its teeth.

FLEXIBLE FINGERS

Many early dinosaurs had five fingers, like a human. *Plateosaurus* used its five flexible fingers like toes by bending them back to rest on the ground. The prosauropod could also bend its fingers forwards to grasp, and perhaps to dig into the ground to search for juicy roots.

THUMB THREAT

Iguanodon had four fingers and an amazing thumb. The fingers were broad with hoof-like nails which helped the dinosaur to walk. Its fourth finger stuck out at right-angles to its wrist and was used for grasping branches. *Iguanodon*'s thumb was a deadly spike which the plant-eater used to defend itself.

GOOD GRIPPERS

Intelligent *Dromiceiomimus* was a speedy dinosaur that preyed on small, fast-moving mammals. It had long, three fingered hands which it used to hold its wriggling victim in a firm grasp. It is possible that *Dromiceiomimus* pulled down fruit and berries with its clawed fingers to add to its varied diet.

19

The story book in the rocks

How do scientists read the rocks beneath our feet and what do they discover?

It is usually geologists, rather than biologists, who study dinosaurs. Why should scientists who study the Earth be better able to find out about dinosaurs than scientists who study living things?

FOSSIL CLUES

The reason is that dinosaurs are found as fossils, embedded in rocks. Geologists can explain the processes that have turned bones into minerals. They can also tell what conditions were like at the time.

THE SANDS OF TIME

The rocks that contain fossils are called sedimentary rocks. That means that they are formed from beds of loose material, called sediment, that have built up layer by layer over thousands of years and have later turned to stone.

FUSSY FOSSILS

Some animals are quite fussy about where they live. In a rock we may find a fossil of a shellfish that we know did not live in salt water. We can then tell that these sediments were formed in fresh water – a river, stream or a lake. Geologists call such a fossil a 'facies fossil'.

Dangerous work! A geologist searches for fossils on a cliff face.

20

This red desert sandstone has been worn away by the wind, showing clearly the layers of rock from which it was formed.

We can tell this sandstone rock was formed from a beach because the ripple marks made by the waves can still be seen.

These shapes in the sandstone were formed by river currents. We call this 'current bedding'.

Mudcracks preserved in the rock tell us where a pond dried out in the sun.

FLY-BY-NIGHT FOSSILS

Some species of animals only lived for a very short period of time – maybe a million years or so (that's a short time to a geologist). Fossils of such creatures – called 'index fossils' – can be used for dating the rocks in which they are found. The best index fossils are of those animals that drifted throughout the world's oceans, like ammonites and graptolites.

SEA SKELETONS

So, in what kinds of rocks do we find dinosaur fossils? Rocks formed under the sea are not a good place to look for fossils of land animals. Because if a dinosaur was washed into the sea the bones would have been scattered before they settled.

DINOSAUR GRAVES

River siltstones and desert sands are the best place to find dinosaur fossils. If a dinosaur drowned in a river, or was engulfed by a sandstorm, and the body was buried quickly before scavenging animals could get at it, then it had a good chance of becoming a fossil.

TIME DETECTIVE

Reading the rocks

Follow the clues to discover the story hidden in the rocks.

Here is a cliff face by the seaside. Can we use the rocks to tell us what the landscape was like in the past?

CLUE (1) The beds are tilted. These rocks would have been laid down in horizontal layers. So there must have been great earth movements since they were formed.

CLUE (2) The first rock that we come to is a massive limestone. Because it is so thick it must have been formed over a long period of time.

CLUE (3) The limestone has fossils of seashells and starfish-like creatures called sea lilies. These animals lived in shallow seas during the Carboniferous period. The limestone must have been laid down in shallow water about 300 million years ago.

CLUE (4) Beds of shale come next. This soft flaky rock is formed from mud. Nearby rivers must have poured mud into the limy sea at this time.

CLUE (5) Then there is a bed of sandstone. It has current bedding showing that it was deposited by rivers. When this formed, the river must have been building sand banks out into the sea.

CLUE (6) A bed of coal on top of the sandstone shows that swampy forests grew on the sandbanks. Tree roots may be seen in the sandstone immediately beneath.

CLUE 7 The whole sequence of shale-sandstone-coal repeats itself several times. The river must have built sandbanks out into the sea, which were then flooded, and then built up, time and time again.

CLUE 8 The last rock type is a massive red sandstone. It has huge curved beds which show that this sandstone was formed from sand dunes.

CLUE 9 Through a magnifying glass we can see that sandstone grains are rounded – rolled about by the wind – and coated with the rusty mineral iron oxide. This means that they were laid down in dry desert conditions.

CLUE 10 A bed of finer siltstone in the middle of the sandstone has mudcracks and reptile footprints. There must have been water holes here that kept drying up.

GOT IT!

By following the clues in the rocks we can tell that 300 million years ago this area was at the bottom of the sea. A nearby river formed sandbanks that built out into the sea several times. Eventually the sea retreated and the area became a desert. Finally, after a long time, when the sediments had turned to stone, the whole rock sequence was tilted and worn away until it became as we see it today.

A DAY IN THE LIFE OF LIOPLEURODON

DURING THE LATE JURASSIC PERIOD, 150 MILLION YEARS AGO...

...FEMALE LIOPLEURODON CRAWL CLUMSILY OUT OF THE WATER AND PLOD ACROSS THE SAND TO LAY THEIR EGGS.

ONCE THE NESTS ARE DUG AND THE EGGS LAID, THE ENORMOUS BEASTS SHUFFLE BACK TO THE SAFETY OF THE SEA...

THE YOUNG LIOPLEURODON ATTRACT A FLOCK OF RAVENOUS PTEROSAURS WHICH SWOOP DOWN.

THE LITTLE LIOPLEURODON ARE DEFENCELESS.

ALTHOUGH MANY HATCHLINGS FALL PREY TO THE PTEROSAURS, EVEN MORE REACH THE SHORELINE.

BUT THEY ARE STILL NOT SAFE.

...AND OTHER SLEEK CREATURES OF THE SEA KNOW OF THE EASY TAKINGS TO BE HAD IN THE SHALLOW WATERS. CRYPTOCLEIDUS IS A PREDATORY PLESIOSAUR WITH AN INSATIABLE APPETITE...

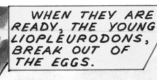

WHEN THEY ARE READY, THE YOUNG LIOPLEURODONS, BREAK OUT OF THE EGGS.

THE HATCHLINGS CANNOT SURVIVE LONG ON LAND. THEY HAVE TO GET TO THE SEA AS QUICKLY AS THEY CAN.

...NEVER AGAIN TO SEE THEIR EGGS OR TO RECOGNISE THE YOUNG THAT WILL HATCH FROM THEM.

NOW THEY FACE THE MOST HAZARDOUS JOURNEY OF THEIR LIVES.

LIKE LEMMINGS, THEY CASCADE DOWN THE BEACH TOWARDS THE WAVES. BUT SOME WILL NEVER MAKE IT.

MANY WILL DIE IN THE CRUSHING JAWS OF METRIORHYNCHUS...

...AND HYBODUS, A PRIMITIVE SHARK, IS AS DEADLY A KILLER AS MANY OF ITS MODERN DESCENDANTS.

BUT MANY LIOPLEURODON ESCAPE THE PERILOUS WATERS AND SWIM TO SAFETY.

PRODUCING SO MANY YOUNG LIOPLEURODON IS NATURE'S WAY OF ENSURING THAT THE SPECIES SURVIVES. WHEN THEY HAVE MATURED, THE FEMALES WILL RETURN TO THE BEACH TO LAY THEIR OWN EGGS, AND SO THE CYCLE WILL CONTINUE.

Improve and test your knowledge with...

FACT FILE

Fascinating facts
to read and
10 fun questions
to answer!

Stamp controversy

We have mentioned before that dinosaurs have been used on postage stamps. Very recently, the American postal service produced a set of stamps which included Brontosaurus. This caused a great deal of correspondence because, as we all know, the real name for Brontosaurus should be...Apatosaurus!

1 *Arrhinoceratops* had:
a) no nose horn
b) a small nose horn
c) a large nose horn

2 Which dinosaur had only two fingers?
a) *Tarbosaurus*
b) *Dromiceiomimus*
c) *Plateosaurus*

3 Geologists learn about dinosaurs by studying:
a) living animals
b) trees and flowers
c) rocks and fossils

4 *Basilosaurus* was mistakenly named:
a) king reptile
b) king mammal
c) king prawn

5 *Aepyornis* is called the:
a) elephant bird
b) brain bird
c) big bird

6 *Ictitherium* was one of the first:
a) hyenas
b) bears
c) dogs

7 *Liopleurodon* laid lots of eggs to try and:
a) feed hungry sea creatures
b) ensure the species survived
c) to get in the record books

8 The Jurassic Period was named after:
a) the film 'Jurassic Park'
b) the Jura Mountains
c) the flying reptile, *Jurapteryx*

9 *Iguanodon* had an amazing:
a) head frill
b) big toe
c) thumb

Dine like a dino

Today, there are some people who eat the same food that dinosaurs did! In the northern USA and southern Canada, young fern fronds are sold as vegetables in early spring. Some are sold fresh, others are canned and sold in stores. These young curled-up fronds are called 'fiddle heads' and lots of people consider them a dining delicacy.

Cornish tomb

Cromhall quarry is a famous 'fissure site' in south-west England. Some of the oldest known mammal fossils have been found there. A fissure is a crack in the rocks. If small creatures fall down a fissure, they usually can't get out. They become buried in the sediment that is washed down into the cracks when it rains, creating the perfect conditions for preserving bones.

As small as an elephant?

Mammoth

Elephas falconeri

Elephants may have evolved their large size as a defence against predators. This idea is supported by the discovery that dwarf elephants lived on Mediterranean islands such as Sicily and Malta. Elephas falconeri was only one metre tall at the shoulder. The islands were largely free of any large land predators such as lions so elephants no longer had to be huge in order to be safe. On average, they were only one quarter the size of their mainland ancestors.

10 *Megistotherium* **had a head like a:**
a) mouse
b) tiger
c) weasel

Fish on a bicycle

Coelacanth, the large scaly fish which scientists thought had died out millions of years ago, was discovered off the coast of South Africa this century. They later found that the people on the Comoros Islands had been catching them for years! Fishermen were using the scaly skin to roughen the inner tubes of bicycle tyres when mending a puncture!

ASK THE EXPERT

Dr. David Norman of Cambridge University answers your dinosaur questions

How can you become a palaeontologist?

So many of you ask about this that I am happy to explain again. First you need to study science at school. If you do well, you can go to university to study Geology and Zoology. These subjects allow you to study palaeontology. Not all people do this; some enjoy palaeontology as a hobby.

How did time periods get their names?

The names were often chosen for local reasons. The Jurassic Period was named after the Jura mountains in France. Devonian rocks are found in Devon, England, and the Silurian is named after the Silures, a Welsh tribe that lived in the region dominated by this age of rock. The Cretaceous Period was named from 'creta' meaning chalk, and the Carboniferous Period is named after the carbon or coal found in rocks of this time period.

Which dinosaur had the most armour?

I do not really know. My best guess would be one of the ankylosaurs such as *Euoplocephalus*. Unfortunately we do not often find complete dinosaurs, so it is impossible to be certain which had the most armour.

Were shellfish able to swim?

The simple answer is yes! But only a few. Ammonites probably swam by jet propulsion, squirting water out of a nozzle under the head. Scallops today, like their fossil ancestors, can swim to escape from predators such as starfish. They swim by clapping their shells together. To see these animals swimming along is a truly amazing sight. Very few other shellfish were able to swim to escape predators.

DINOSAURS!
DISCOVER THE GIANTS OF THE PREHISTORIC WORLD

DIATRYMA

This huge, flightless bird, taller than the average man, preyed on small plant-eating mammals.

NO NEED TO FLY

Without an enemy to chase it, the big bird had no need of a pair of working wings to give it a quick means of escape.

fter the dinosaurs disappeared from the Earth, new predators emerged to take their place. About 50 million years ago the biggest hunters were massive birds – 'terror cranes' – which could not fly. For millions of years, *Diatryma* had no real rival amongst other predators. It usually hunted little plant-eating mammals, although some experts suggest that it was fierce enough to attack and kill a small horse!

ON THE RUN

Diatryma sped along on two strongly built legs which were perfectly designed for a fast-running animal. It took long, powerful strides as it pursued its prey. Like some predatory dinosaurs, it used its large, clawed feet as a weapon to help subdue its victim.

PLAIN LIVING

Diatryma probably lived on open plains. It could do this quite safely as it had little to fear from other animals. No other large predators existed at the same time.

29

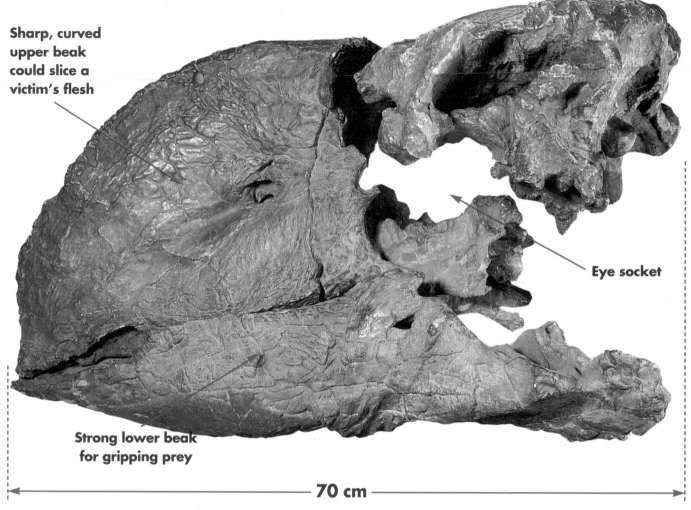

Sharp, curved upper beak could slice a victim's flesh

Eye socket

Strong lower beak for gripping prey

◄—————— **70 cm** ——————►

LIGHT AS A FEATHER

A thick covering of feathers made *Diatryma*'s body look bigger than it really was. In reality its feathered plumes made the bird very light so that it was able to run swiftly.

Today's flightless cassowary can kill a man with its powerful kicking legs.

DEADLY DAMAGE

Diatryma had three long, clawed toes on each foot and a fourth toe which pointed backwards. As its victim was held in the firm grip of *Diatryma*'s beak, the sharp talons ripped at the skin until the creature was too weak from loss of blood to resist.

MONSTER FACTS

- **NAME:** *Diatryma* (<u>die</u>-a-try-ma) means 'through hole'
- **GROUP:** bird
- **SIZE:** about 2m tall
- **FOOD:** meat, mostly small mammals
- **LIVED:** about 50 million years ago in the Eocene Epoch in Europe and North America

HUGE HEAD

Unlike the emu or ostrich of today, *Diatryma* had a huge head for the size of its body. From its neck to the tip of its beak the head was almost as long as that of a horse. At the front was an enormous, curved beak which was immensely hard and strong. As *Diatryma* snatched up its prey it clamped down with its beak to crush the body and tear it to pieces. Although, like modern birds, *Diatryma* had no teeth, its beak was sharp enough to slice the flesh from its victim.

IT'S A FACT

The largest prehistoric bird was *Dromornis stirtoni*. This huge emu-like flightless bird was as tall as a polar bear and four times heavier than an ostrich. The fossilized remains of its leg bones were found at Alice Springs, central Australia in 1974. *Dromornis stirtoni* lived over 11 million years ago.

Diatryma could probably run fast enough to catch *Hyracotherium* – a small horse – and plant-eating mammals such as sheep-sized *Phenacodus*.

EUSKELOSAURUS

***Euskelosaurus* was one of the first dinosaurs to be discovered in Africa.**

onger than an elephant, and with large, powerful legs, *Euskelosaurus* roamed the ancient forests of South Africa and fed on ferns and horsetails.

SIZE WISE

8m

MONSTER FACTS

- **NAME:** *Euskelosaurus* (yoo-skell-oh-<u>saw</u>-rus) means 'true leg reptile'
- **GROUP:** dinosaur
- **SIZE:** up to 8m long
- **FOOD:** plants
- **LIVED:** about 210 million years ago in the Late Triassic Period in Africa

HEADLESS REMAINS

Since 1866, when the first set of leg bones were sent to England from Africa, many more remains of *Euskelosaurus* have been found. This suggests that 210 million years ago, it was probably a very common dinosaur. Unfortunately, none of these skeletons include a skull and so, up until now, experts could only presume that it had a small head like other prosauropods.

HEAD FOUND

A group of palaeontologists working in the Orange Free State in South Africa has just reported the discovery of the first skull of *Euskelosaurus*. Soon we will know more about their findings!

WATCH OUT – FLESH-EATERS ABOUT!

As it walked, *Euskelosaurus* probably balanced its long neck by holding its tail stiffly above the ground. Like other prosauropods, *Euskelosaurus* had to be constantly on the alert for predators as it grazed on leaves and shrubs. Some experts think that dinosaurs like *Euskelosaurus* probably gathered together in large groups for extra protection from flesh-eaters.

HYLONOMUS

One of the oldest known reptiles, *Hylonomus* was about as long as this page is wide.

Several skeletons of this lizard-like creature were found in fossilized tree stumps in Nova Scotia, Canada. *Hylonomus* probably scampered along the branches and became trapped inside hollow tree trunks. For many years, experts thought that it was the oldest of all reptiles. But in 1988, another ancient creature, nicknamed 'Lizzie', was discovered in Scotland. It is probably about 40 million years older than *Hylonomus*.

SOLID SKULL

Although *Hylonomus* had the sprawled legs and small, darting head of a lizard, it was actually a 'stem reptile' or cotylosaur. This first known family of reptiles had simple skulls, which were only broken by eyeholes and nostrils. Its fossilized remains show that it had a long tapering tail and slender fingers and toes.

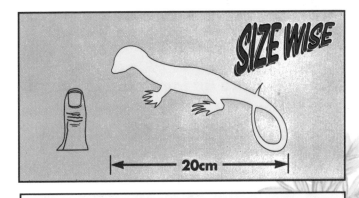

SIZE WISE

20cm

MONSTER FACTS

- **NAME:** *Hylonomus* (<u>hy</u>-lo-<u>nome</u>-us) means 'wood law'
- **SIZE:** about 20cm long
- **GROUP:** reptile
- **FOOD:** large insects
- **LIVED:** about 310 million years ago in the Middle Carboniferous Period in Nova Scotia, Canada

TIGHT GRIP

Hylonomus moved stealthily around the forest floor and preyed on large insects and centipedes. As it snatched up small creatures, *Hylonomus* gripped them with a row of small, sharp teeth which ran along the edge of its long jaw.

Success in the sea

Trilobites were an important group of animals for 160 million years, and we know of about 2,000 different types.

O ver 500 million years ago – long before the Age of Dinosaurs – the continents were bare and lifeless. There was no movement but the drift of sand over rocks, no sound but the wind, no plant shoots peeping through the sterile soil. In the ancient seas, however, it was a very different story.

Only very rarely do we find a complete fossil trilobite, legs and all.

IT'S A FACT

FOSSIL RECORDS
The oldest useful fossils date from the beginning of the Cambrian Period. Before this, animals had no hard shells, and so did not leave good fossils. Then hard shells developed amongst all kinds of animals, and we have good fossil records from then on.

SEA STORY
A sudden flush of evolution had filled the waters with all sorts of swimming, crawling, wriggling things – all with some kind of hard shell or skeleton. One of the most successful of these groups were the animals we call the trilobites.

SHAPED TO SURVIVE
Imagine an animal like a woodlouse with a body divided into segments. Give it a semi-circular shield at the head end, with a mouth, a pair of eyes and a pair of feelers. Give it another shield at the tail end, and give each segment of the body a pair of legs to use for crawling, swimming and eating. This is the basic shape of a trilobite.

The trilobite shed its shell several times throughout its life. That is why parts of the shell are found as fossils more often than complete trilobites.

Trilobite: top view

Trilobite: underneath view

Feelers

Semicircular shield

Eye

Heavy, jointed part of leg for walking on

Feathery gills used for breathing and to help with swimming

Toothy part of legs carried food to the mouth

TRI MEANS THREE

Down the middle of the trilobite's back, from head to tail, was a raised ridge. This ridge, and the parts of the body lying to each side, gave the animal a 'three-lobed' appearance, hence the name 'trilobite'.

LONG-LIVED LINE

Cambrian, Ordovician and Silurian rocks are full of trilobite fossils. Then they began to die away and by the end of the Permian they are completely extinct.

From above a trilobite looked rather like this modern sea creature called a sea slater or gribble, but with a ridge down its back.

NEW SHELLS FOR OLD

Trilobites were arthropods – the group of joint-legged animals to which today's shrimps, crabs and lobsters belong. Like these animals they were covered by shells. These shells could not grow with the animal. Every now and again the trilobite would throw off its shell and then grow another one.

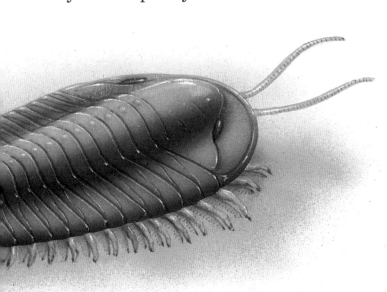

DIFFERENT SHAPES, DIFFERENT LIFESTYLES

As with most animals, we can tell how particular trilobites lived by looking at their shapes.

LIFE AT THE BOTTOM

We can tell a trilobite that lived on the sea bed, because it is quite lumpy and heavy-looking, and has its eyes on stalks so that it can see around it. *Encrinurus* from the Silurian was a typical bottom-dweller.

SWIMMING FREE

A swimming trilobite was lightly-built, with less shell than other trilobites. Feathery-looking *Paracybeloides* may have been an Ordovician swimmer.

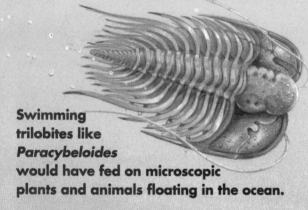

Swimming trilobites like *Paracybeloides* would have fed on microscopic plants and animals floating in the ocean.

Is it true

that there are no trilobites left?

The last trilobite died out 250 million years ago. The nearest living relative is the horseshoe crab *Limulus* from the shallow waters around North America. In its young stage *Limulus* looks very much like a trilobite.

BIG EYES

We know other trilobites were swimmers because of their big eyes that could look all around and could also look downwards. *Cyclopyge*, also from the Ordovician Period, had big eyes like this.

BURROWER

Any burrowing animal has a streamlined body shape – look at a mole. Trilobites were no exception. Silurian *Trimerus* had a head shield that was distinctly spade-like, and had tiny eyes. It probably burrowed through the sand.

THE SMALLEST

The Cambrian trilobite *Agnostus* was smaller than your little finger nail. It consisted of a head shield and a tail shield which were about the same size, and only two body segments between them. It had no eyes, so it may have lived in the deep sea where there was no light.

AND THE BIGGEST

The biggest trilobite that we know was *Uralichas* which lived in Ordovician times. It was 70cm long. It was a harmless but an impressive beast!

Bottom-dwelling trilobites like *Encrinurus* crawled across the seafloor eating the food particles lying there.

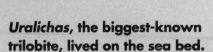

Uralichas, the biggest-known trilobite, lived on the sea bed.

Many trilobite fossils are of the empty shell – left behind when the trilobite moulted and grew a new, bigger shell.

Today's horseshoe crab may be related to the trilobites. It looks a bit like a trilobite and its young look like young trilobites.

Burrowing trilobites like *Trimerus* may have spent their time digging into loose sand in search of food. Fossilized trilobite trails – the marks left as trilobites travelled across the sea bed – are sometimes found.

37

GIANTS OF THE PAST

DIATRYMA

Huge, meat-eating *Diatryma* out-runs and
catches *Hyracotherium*. The little horse has
unwisely ventured out into the open where it is
no match for the immensely strong legs and
vicious beak of the gigantic flightless bird. Other
Diatryma look on, hoping to scavenge a few
morsels for themselves.

39

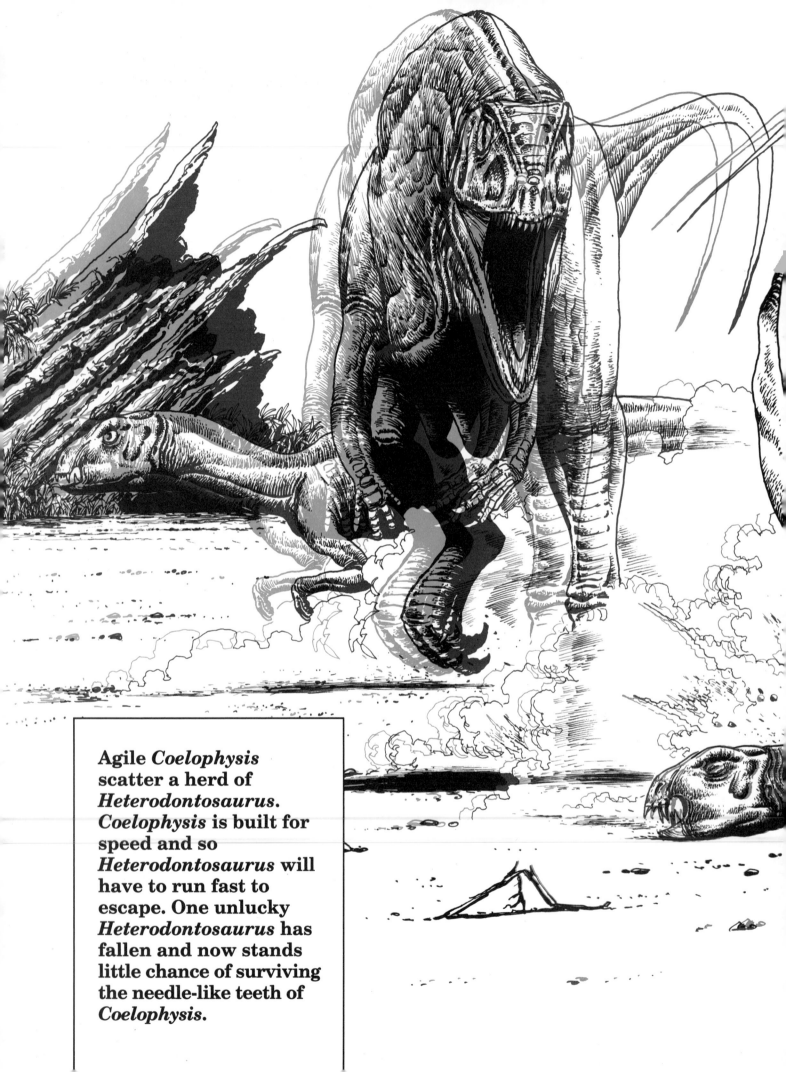

Agile *Coelophysis* scatter a herd of *Heterodontosaurus*. *Coelophysis* is built for speed and so *Heterodontosaurus* will have to run fast to escape. One unlucky *Heterodontosaurus* has fallen and now stands little chance of surviving the needle-like teeth of *Coelophysis*.

3-D Gallery 63

HETERODONTOSAURUS

AMAZING

Antlers are the fastest growing structure in the animal world.

In one hundred days, an antler could grow to about the length of your arm! Growing antlers at such a tremendous rate takes lots of energy. Some scientists think a male may use as much energy when its antlers are growing as a female does when bringing up young deer.

This magnificent red deer is called a 'royal stag' because it has antlers with 12 branches.

RECORD-BREAKER

Imagine a pair of antlers wider than a car is long. The owner of this extraordinary headgear, the prehistoric deer *Megaloceros* (<u>meg</u>-al-oh-<u>ser</u>-os), had the largest antlers of any known deer. This herbivore lived in Europe and Asia about 20,000 years ago. The largest pair of *Megaloceros* antlers yet found measure an amazing 4.3m, end to end.

BRANCHING OUT

Eucladoceros (<u>yoo</u>-klad-oh-<u>ser</u>-os), now extinct, also had magnificent antlers with many branches which sprouted in different directions. This spread of antlers is called a rack.

Eucladoceros

BIG HEAD

Eucladoceros' name means 'well-branched antler', a good name for a deer whose antlers could reach a span of 1.7m.

ANTLERS

Megaloceros' antlers could weigh as much as 45kg – one seventh of its total weight.

A RANGE OF RACKS

Cranioceros (cran-ee-oh-<u>ser</u>-os) lived in North America from the Miocene to the Pliocene. It had antlers that looked more like pronged horns. Two rose straight up and a third curved back between its ears. *Hoplitomeryx* (hop-<u>light</u>-o-mer-rix) had five horn-shaped antlers. Three of these pointed backwards and two smaller ones curved forwards. *Hoplitomeryx* also had two distinctive fangs.

NEW FOR OLD

Megaloceros, like the deer of today, grew new antlers each year. These begin to grow in the summer and reach their full size in the autumn.

Cranioceros

VELVET SOFT

As the antlers grow they are protected by a layer of soft skin called velvet. In spring, the old antlers are shed and the base of the new growth revealed.

Hoplitomeryx

IT'S A FACT

Who has antlers?

Deer have antlers. Cattle and antelope have horns. It is usually only the male deer that carry these large antlers although some female caribou and reindeer also have them. Unlike horns, antlers are made of solid bone and are shed each year. Carnivores do not need antlers as they have teeth and claws for protection.

Dinosaur weather

What was the weather like hundreds of millions of years ago? And how did the dinosaurs cope?

Dinosaurs had to adapt themselves to days of blazing sunshine and nights of chilly darkness. They were also plagued by huge volcanic eruptions, violent storms and flash floods.

ALL CHANGE

Why did the climate change so much during the Dinosaur Age? One reason was that when the first dinosaurs appeared, all the continents were joined together. That meant there were vast inland regions cut off from rain-bearing ocean winds. So the climate was drier. But as the continents continued to move, the climate gradually changed.

OUTLOOK UNSETTLED

Shallow seas invaded the land in the Jurassic Period and seaborne winds brought rain to areas that had been deserts. By Cretaceous times, the continents looked more like they do today. The climate was cooler and the different seasons began to emerge.

HOT AND DRY

How did dinosaurs survive in the deserts of Triassic times? The early plant-eating dinosaur *Lesothosaurus* may possibly have aestivated, or slept, through long periods of drought just as some desert animals do today.

This dew-drinking thorny devil lizard (above) lives in the deserts of Australia.

***Lesothosaurus* (left) may have slept during long dry spells and became active again when the rains started.**

A *Diplodocus* herd enjoys the warm rains of the Jurassic Period.

WARM AND WET

More rain fell in the Jurassic Period. A tropical rainstorm was probably just as threatening to animal life as it is today. Modern birds and insects cannot fly through the heavy drops. But reptiles, such as crocodiles, alligators and turtles are much better adapted. Dinosaurs probably behaved in a similar way to today's reptiles. Fossil footprints reveal that the giant sauropods of the time were water-loving creatures which could swim as well as walk.

COOL AND OPEN

Earth was cooler and drier in Cretaceous times. The forests thinned and open plains of ferns and horsetails appeared. Long-necked sauropods were replaced by plant-eating dinosaurs which browsed closer to the ground. Low-lying plains could have flooded badly after violent rainstorms.

DEW DRINKER

Some desert dinosaurs might have had a special spiny covering like today's thorny devil lizard. This lizard's spines become covered in dew at night, which condenses and runs down grooves towards its mouth.

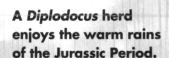 **WEATHER**

The air in which we live and breathe is forever on the move. As the Sun warms the Earth's surface, hot air rises and cold air sinks to take its place. Air masses also move around the world. They can be cold, hot, wet or dry. This constant swirling and stirring of air gives us everything we call weather.

Today's wildebeeste migrate across the grasslands of East Africa in search of food. Some dinosaurs may have migrated and, like the wildebeest, lost members of the herd in flooded rivers.

45

FOREST FIRE

Large groups of dinosaurs such as *Lambeosaurus* may have perished together as a result of forest fires. A bolt of lightning or a shower of volcanic sparks could have triggered a blaze. Whatever the cause, the flames would have created instant panic. Just like creatures caught in a forest fire today, many dinosaurs might have been fatally injured trying to escape.

RIVERS OF ROCK

The end of the Dinosaur Age was a time of great volcanic activity. Liquid rock, or lava, gushing down a mountain would have destroyed everything in its path. And the clouds of poisonous gases, which billowed up into the air, also caused death and destruction. A bone bed containing a huge herd of *Hypacrosaurus* has been found in a volcanic region in North America. Perhaps they perished in a giant eruption.

An enormous herd of *Hypacrosaurus* may have perished together in a volcanic eruption in North America. A bone bed has been found with thousands of *Hypacrosaurus* bones.

An erupting volcano destroys animal life both because of the red hot lava gushing from it, and because of the poisonous gases and

A herd of *Lambeosaurus* is caught in a forest fire and panics.

THE BIG FREEZE

A drastic change in the world's weather could have caused the death of the dinosaurs. Fossil evidence shows that the Earth might have been hit by a massive meteorite. Or there could have been an immense volcanic eruption. Either catastrophe could have blanketed the world in a deadly dust cloud. Dinosaurs would have been too big to burrow to escape frost, and they probably had no hair or feathers to keep them warm. So they could have been wiped out by the cold.

IT'S A FACT

THUNDERSTRUCK

Big thunderclouds tower 16km high. They churn up enough energy to light a small town for a year. Huge electric sparks fly between thunderclouds. They are lightning flashes. They heat the air so much it expands at great speed. That produces the sonic bang we call thunder.

Today's furry dormouse can curl up and hibernate to sleep away cold spells. Some dinosaurs may have been able to hibernate too.

47

THINGS WERE NO BETTER AT CAMBRIDGE UNIVERSITY, WHERE HE STUDIED THEOLOGY. THEN, IN 1831, AN OLD FRIEND, ROBERT FITZROY INVITED HIM TO JOIN AN EXPEDITION ON H·M·S· BEAGLE, TO THE SOUTH PACIFIC.

I'M GLAD YOU ACCEPTED OUR INVITATION CHARLES!

I WON'T SEE ENGLAND FOR A LONG TIME.

FIVE YEARS WILL SOON PASS!

DARWIN CAME ACROSS MANY THINGS THAT PUZZLED HIM IN SOUTH AMERICA. HE DUG UP THE FOSSIL OF A GIANT EXTINCT ARMADILLO.

OUCH! PESKY INSECT!

HOW COME EXTINCT ANIMALS WERE SO LIKE EXISTING ANIMALS?

WHEN THEY RETURNED TO ENGLAND, DARWIN MARRIED AND SPENT THE NEXT 20 YEARS TRYING TO SOLVE THE PUZZLES HE HAD ENCOUNTERED ON HIS JOURNEY.

WHO'S THE LETTER FROM, CHARLES?

SOMEONE CALLED ALFRED WALLACE. HE'S REACHED THE SAME CONCLUSIONS AS I HAVE.

DARWIN AND WALLACE HAD EACH REALISED THAT, OVER MILLIONS OF YEARS, SPECIES CHANGE AS FEATURES OF THE STRONGEST ANIMALS ARE PASSED ON TO THE NEXT GENERATION. DARWIN HAD DISCOVERED **EVOLUTION!**

HE PUBLISHED HIS WORK IN A BOOK CALLED "ON THE ORIGIN OF SPECIES." IT WAS DENOUNCED IN CHURCHES AND THE BOOK WAS PUBLICLY BURNED!

THAT'S ALL IT'S FIT FOR!

IT'S DARWIN WE SHOULD BE BURNING!

DARWIN'S THEORY EXPLAINS HOW DINOSAURS EVOLVED, AND WHY THEY RULED THE EARTH FOR SO LONG. IT ALSO SUGGESTS THAT SOME DINOSAURS BECAME THE ANCESTORS OF TODAY'S BIRDS.

DARWIN DIED IN 1882, HAVING SUFFERED FOR MANY YEARS FROM A MYSTERIOUS ILLNESS. WE NOW KNOW THAT THE INSECT BITE IN SOUTH AMERICA WAS RESPONSIBLE FOR HIS ILL-HEALTH. HE WAS BURIED IN WESTMINSTER ABBEY.

Improve and test your knowledge with...

FACT FILE

Dimetrodon holds all the answers. See how you score in the quiz.

Misidentified corpse

Sometimes people think that they have found a dead plesiosaur on the beach, when all they have found is a basking shark! When a dead shark decays, its enormous jaws fall off. This leaves a tiny skull at the end of a long backbone, looking for all the world like a plesiosaur's head and neck.

Change of name

Dinosaurs were not always called that. In 1832, the German scientist Hermann von Meyer suggested the name 'pachypoda' (thick feet) for the group containing Iguanodon and Megalosaurus – the only dinosaurs then known. About ten years later, British scientist Richard Owen suggested the name 'dinosauria' and this is the name that stuck.

5 *Coelophysis* had teeth like:
a) nails
b) staples
c) needles

4 The largest prehistoric bird was:
a) *Dromornis stirtoni*
b) the ostrich
c) *Dromiceiomimus*

3 *Diatryma* had a thick covering of:
a) fur
b) feathers
c) scales

2 When the dinosaurs first appeared the continents were:
a) like they are today
b) joined by bridges
c) all joined together

1 A spread of antlers is called:
a) a mantelpiece
b) a rack
c) a tree

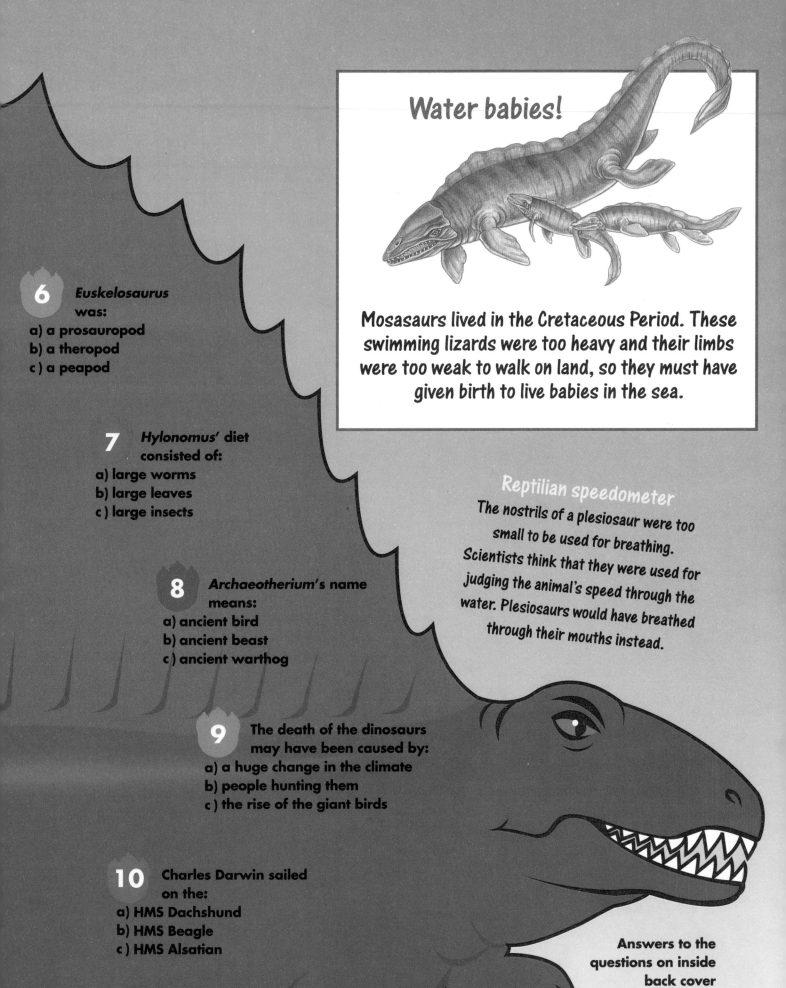

Water babies!

Mosasaurs lived in the Cretaceous Period. These swimming lizards were too heavy and their limbs were too weak to walk on land, so they must have given birth to live babies in the sea.

6 *Euskelosaurus* was:
a) a prosauropod
b) a theropod
c) a peapod

7 *Hylonomus'* diet consisted of:
a) large worms
b) large leaves
c) large insects

8 *Archaeotherium's* name means:
a) ancient bird
b) ancient beast
c) ancient warthog

9 The death of the dinosaurs may have been caused by:
a) a huge change in the climate
b) people hunting them
c) the rise of the giant birds

10 Charles Darwin sailed on the:
a) HMS Dachshund
b) HMS Beagle
c) HMS Alsatian

Reptilian speedometer
The nostrils of a plesiosaur were too small to be used for breathing. Scientists think that they were used for judging the animal's speed through the water. Plesiosaurs would have breathed through their mouths instead.

Answers to the questions on inside back cover

ASK THE EXPERT

Dr. David Norman of Cambridge University answers your dinosaur questions

Did dinosaurs have hair?

Scientists do not think that dinosaurs were hairy. Some fossil dinosaur skeletons – including several hadrosaurs, and some theropods and sauropods, have now been found which include impressions of the skin. All these show that the skin was scaly like that of modern reptiles, so it seems most probable that dinosaurs were scaly rather than hairy.

What is the largest known carnivorous mammal ever?

One of the largest carnivorous fossil mammals that I know of was *Basilosaurus*. This was a huge early whale which grew up to 20m long. It had large saw-shaped teeth, which it would have used to cut up its prey once it had killed it with the large stabbing teeth in the front of its mouth. The largest carnivorous mammal alive today is the huge sperm whale.

Which prehistoric animal had the longest tusks?

The Ice Age mammoths seem to have had the longest tusks of all. They may have used them as shovels to clear snow and get to the grass beneath. Tusks have been found reaching lengths of 3.5m measured along their curved edges.

Did the Earth look the same millions of years ago as it does today?

The Earth looked very different millions of years ago. About 250 million years ago, all the continents were joined together in one large land mass. So animals could literally walk right across the world! The continents have gradually drifted apart to the position you see them on maps today. But they are still moving so hold on tight!

ULTRASAUROS

As long as three buses, *Ultrasauros* was probably one of the tallest of all the dinosaurs.

Until recently this gigantic dinosaur from Colorado, North America, was called '*Ultrasaurus*' ('us' at the end of its name). But, unknown to the American palaeontologists who found it, another sauropod dinosaur discovered in South Korea had been given the same name. To prevent any confusion, the dinosaur from Colorado has been renamed *Ultrasauros* ('os' at the end of its name).

SUPERSTARS

Ultrasauros was found in the same area of North America as gigantic *Supersaurus*. These giants were both plant-eaters. With *Brachiosaurus,* these amazing creatures are among the heaviest and tallest dinosaurs that ever lived.

WELL-SUPPORTED

Although it was shaped like many other sauropods, *Ultrasauros* was built on a huge scale. It was about 25 times heavier than a modern giraffe and taller than a four storey building. Its incredibly long neck and tail were supported by a girder-like spine. Gaps in the sides of each vertebra reduced *Ultrasauros'* weight without weakening its back.

WEIGHT BEARING BONE

Most of the dinosaur's weight was taken by its gigantic limbs. So one of the most important bones was the shoulder blade, which joined its front legs to its body. In *Ultrasauros* it was both large and strong. Held upright, this dinosaur's shoulder blade was taller than a soccer goal post!

BEST OF BOTH WORLDS

Ultrasauros' body sloped down from its high shoulders as its back legs were shorter than the forelimbs. It swung its long neck up and down and from side to side as it browsed on plants and shrubs. It could reach both the juicy leaves at the very top of trees and low-growing ferns.

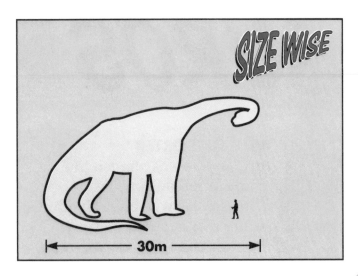

SIZE WISE

|← 30m →|

These huge herbivores had to eat enormous quantities of vegetation to stay alive.

STONES AND VEGETABLES

Ultrasauros needed a plentiful supply of vegetation which it cut with its chisel-like teeth. To help it digest this, *Ultrasauros* probably swallowed small stones which lay in its gut to help grind plant food to a pulp.

SLOW-MOVING HERDS

Although it is hard to imagine, experts have suggested that brachiosaurids like *Ultrasauros* wandered around in slow-moving herds. The ground must have trembled beneath their feet!

Is it true

that some sauropods ate all day?

Experts have estimated that if a large sauropod such as *Brachiosaurus* was endothermic (that is it generated its own body heat like mammals and birds) it would need about 200kg of plant food per day to keep alive and healthy. That's about the same weight as 260 large boxes of cornflakes.

TOO BIG TO TACKLE

The sheer size and bulk of an animal like *Ultrasauros* probably put off most predators that lived at the same time. But if one became isolated from the rest of a herd, it was exposed to danger.

'Dinosaur Jim' – James Jensen – with the gigantic leg bones of *Ultrasauros*.

MONSTER FACTS

- **NAME:** *Ultrasauros* (<u>ull</u>-tra-<u>saw</u>-ros) means 'ultra reptile'
- **GROUP:** dinosaur
- **SIZE:** up to 30m long
- **FOOD:** plants
- **LIVED:** about 145 million years ago in the Late Jurassic Period in Colorado, North America

HIDDEN WEAPON

On the inside of its elephant-like foot, *Ultrasauros* had a sharp claw. With a well-aimed kick and a swipe of its whiplash tail, *Ultrasauros* could send its enemy flying back into the bushes.

55

MESOSAURUS

Little *Mesosaurus* helped a scientist to prove an important theory about how our Earth developed.

n 1911, a German scientist called Alfred Wegener noticed that the small reptile, *Mesosaurus*, had been found in Permian rocks in both South America and Africa. But it did not appear anywhere else in the world. When he had collected more evidence, Wegener put forward his idea that all continents were once joined together in one 'supercontinent' which he called Pangaea.

FISHY DINNERS

Mesosaurus was a small reptile, about as long as an adult human's arm. It swam in freshwater lakes and ponds about 265 million years ago. *Mesosaurus* preyed on fish and water animals and needed to move with great speed to catch them.

MONSTER FACTS

- **NAME:** *Mesosaurus* (<u>me</u>-zoh-<u>saw</u>-rus) means 'middle reptile'
- **GROUP:** reptile
- **SIZE:** 71cm long
- **FOOD:** small freshwater fish and water creatures
- **LIVED:** about 265 million years ago in the Permian Period in the freshwater lakes and ponds of Brazil and South Africa

SUPER SWIMMER

Its long, slender body gave the reptile a streamlined shape which was perfect for fast swimming. When you swim, you turn your hands out to push through the water with the greatest force. *Mesosaurus'* hands and feet were shaped like little paddles which scooped away water in the same way. Its tail was narrow and deep so that it did not slow the reptile's body

SIZE WISE

71cm

down as it cut swiftly through the water in search of food.

SUDDEN SNAP

Mesosaurus had long, slender jaws like a crocodile. They were full of needle-like teeth. As it glided through the water, it took mouthfuls of tiny water creatures and fish and strained the water away through its teeth before it swallowed its prey.

HARPYMIMUS

Speedy *Harpymimus* could pluck flying insects from the air and chase fast-moving lizards.

One of the earliest ornithomimosaurs, *Harpymimus*, had a unique feature which none of its relatives shared. At the front of its upper and lower jaw were ten or more tiny teeth.

ON THE LOOKOUT

Harpymimus had large eyes set on either side of its head. Always on the alert, it twisted its neck and head from side to side so that it could look all around. If attacked by a predator, *Harpymimus* relied on its two long legs to make a quick getaway.

LEAVES AND LIZARDS

Harpymimus ate all sorts of food. It probably browsed among trees and shrubs and could also run fast enough to catch insects, lizards and even small mammals in its narrow jaw.

MONSTER FACTS

- **NAME:** *Harpymimus* (har-pih-mime-us) means 'harpy mimic'
- **GROUP:** dinosaur
- **SIZE:** about 2m long
- **FOOD:** lizards, insects and possibly plants
- **LIVED:** about 100 million years ago in the Cretaceous Period in Mongolia

SIZE WISE

2m

57

Fantastic fishes

Fishes have been the masters of rivers, lakes and seas for nearly half a billion years. What were the early fishes like?

I n the world today, there are over 21,000 kinds of fishes. That's over twice the number of bird species, and five times the number of mammals.

Arandaspis

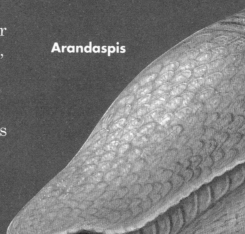

THE FIRST VERTEBRATES

Fishes were the first vertebrates – animals with backbones. The vertebrates include all fishes, amphibians, reptiles, birds and mammals. The fishes appeared in the oceans over 500 million years ago.

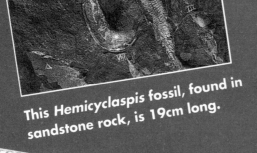

This *Hemicyclaspis* fossil, found in sandstone rock, is 19cm long.

LOOK, NO JAWS

The first fish had no proper fins. They had no proper jaws either. They were called agnathans, or jawless fishes. They had round mouths and sucked up small bits and pieces of food from the sea bed. Some grubbed in the mud, some sucked the meat off dead sea creatures, and some filtered tiny animals from the water.

THE 'SHELL SKINS'

Many jawless fishes had protective plates of bone over their bodies. These plates made good fossils. One of the first jawless fishes was *Arandaspis* which lived about 470 million years ago in the Ordovician Period, in seas that covered Australia. It was about 15cm long, with a strong back shield covered by tiny studs, and two tiny eyes near the front.

Hemicyclaspis

Close-up view of a modern lamprey's circular mouth showing its horny teeth.

IT'S A FACT

THAT THERE ARE STILL JAWLESS FISHES TODAY

There are two main kinds of fishes today that have no jaws: lampreys and hagfishes. A lamprey clamps its mouth on to a larger fish, and sucks out the blood and fluids. The hagfish looks like a slimy, eye-less worm. It has a rasping tongue and can eat its way into a dying fish.

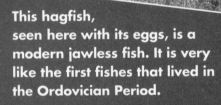

This hagfish, seen here with its eggs, is a modern jawless fish. It is very like the first fishes that lived in the Ordovician Period.

Pteraspis

LIFE ON THE BOTTOM

Another jawless fish was *Hemicyclaspis*, which lived about 400 million years ago. Again, it was small – up to 19cm long. It had a rounded head shield and eyes on the top of its head. It was covered in scales, and had the beginnings of a tail. It probably lived on the sea bed, sucking food from the ooze.

STRANGE SHAPES

During the Silurian and Devonian Periods, fishes evolved all manner of strange shapes. *Pteraspis* had about eight sets of plates of bony armour on its head, and a long snout like a pointed beak. It also had a large spine on its back. Many of the early fishes were small, but *Pteraspis* was tiny, only about as long as your finger. All of these fishes had mouths like suckers or files. Jaws were to be the next great evolutionary invention.

Macropoma

Bothriolepis

Climatius

Is it true

that jaws evolved from gills?

Probably. The first fishes had arches of cartilage or bone on each side of the head. These supported the gills, through which fishes breathed. Over millions of years, these arches changed and developed. The first arch formed part of the skull. The second arch developed into the jaws and the third one formed the jaw joint. And hey presto, biting was invented!

THE COMING OF JAWS

Another big group of early fishes were the acanthodians. They evolved about 400 million years ago and flourished for about 150 million years. They were small and lived in fresh water. They were probably the first of all vertebrates to have jaws. Now fishes could open their mouths!

FISH-FINGER-SIZED FISH

Climatius was a small acanthodian, about the size of a fish-finger. It had two curved, shark-like fins on its back, front and back fins on its belly, and also five extra pairs of fins along its underside. *Acanthodes*, which lived during the Devonian Period, was about 30cm long and had only three sets of fins. It also had fewer, smaller scales, and looked more like today's eel.

The first jawless fishes had nine arches of bone that protected their delicate gills.

Gradually, over millions of years these bones altered to form part of the skull and the jaws of later fishes.

MORE ARMOURED FISHES

The placoderms, or 'plated skins', also had jaws and bony armour over their heads and the fronts of their bodies. But this armour was jointed, so they could twist their heads and necks. With several sets of fins, they looked more like modern fishes. They lived over 400 million years ago.

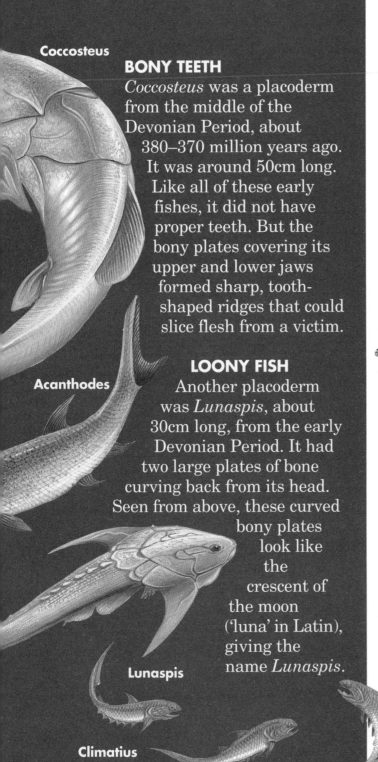

Coccosteus

BONY TEETH

Coccosteus was a placoderm from the middle of the Devonian Period, about 380–370 million years ago. It was around 50cm long. Like all of these early fishes, it did not have proper teeth. But the bony plates covering its upper and lower jaws formed sharp, tooth-shaped ridges that could slice flesh from a victim.

Acanthodes

LOONY FISH

Another placoderm was *Lunaspis*, about 30cm long, from the early Devonian Period. It had two large plates of bone curving back from its head. Seen from above, these curved bony plates look like the crescent of the moon ('luna' in Latin), giving the name *Lunaspis*.

Lunaspis

Climatius

CRAB-LEG FINS

Bothriolepis, also a placoderm, had front fins that looked like crab's legs. They were rounded, hollow tubes each with two joints. No other vertebrate animal had such limbs. *Bothriolepis* was about 35cm long and had a small, weak mouth, so it probably fed on small, soft bits of food.

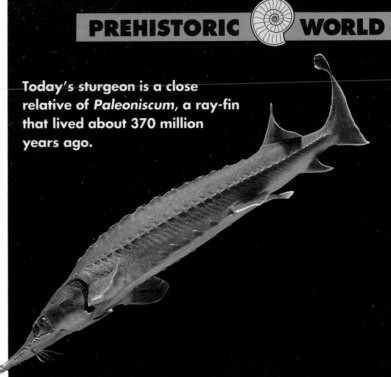

Today's sturgeon is a close relative of *Paleoniscum*, a ray-fin that lived about 370 million years ago.

BEGINNINGS OF BONY FISHES

Most fishes alive today are bony fishes. These appeared about 370 million years ago. Most belong to a group called ray-fins. *Paleoniscum*, an early ray-fin, was related to today's sturgeon. *Lepidotes* swam in the seas during the Jurassic, when dinosaurs ruled the world, as did *Leptolepis*.

THE LOBE-FINS

Another group of bony fishes was the lobe-fins. *Eusthenopteron* was probably a link in the evolution from fishes to amphibians. *Macropoma* was an early coelacanth. Coelacanths were thought to have died out over 60 million years ago until one was discovered in the 1930s, swimming in the seas near south-east Africa. A fossil had come back to life!

Today's coelacanth is a living fossil!

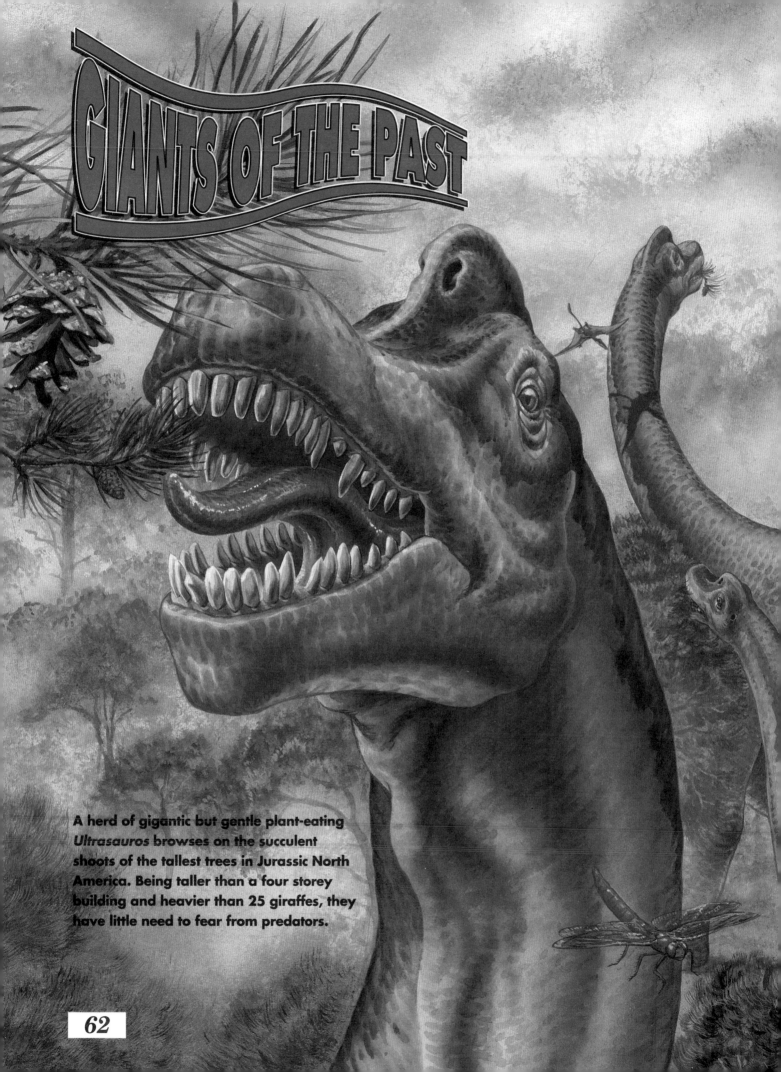

GIANTS OF THE PAST

A herd of gigantic but gentle plant-eating *Ultrasauros* browses on the succulent shoots of the tallest trees in Jurassic North America. Being taller than a four storey building and heavier than 25 giraffes, they have little need to fear from predators.

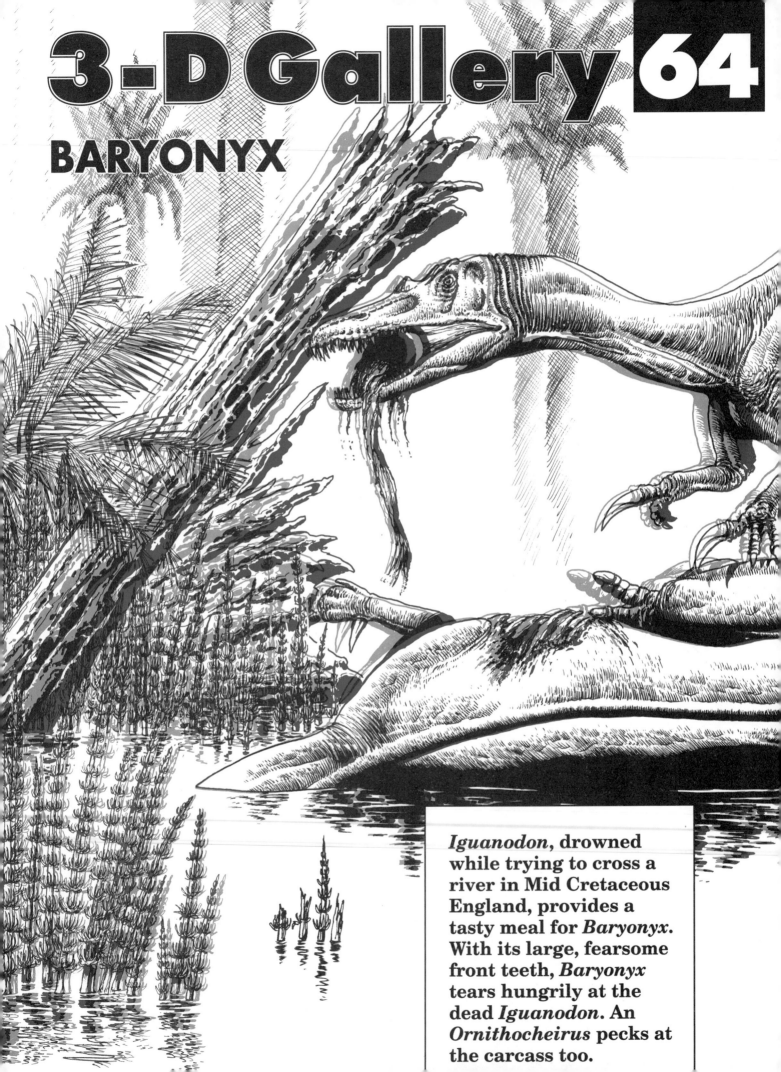

3-D Gallery 64

BARYONYX

Iguanodon, drowned while trying to cross a river in Mid Cretaceous England, provides a tasty meal for *Baryonyx*. With its large, fearsome front teeth, *Baryonyx* tears hungrily at the dead *Iguanodon*. An *Ornithocheirus* pecks at the carcass too.

In the swim

Water is much thicker than air. To move in water, animals such as fishes have evolved special equipment.

When you dive into water you stretch your arms above your head, hands touching and make a pointed shape. As you hit the water your hands cut through it easily so that you travel faster and further.

Eye

Gill cover protects delicate gills

Rows of teeth for catching prey

Enchodus appeared just as the dinosaurs died out. Designed for hunting in the open seas, it was lightweight and streamlined. *Enchodus* was a skilled hunter and probably caught fishes in its teeth-lined jaw

CUTTING THROUGH
Think of all the good swimmers in the animal kingdom – fishes, seals, dolphins. They all have the same basic shape: pointed at the front, thicker in the middle, tapering towards the back and finishing in fins or flippers. This streamlined shape is perfect for cutting through water. Submarines copy this shape from nature.

Dolphins, sea lions and submarines all share a streamlined shape. They can move through water easily.

POWERING ALONG
The tail of a fish is its engine room. Strong muscles move the tail from side to side and this movement pushes the fish forward through the water.

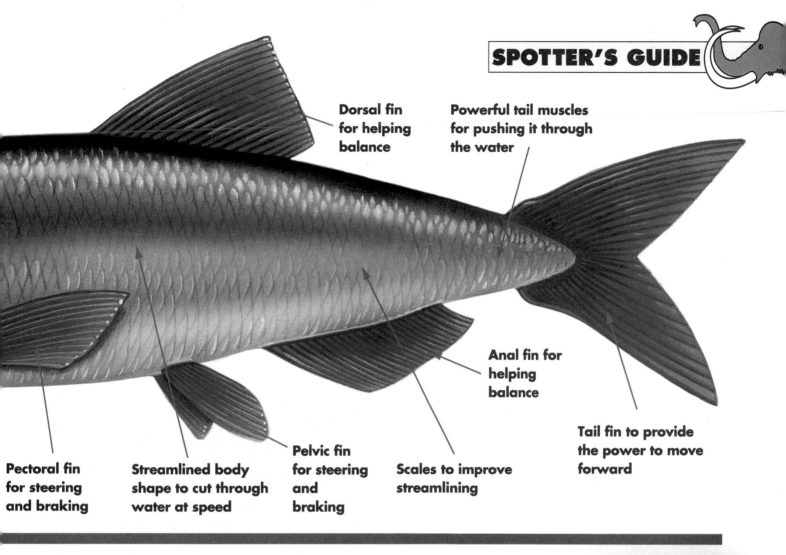

Dorsal fin for helping balance

Powerful tail muscles for pushing it through the water

Anal fin for helping balance

Tail fin to provide the power to move forward

Pectoral fin for steering and braking

Streamlined body shape to cut through water at speed

Pelvic fin for steering and braking

Scales to improve streamlining

FIN AND SCALE POWER

So what are fins for? To steer, so that fishes can turn sharply to catch prey or avoid being eaten; to keep the right way up, and to brake. Early fishes had heavy armour or thick scales that slowed them down. But later fishes had thinner, closer fitting scales which made them lighter and more flexible so they could swim better and faster.

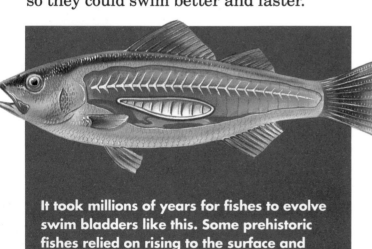

It took millions of years for fishes to evolve swim bladders like this. Some prehistoric fishes relied on rising to the surface and taking gulps of air to keep themselves afloat.

Most fishes use their fins to help them change direction.

BAGS OF GAS

Staying afloat can be difficult. It usually means swimming non-stop. But most fishes have solved this problem. They have a bag of gas in their bodies called a swim bladder. The gas is taken directly from the fishes' blood. It is lighter than water and helps keep the fish afloat. To move up and down in the water, fishes can empty the gas out of the swim bladder (they go down) or fill it (they go up).

Dinosaur detectives

Deinonychus

Finding dinosaur fossils isn't easy. All the palaeontologists shown here have been lucky enough to make important discoveries.

Dinosaur detectives have to be quite tough. They work in some of the most remote places in the world – deserts and mountains. They travel great distances and face many dangers and discomforts to get the fossils. On top of all this, most dinosaur detectives have spent years at university studying sciences such as geology, zoology and palaeontology.

ENVIRONMENTAL SPECIALIST
Palaeontologists are not just interested in the animals themselves, but in where and how they lived. Peter Dodson, of the University of Pennsylvania, USA, has made a study of the environments in which dinosaurs lived, died and were buried. This has helped palaeontologists to a far better understanding of how dinosaurs lived. Dodson named *Avaceratops*, the small ceratopian dinosaur, after his wife.

DEINONYCHUS DETECTIVE
John Ostrom, of Yale University's famous Peabody Museum in the USA, has discovered many fossils, but his most important find was *Deinonychus* in 1964. Ostrom loves to think about tricky problems such as whether dinosaurs

John Ostrom with *Deinonychus!*

were endothermic ('warm blooded'). He has also done some very important work on the link between birds and dinosaurs.

NEW IDEAS MAN
Dressed in a stetson (cowboy hat), check shirt and boots, Robert Bakker loves to stride about the hills with his dog, searching for dinosaurs. His kitchen is full of dinosaur bones! He is based at Denver Museum, Colorado, USA. Bakker is a dinosaur detective who is always coming up with new ideas.

LIVELY DINOSAURS?

One of Bakker's most famous theories is that dinosaurs were not lumbering plodders but energetic and agile. With other experts, he named the dinosaur *Nanotyrannus*.

CHINESE EXPERT

Dong Zhiming has found at least nine new species of dinosaur. One of his most exciting finds was a huge number of massive *Shunosaurus* in a quarry in central China. They probably died in a great flood. Dong, who is head of Beijing University's Institute of Palaeontology, China, also discovered the carnivore *Yangchuanosaurus*.

Dong Zhiming at work.

Nanotyrannus

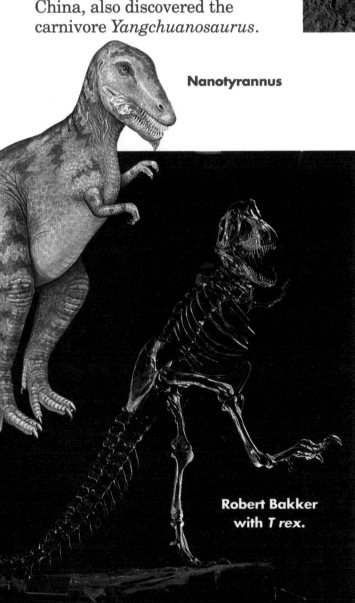
Robert Bakker with *T rex*.

DINOSAUR JIM

Jim Jensen is different from most dinosaur detectives because, instead of going to university, he taught himself about palaeontology. He went on to become curator of Brigham Young University's Earth Science Museum in the USA. He found so many fossils that he was nicknamed 'Dinosaur Jim'. Before he retired, his biggest find was the gigantic dinosaur *Ultrasauros*.

Jim Jensen with the front leg bone of *Ultrasauros*.

69

TROODON EXPERT

Philip Currie's dinosaur hunts have taken him across the world from Canada to Inner Mongolia. Currie, from the famous Royal Tyrrell Museum in Alberta, Canada, is one of the most successful dinosaur hunters in North America. With other fossil hunters, he made an enormous number of finds in Alberta, in the area now called Dinosaur Provincial Park. He has found large numbers of *Hadrosaur* babies, including nests and eggs. He is an expert on the highly intelligent, bird-like *Troodon*.

Troodon

Philip Currie

EGGSPERT HUNTER

Jack Horner is best known for discovering that *Maiasaura* looked after its young after they hatched. *Maiasaura* means 'good mother lizard'. Horner (of the Museum of the Rockies, USA) and his team discovered 14 *Maiasaura* nests, with 42 eggs and 31 babies in the rocks of Montana, USA. So many finds were made, this place is now called 'Egg Mountain'.

DESERT DETECTIVE

The French dinosaur expert Philippe Taquet, has made several expeditions to the great Sahara Desert in North Africa. There, in the sweeping sands, he discovered the extraordinary dinosaur *Ouranosaurus*, a plant-eater with a huge fin-like sail on its back.

Philippe Taquet

Ouranosaurus

Jack Horner

Maiasaura

71

A DAY IN THE LIFE OF PTERANODON

ITS OUTSTRETCHED WINGS CATCH THE WIND AND IT IS CARRIED INTO THE AIR LIKE A KITE.

KANSAS, USA, DURING THE CRETACEOUS PERIOD. A MOTHER PTERANODON HAS JUST LEFT ITS EGGS AND IS ABOUT TO RETURN TO THE SKIES IN SEARCH OF FOOD.

THE HUGE, FLYING REPTILE STANDS ON THE CLIFFTOP, ITS WINGS OUTSTRETCHED, FACING THE WIND.

ON THE GROUND, PTERANODON IS SLOW AND AWKWARD, BUT IN THE AIR, IT IS AS GRACEFUL AS AN ALBATROSS. IT USES AIR CURRENTS TO SOAR UPWARDS...

BUT SUDDENLY, A GIANT PLESIOSAURUS TORPEDOES TOWARDS THE FLYING REPTILE AND CATCHES ITS WING.

MOSASAURUS ATTACKS AGAIN, AND SURPRISED PLESIOSAURUS LOOSENS ITS GRIP ON PTERANODON'S WING.

THE STRICKEN PTERANODON DESPERATELY FLAPS ITS GOOD WING AND CATCHES A GUST THAT BEARS IT UPWARDS.

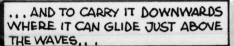

... AND TO CARRY IT DOWNWARDS WHERE IT CAN GLIDE JUST ABOVE THE WAVES...

LIKE A PREHISTORIC PELICAN, PTERANODON SPEARS A FISH IN ITS BEAK...

JUST AS MOSASAURUS IS ABOUT TO CRUNCH PTERANODON IN ITS JAGGED JAWS, A GUST OF WIND CATCHES THE PTEROSAUR'S WINGS AND IT IS CARRIED TO SAFETY.

... EVER ON THE LOOKOUT FOR FISH.

... BUT AS IT STRETCHES ITS WINGS AGAIN, A FEROCIOUS UNDERWATER KILLER SLAMS THROUGH THE WAVES.

BUT PLESIOSAURUS HAS CRUNCHED THE BRITTLE BONES IN PTERANODON'S WING AND PTERANODON CAN DO NOTHING TO STOP ITSELF SPIRALLING DOWNWARDS AND DOWNWARDS TOWARDS THE SEA.

BUT EVEN IF PTERANODON IS DEAD...

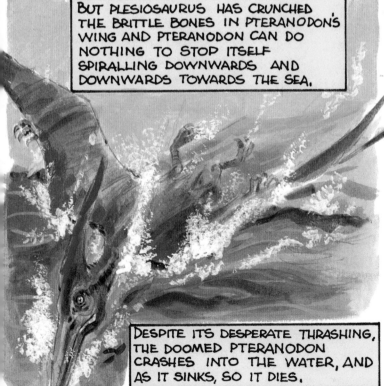

DESPITE ITS DESPERATE THRASHING, THE DOOMED PTERANODON CRASHES INTO THE WATER, AND AS IT SINKS, SO IT DIES.

... ITS EGGS HAVE HATCHED AND AT LEAST ONE OF THE YOUNG HAS SURVIVED LONG ENOUGH TO HOBBLE TO THE CLIFFTOP. IT INSTINCTIVELY STRETCHES ITS WINGS AND WAITS FOR THE WIND TO CARRY IT OFF.

Improve and test your knowledge with...

FACT FILE

Ichthyosaurus holds all the answers. See how you score in the quiz.

Rubber bones
In the Triassic sandstones of Scotland the fossil reptile bones have dissolved away, leaving holes in the rock. Scientists can fill these holes with liquid rubber, and when it hardens they can chip away the sandstone and study the rubber casts of the bones.

1 *Ultrasauros* was taller than:
a) a four storey building
b) a football post
c) the Empire State Building

2 The first fish did not have:
a) eyes
b) fins
c) tails

3 How did the prehistoric fish *Lunaspis* get its name?
a) it swam like a lunatic
b) its bony plates were moon-shaped
c) it was named after a fisherman

4 *Mesosaurus* was a small swimming:
a) dinosaur
b) reptile
c) mammal

5 What are fins for?
a) eating and drinking
b) steering, balancing and braking
c) fetching and carrying

6 What did *Ultrasauros* have to protect itself?
a) sharp teeth
b) bony armour
c) sharp claws

7 The dinosaur *Harpymimus* had:
a) big feet
b) big ears
c) tiny teeth

8 *Astrapotherium* probably had:
a) a flexible trunk
b) a long tail
c) a pair of horns

Dainty feet
Dinosaur footprints only 1cm long have been found in the USA. They have four toes and so probably came from a dinosaur related to Fabrosaurus.

74

Red or black?

Most pictures of mammoths show them with reddish hair. This is because the mammoth hair found preserved in frozen mud is red. Experts now think the colour changed over the centuries, and the original mammoth hair colour was black.

Creepy zoo

In the Carboniferous coal forests there were dragonflies as big as macaws, centipedes as big as crocodiles, and scorpions the size of cats!

9 **Who discovered *Deinonychus* in 1964?**
a) Dinosaur Jim
b) Robert Bakker
c) John Ostrom

10 **What sort of animal was *Arthropleura*?**
a) a giant spider
b) a giant millipede
c) a giant dragonfly

Flying Stegosaurus

Edgar Rice Burroughs, who created Tarzan, wrote many adventure books about dinosaurs in the 1920s. In one he had a Stegosaurus flying, using its plates as wings!

ASK THE EXPERT

Dr. David Norman of Cambridge University answers your dinosaur questions

Did prehistoric mammals protect their young after they had been born?

Yes. One of the characteristics of mammals is that they rear their young from birth. The mother gives birth to her babies and then suckles them on her milk. During this time the young grow very quickly (mother's milk is very nutritious) and get an education in how to survive.

Why did amphibians like Ichthyostega lay their eggs in water?

Ichthyostega was one of the first animals capable of walking on land. It had evolved from fishes, and it simply kept the habit of reproducing in water. It is also the case that animals such as *Ichthyostega* spent a great deal of time in water. They still used gills for breathing for at least part of the time, and had a long fin on their tail which shows that they were accomplished swimmers. So animals like *Ichthyostega* laid eggs in water because it was the obvious thing to do!

Why have no 'giant' mammals survived while smaller ones have?

It is a very sad fact that when humans first appeared in significant numbers in the fossil record about 10,000 years ago, the larger mammal groups declined very rapidly. It seems likely that early human hunters killed all the large mammals and that is why mammoths the size of dinosaurs are no longer with us.

Has the crest of Dilophosaurus ever been found in one piece?

Dilophosaurus' crest, probably used to frighten enemies or to attract mates, was very delicate. We have not found a complete pair of these ridges on any skull so far. Since we only know the shape of the base of the crest, we can only guess at its exact shape.

DINOSAURS!

DISCOVER THE GIANTS OF THE PREHISTORIC WORLD

ICHTHYOSTEGA

Ichthyostega was one of the first animals to leave the water and walk on four legs.

A bout 340 million years ago, before the continents began to drift apart, Greenland was closer to the Equator and the climate there was quite warm. *Ichthyostega* lived in Greenland, and early this century a few skeletons were found.

A FISH ON LEGS

This fish-like animal moved slowly on land and kept close to freshwater lakes and rivers where it found plenty of food. *Ichthyostega* was slightly longer than a badger of today. It looked rather like a fish on legs! As well as its fishy tail, *Ichthyostega* had many other features that show links with its fishy ancestors. Its slender, tapering shape was streamlined like the body of a swimmer and its head was low and pointed.

FISHY TAIL

Ichthyostega's tail was quite long with a thin fin running along the top and bottom, a bit like that of a fish. Experts have also found that the shape of the bones of its back are very like those of early fish such as *Eusthenopteron*.

Pointed, streamlined head indicates it was a swimmer

Eye socket

25cm

The skull of an *Ichthyostega* (left).

These two *Ichthyostega* have crawled out of the water and lay in wait for a meal. When a fish swims past, one of the amphibians will slide into the water to devour its prey.

SIZE WISE

1m

MONSTER FACTS

- **NAME:** *Ichthyostega* (ik-thee-o-stee-ga) means 'skull like a fish'
- **GROUP:** amphibian
- **SIZE:** about 1m long
- **FOOD:** fish and occasionally worms
- **LIVED:** about 340 million years ago in the Late Devonian Period in Greenland

FISH OUT OF WATER

As one of the earliest known amphibians, *Ichthyostega* could live on land and swim in water. Experts think that its scaly skin was not very waterproof but it still needed to swim in search of prey. On land, it needed a moist atmosphere in which to survive. As it crawled along the shore, a glimpse of a darting fish was likely to tempt it into shallow waters.

WIDE MOUTH

Ichthyostega had long, broad jaws lined with little spiky teeth. As it swam, it probably opened its mouth, scooped up its prey and snapped the jaw shut over the trapped victim.

SPRAWLING CRAWLER

The biggest clue to *Ichthyostega*'s lifestyle lies in the fact that it had four limbs where a fish has fins. These were fully formed like a land animal's legs and attached to the body by strong bones. This shows that *Ichthyostega*'s weight could be supported on dry land. Like a modern newt or salamander, it had sprawling limbs on either side of its body. *Ichthyostega* is one of the earliest known tetrapods or four-limbed animals.

Is it true

that amphibians sometimes have special types of tongue?

Yes, amphibians were the very first creatures that had tongues which could shoot out to catch insects. Some of today's amphibians, such as salamanders, have tongues that are sticky. With a sticky tongue a salamander can easily catch an insect flying past. Perhaps *Ichthyostega* also had a sticky tongue?

ARALOSAURUS

Aralosaurus had a ridge above its eyes like Hadrosaurus, and probably grew to be longer than today's elephant.

xperts think that *Aralosaurus* was related to *Maiasaura*. Like the 'good mother' dinosaur, *Aralosaurus* probably lived in large herds and laid its eggs in shared nesting sites.

DEEP END
Aralosaurus walked among the flowers and trees of the Cretaceous on two strong legs. Its head and front legs were balanced by a long, deep tail.

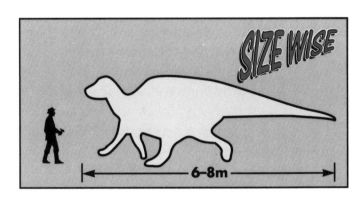

MONSTER FACTS

- **NAME:** Aralosaurus (a-ral-o-saw-rus) means 'Aral reptile' as it was found near the Aral Sea
- **GROUP:** dinosaur
- **SIZE:** about 6–8m long
- **FOOD:** plants
- **LIVED:** about 75 million years ago in the Late Cretaceous Period in Kazakhstan, central Asia

TWIG CRUSHER
Aralosaurus could bite into tough twigs with its wide, toothless beak. But it never suffered from indigestion! Evidence from its skull shows how its teeth were arranged in rows to form a flat, grinding surface. With the help of its strong jaw muscles, *Aralosaurus* could crush and slice even the toughest food.

FLOWER POWER
Many other hadrosaurids lived at the same time as *Aralosaurus* and some experts think that their numbers increased because they could eat the new flowering plants that flourished 75 million years ago.

EUSTHENOPTERON

Eusthenopteron was a fish that could survive out of water because it had lungs as well as gills.

The seasonal hot, dry weather of the Devonian Period held great dangers for water-living creatures. As lakes and pools dried up, fishes were left stranded, and died. The only survivors were animals such as *Eusthenopteron* that could breathe air until they found more water in which to live.

FOOT FINS

Eusthenopteron's back and skull were very like those of early amphibians. Inside its fins there were a number of small bones. These later evolved into the leg bones and feet of amphibians. Such strong fins helped *Eusthenopteron* drag itself along the ground when it needed to find a new source of water.

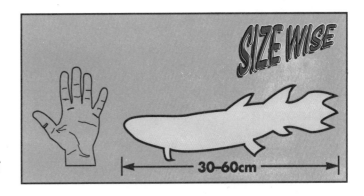

SIZE WISE

30–60cm

MONSTER FACTS

- **NAME:** *Eusthenopteron* (yoos-then-<u>op</u>-ter-un) means 'strong fin'
- **GROUP:** fish
- **SIZE:** about 30–60cm long
- **FOOD:** fish
- **LIVED:** about 350 million years ago in the Late Devonian Period in fresh and salt waters of Europe and North America

BACK FLIP

As it lurked in shallow waters, *Eusthenopteron* lay in wait for other, smaller fish to swim by. An adult may even have been tempted to eat its own young. If a quick escape was necessary, a young *Eusthenopteron* may have flipped its body on to dry land to avoid an early death.

THREE-PRONGED

Eusthenopteron had paired fins along the back half of its long body. It grew to be twice as long as this page and had a tail fin that was unusual and quite distinctive. This fin curved into three prongs like Neptune's trident.

Sharks rule – okay!

Sharks have ruled the seas since the Age of Dinosaurs.

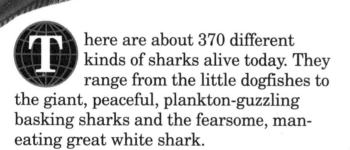

Xenacanthus

There are about 370 different kinds of sharks alive today. They range from the little dogfishes to the giant, peaceful, plankton-guzzling basking sharks and the fearsome, man-eating great white shark.

IT'S A FACT

SHARKS HAVE TO KEEP SWIMMING

To keep afloat sharks have to keep swimming, otherwise they sink to the sea bed. Unlike other fishes, they do not have a swim bladder full of gas to keep them afloat, so they propel themselves along with the powerful thrust of their tails. If they stop beating their tails, they sink. Unlike other fishes, sharks cannot use their fins as brakes either. If a shark charges, it has to swerve aside to avoid a collision.

SPECIAL FISHES

Sharks are fishes. But unlike all the bony fishes, they have a skeleton made of cartilage, not bones, and they have scales shaped like tiny teeth. All the bony fishes have flat scales. Another difference from bony fishes is that sharks do not have swim bladders and have to keep moving all the time.

NO BONES ABOUT IT

Along with their close relatives, the skates and rays, sharks form a group called the cartilaginous fishes. Their skeletons are made of cartilage, not of bone. Cartilage is tough and gristly, but also flexible. It works well as a shark's skeleton but it decays more quickly, so it is less likely to form fossils.

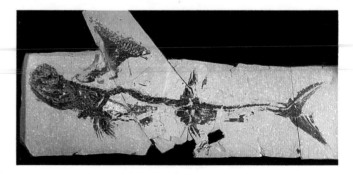

This *Stethacanthus* fossil clearly shows the shark's curious crest.

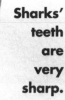
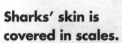

Sharks' teeth are very sharp.

Sharks' skin is covered in scales.

EARLY-BIRD SHARK

Some of the earliest shark fossils yet discovered were found by an American fossil hunter, Dr William Kepler, in the 1880s. He discovered impressions of teeth, the harder bits of cartilage, the skin and body outline, and even some of the muscles. This very early shark is called *Cladoselache*. It was up to 2m long and had the typical streamlined shark shape.

Cladoselache

EEL-LIKE SHARK

Xenacanthus was another early shark from the Devonian and Permian Periods. It looked like a cross between a shark and an eel. It had a long body, one long fin along its back, and a tail tapering to a point. Like many prehistoric sharks, it had a spine on its head.

TONNES OF TEETH

On the other hand, shark teeth often get preserved as fossils. All sharks constantly grow new teeth. They form in rows around the back of the jaw, and as the old ones drop out, the new ones move towards the front, ready to take their first bite.

ROUGH SKIN

Other bits that fossilized include the spines that stuck out from the bodies of some prehistoric sharks, and also the shark's tiny, tooth-shaped skin scales. These are called denticles, and they are different from the thin, flat scales of other fishes. Denticles make a shark's skin very tough, and rough to touch.

Today's dogfish is actually a small shark.

Today's Blue Shark (left) has to keep moving to stay alive.

Stethacanthus

HITCH-HIKER SHARK?

Stethacanthus was another Carboniferous shark with head-gear. It had a crest sticking up from its head, which could have been a sucker for sticking to larger fish so that this 1m-long shark could hitch a ride!

SHARKS WITH SUNSHADES

There were some very strange sharks during the Carboniferous Period, around 350–280 million years ago. *Falcatus* was a tiny shark, only about 15cm long. It had a weird spine that stuck up from its neck and bent over its head, like a flat sunshade! Only adult males grew this odd spine, so it may have been for displaying to females when breeding.

SHARK 'ANTLERS'

About 325 million years ago, *Harpagofutator*, the owner of another weird head-dress, sped though the seas. It had two forked branches on its head. Scientists have discovered that only the males had these fishy 'antlers', so perhaps they too were used to attract females when it was time to mate.

Harpagofutator

Six people may have been able to fit inside this prehistoric shark's jaws.

INTO THE CRETACEOUS

As dinosaurs spread on land during the Jurassic and Cretaceous Periods, sharks were still at large in the seas. *Hybodus* was over 2m long and looked incredibly similar to the Bull Shark of today.

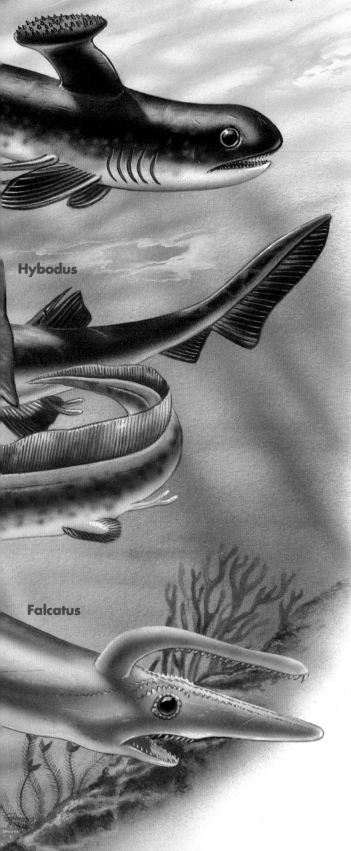

Hybodus

Falcatus

MEGA SHARK

The biggest killer shark that ever lived was probably an extinct relative of today's Great White Shark. This prehistoric killer lived about 50 million years ago and was called *Carcharadon megalodon*, the mega-great-white. This giant is known only from its teeth. Each tooth was up to 15cm long, almost as big as an adult human hand.

Today's Great White Shark is related to the mega-shark, *Carcharadon megalodon*, which was the biggest shark ever to have lived.

A FAIRLY BIG GIANT

Years ago, experts compared the teeth of the modern Great White to its fossil mega-relative. They estimated that the mega-shark was up to 24m long, with a mouth 2.7m across that could open 1.8m and fit about six people inside! But this is probably too big. Modern estimates put the length of this extinct mega-great-white at 13m, compared to today's great white at about 9m, and the biggest of all sharks, the whale shark, at 17m.

Is it true

that sharks came before dinosaurs?
Yes. Sharks appeared in the Devonian Period, more than 140 million years before the dinosaurs. They have lived in the seas of the world for about 400 million years and are one of the great success stories of life on Earth.

GIANTS OF THE PAST

In the swampy, damp atmosphere of the Devonian Period, 340 million years ago, these *Ichthyostega* are lying in wait for their dinner – unsuspecting fish. One has already caught a tasty morsel in his broad jaws and is about to devour it. These scaly amphibians were equally happy living on swampy land or in the water.

3-D Gallery

PSITTACOSAURUS

A herd of *Psittacosaurus* takes shelter in a sandstorm about 100 million years ago in Mongolia. They are disturbed by the presence nearby of a passing *Shamosaurus*. On the alert, they can, if necessary, run away speedily on their strong back legs.

Horns

Horns, whether big or small, were an important form of defence for many of the prehistoric plant-eaters.

Some animals can rely on their speed to escape danger. Slow, lumbering creatures need more protection. From *Elasmotherium*'s spectacular horn to the six strange knobs on *Uintatherium*'s head, these weapons were an asset to their owners. They often used them to frighten away enemies.

Elasmotherium

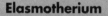

CHARGE!

Imagine *Elasmotherium* charging at you with its head bent. It would be terrifying! This early rhinoceros lived in Europe and Asia during the Pleistocene. It was as big as a modern elephant and its single horn stood high above its head.

CATAPULT HORNS

Halfway between an elephant and a rhinoceros in size, huge *Brontotherium* lived on the open plains of North America about 35 million years ago. Its catapult-like horns were above its snout. As males had larger horns, experts think that they fought with rivals.

Brontotherium

MULTI-HORNED

Uintatherium had three pairs of horns which sprouted like bony knobs from its gigantic head. It lived where the Uinta mountains stand in Colorado, North America. Males had an extra pair of weapons in the shape of two long, strong 'fangs'. It probably used its 'six-horned' head in defence against enemies and also in battles to win a mate.

Uintatherium

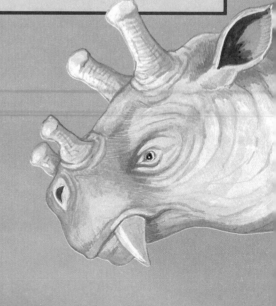

Y HORNS

Synthetoceras was about the same size as a modern deer. It lived in North America about 10 million years ago. The males had bizarre y-shaped horns which grew to be longer than the animal's head.

Synthetoceras

SIDE BY SIDE

Arsinoitherium had two large, flat horns which stood side by side above its snout. The horns were covered with a layer of skin like the knobs on a giraffe's head. *Arsinoitherium*'s horns were light with spaces inside which made them almost hollow.

Arsinoitherium

HAIR HORNS

The horns of the rhinoceros are made from hair. When the hairs become stuck together they are amazingly strong. *Dicerorhinus* was a prehistoric rhinoceros which lived in Central Europe over a million years ago. It had two horns, one above the other, with the longer horn nearest to its snout.

Dicerorhinus

RODENT HORNS

About the size of a small rabbit, *Epigaulus* belonged to the rodent family, which includes mice, rats and beavers. It lived in the mid-west of Miocene North America. This strange little mammal had a short pair of triangular horns right above its nose.

Epigaulus

The horns of today's rhinos resemble their ancestors'.

SPIRAL TOP

Little *Paleoreas* had two spiral horns which stood straight up from the top of its head like the Arabian Oryx of today. Both males and females had horns. *Paleoreas* lived in Europe, Asia and North Africa over seven million years ago.

Arabian Oryx

Paleoreas

91

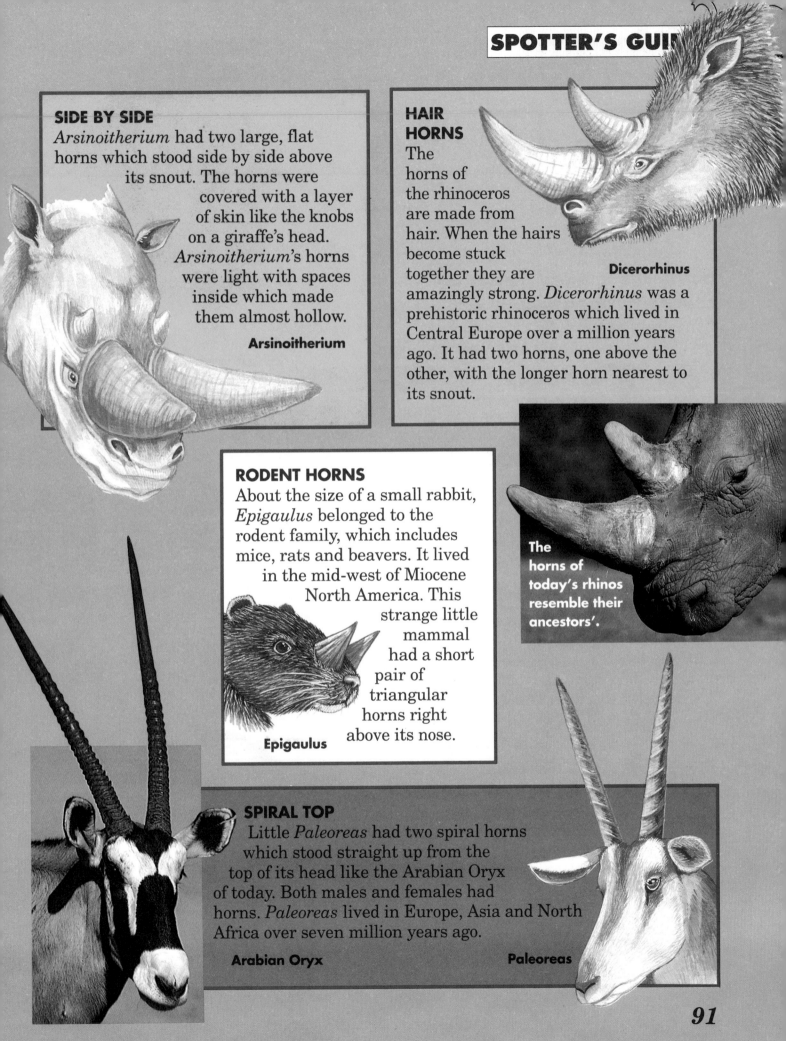

Out of the water

Hundreds of millions of years ago a wonderful thing happened – fishes began to walk!

The first fishes crawled out of the water about 370 million years ago. By doing this they changed the whole course of evolution. All land-living creatures with backbones are descended from these early adventurers. But how and why did this amazing advance occur? Scientists have pieced together the puzzle from the following vital clues.

PLANT POWER

Experts believe it was the water plants that led the way. There was no life on land for many millions of years. Then around 430 million years ago the first plants took root on shore. One of the earliest was a marsh plant called *Cooksonia*.

The skull and forelimb of *Eusthenopteron*, a lobe-fin fish.

With simple lungs, this early lobe-fin slides on to the land where it can feast on insects and mites.

Is it true

that the first fish crawled out of the water on to land to find more water?

It sounds weird but it is one theory. The idea is that when their ponds dried up, the lobe-fins needed to find more water in a hurry. Experts think that could be one of the reasons why they used their fins like legs – to stagger to new ponds in times of drought.

INSECTS APPEAR

Once the first plants had established themselves, insects, mites and spiders followed. Soon worms burrowed in the mud and moist vegetation. A whole new world grew up full of good things to eat.

A FEAST ON LAND

Some fish had simple lungs and so could hunt for insects around the edge of the water. Keen to take advantage of the food on shore, they evolved to feast on land.

LUNG POWER

Fishes that could breathe in the air as well as underwater appeared about 390 million years ago. They were called lobe-fins and were probably the first fishes to venture on to land. *Eusthenopteron* was a lobe-fin. It had lungs like us for breathing air, and gills like a fish for breathing in water.

LEARNING TO WALK

Lobe-fins had bony fins under their bodies, which they used like legs to push their bodies out of the shallows and wriggle their way across the ground.

Today's mudskippers behave like the early lobe-fins, wriggling across the mud.

This rare Australian Lungfish has a single lung as well as gills. It looks very like the lobe-fins did around 390 million years ago.

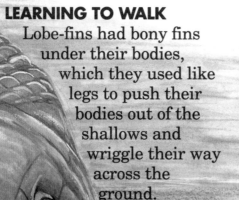

MOVING ON

How did a clumsy lobe-fin survive on land? Over millions of years, its body shape changed. Its fins turned into sturdy legs and it evolved into the first amphibian.

FISH FINGERS

Experts discovered that many lobe-fins had the same bones in their fins as the early amphibians had in their arms and legs. Amphibians were the first creatures with backbones to have fingers and toes. Our arm and hand bones are still the same today.

STRONGER BACKS

Early amphibians still looked like fish. To walk they had to raise their bodies off the ground. So they developed a strong backbone with an arch to hold the body up. One of the first amphibians was *Ichthyostega*. It was powerfully built with a thick backbone and ribs and strong joints to support it legs.

A human hand today has the same bone structure as that of an early amphibian.

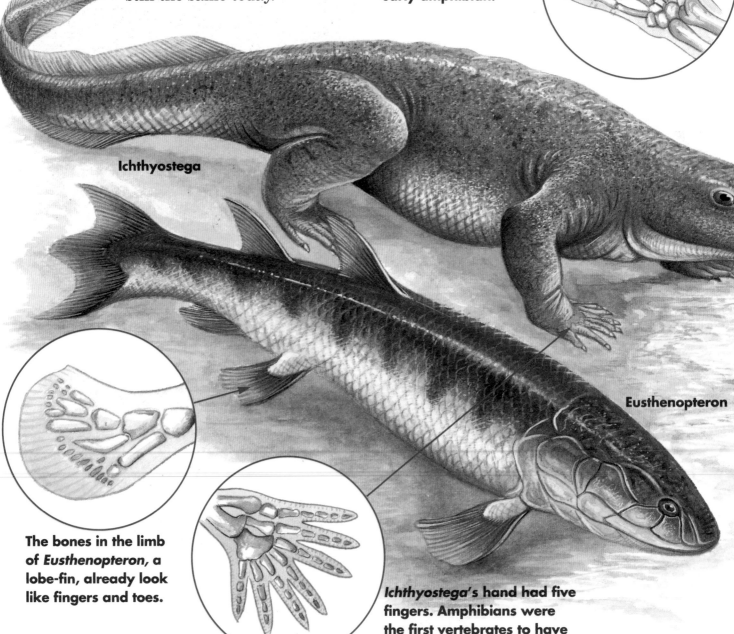

Ichthyostega

Eusthenopteron

The bones in the limb of *Eusthenopteron*, a lobe-fin, already look like fingers and toes.

Ichthyostega's hand had five fingers. Amphibians were the first vertebrates to have fingers and toes.

94

Like the pillars of a bridge, *Ichthyostega's* sturdy legs support the weight of its body

Arched backbone makes *Ichthyostega's* back strong like the arch of this natural bridge

... AND BEFOR
SAFETY, VELO

VELOCIRAPTO
SPOTS A BAB
THAT HAS SHUFF
OFF A LITTLE FR
THE REST OF T
HERD. EASY PR
FOR A FLEET-FOO
THIEF LIKE
VELOCIRAPTOR

DESPITE T
IN ITS CHEST,
STRONG FOR
WRESTLE ITSE

BUT
FROM
ITS CH
SINKS
THE OT

DEEP BREATHS

Lobe-fins had simple lungs. They could breathe when out of water just long enough to snap up insects living on the river banks. But they could not survive in the air for long.

POWERFUL LUNGS

They had to evolve powerful lungs to become amphibians. Experts think *Ichthyostega* probably breathed by lowering the floor of its mouth to draw air in, and raising it to pump air down into its lungs.

FISH FANGS

Experts have found another vital clue to prove that the first amphibian evolved from a fish. They have discovered that early amphibian teeth were almost identical to some lobe-fin teeth.

The shape of *Ichthyostega's* backbone was similar to that of this natural bridge. This curved shape is very strong and allowed this amphibian to raise its body up and walk on land.

IT'S A FACT

AMPHIBIANS CAN HEAR LIKE US

Sound travels in a different way on land than it does in water. Fish 'hear' by sensing the vibrations made by sound moving through the water. But amphibians have developed both pockets of air and pools of water inside their heads. Amphibians hear when sound travels into their ears and vibrates through these pockets of air and pools of water. We hear in the same way.

95

VELOC
AMONG
SMALL N
YESTERD
ALREADY
BONES

BUT E
IS GIVING
IT IS A
SOUND

BEFOR
ONE SI
INTO IT

A D
VE

SCUTOSAURUS

Scutosaurus was a large, lumbering herbivorous reptile with a spiked head and bony armour.

turdy *Scutosaurus* belonged to the pareiasaur family which first appeared in southern Africa during the mid-Permian Period. Several million years later, many pareiasaurs moved into eastern Europe and Asia. *Scutosaurus* and its relatives died out around 245 million years ago.

STRAIGHT LEGS

Scutosaurus walked on four massive, pillar-like legs. Like the bulky dinosaurs which came later, *Scutosaurus* needed its strong legs and broad feet to support its heavy body.

SIZE WISE

2.5m

MONSTER FACTS

- **NAME:** *Scutosaurus* (<u>skoo</u>-toh-<u>saw</u>-rus) means 'shield reptile'
- **GROUP:** reptile
- **SIZE:** 2.5m long
- **FOOD:** plants
- **LIVED:** about 260 million years ago in the Late Permian Period in Russia

THICK SKINNED

Scutosaurus moved slowly through the firs and pines of the Permian landscape. It ate plants and soft shoots, probably using its small, saw-edged teeth to slice through the vegetation. Thick body armour and a spiked head made this reptile safe from predators as it lumbered along hunting for food.

104

PISANOSAURUS

Some experts think that chicken-sized *Pisanosaurus* was the first ornithopod, or bird-hipped, dinosaur.

Unfortunately, not enough is known about this little dinosaur to be certain that it was the earliest of the bird-hipped dinosaurs. Only parts of its backbone, jaw, leg and foot have so far been discovered. Scientists need more evidence before they can be sure of this creature's origins.

AGILE MOVER

Pisanosaurus was less than 1m long and its slender tail made up almost half its length. It was an extremely agile dinosaur and moved swiftly and easily across the fern-covered ground of Triassic Argentina.

SIZE WISE

|← 90cm →|

MONSTER FACTS

- **NAME:** *Pisanosaurus* (pi-<u>zan</u>-o-saw-rus) means 'Pisano's reptile'
- **SIZE:** 90cm long
- **GROUP:** dinosaur
- **FOOD:** plants
- **LIVED:** about 210 million years ago in the Late Triassic Period in Argentina, South America

FREE HANDS

As it walked on its two long back legs, this little dinosaur kept its hands free to tug at low-growing plants and leaves. Like *Lesothosaurus*, it had small, pointed teeth which it probably used to chew up the woody parts of plants.

EXPLODING PLANTS

Once small plants like *Cooksonia* had got a root-hold on the empty land, there was an explosion in plant evolution. Many new groups evolved, some to giant sizes.

ROOT-HOLD

About 370 million years ago lived *Asteroxylon*, a clubmoss, about 1m tall. By Carboniferous times, 300 million years

Asteroxylon

ago, clubmosses such as *Lepidodendron* and *Sigillaria* were like giant trees, 30m high, as were horsetails, such as *Calamites*. Like all plants, whether green or red, they lived by trapping the energy from the sun, using a chemical process called photosynthesis. Both the clubmosses and horsetails survive today, but they rarely grow more than 1m tall.

FORESTS OF FERNS

Since the Carboniferous Period, many types of ferns have evolved, with their feathery-looking fronds. Some are still with us today. Tree-ferns, or marattites, were large ferns with woody stems, resembling modern palm trees. *Psaronius* was up to 10m tall, and shaded the giant amphibians of the Permian Period. Tree-ferns up to 25m tall still grow in some tropical areas.

THE FIRST SEEDS

The seed-ferns, or pteridosperms, were the first plants with true seeds (not spores as in mosses and ferns). They had feathery fronds on a short, woody stem. They flourished during the Carboniferous Period, but then gradually died away. Some, like *Medullosa,* grew to be up to 5m high.

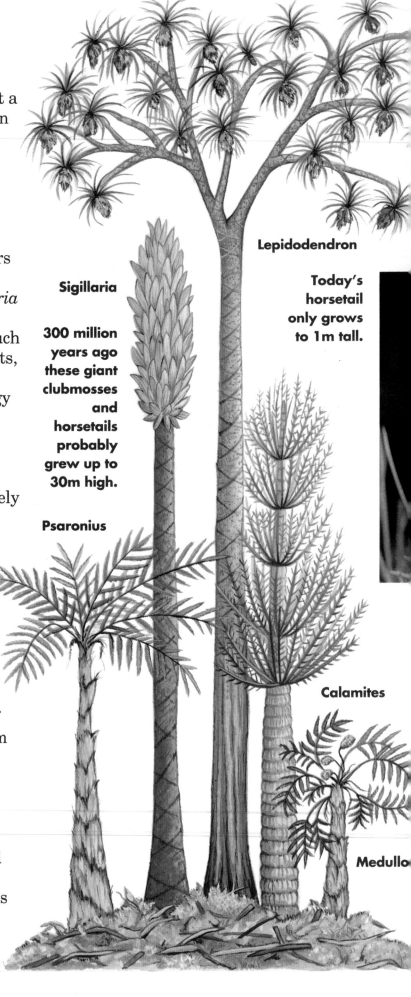

Lepidodendron

Sigillaria

Today's horsetail only grows to 1m tall.

300 million years ago these giant clubmosses and horsetails probably grew up to 30m high.

Psaronius

Calamites

Medullo

108

NAKED SEEDS

Fern-like plants called bennettites, such as *Williamsonia*, appeared at about the same time as the dinosaurs. Bennettites belonged to a successful new group – the gymnosperms, or 'naked-seed' plants.

STILL ALIVE

Cycads were also gymnosperms. They had dumpy, woody stems topped by whorls of palm-shaped fronds. Cycads were very successful during the Age of Dinosaurs.

DINO DINNERS

More gymnosperms evolved that still survive today. They include yew trees and gingkoes. The best-known gymnosperms are the conifers – fir trees, pines and larches. The first ones appeared in late Carboniferous and early Permian Periods. They had fronds arranged like upside-down umbrellas and many dinosaurs must have chomped their leaves.

FLOWERS AT LAST

The last main group, the flowering plants, or angiosperms, probably appeared over 120 million years ago. By 100 million years ago they were taking over the landscape. More than four-fifths of all plants today are flowering plants, from beautiful roses and irritating weeds to towering oak trees. Millions of years ago, the bright petals of magnolias and water lilies brought vivid new colours to the world.

NEW BURST

Plants had one more big burst of evolution. About 20 million years ago, grasses appeared. The arrival of grasslands led to a whole new batch of fleet-footed, grazing mammals.

Tree-ferns like *Williamsonia* (left) and cycads (right) provided food for plant-eating dinosaurs.

What is? PHOTOSYNTHESIS

It means 'building with light'. Special chemicals in the plant take in energy from the sun's light rays. They use this to join together simple nutrients, which the plant absorbs from the water or soil. The nutrients are built up into the plant's new roots, stems and leaves. The main photosynthetic pigment is chlorophyll, which is green – and that's why most plants are green. Red algae have carotenoids which makes them red. This is what makes carrots red too!

109

GIANTS OF THE PAST

ARCHAEOPTERYX

It is the Late Jurassic Period and central Europe is a land of hot, steamy forests. Here, *Archaeopteryx* glides through the trees searching for food. With its fiercesome beak lined with sharp, spiky teeth, the clawed fingers on its wings, and its large eyes, *Archaeopteryx* can easily catch and kill this dragonfly.

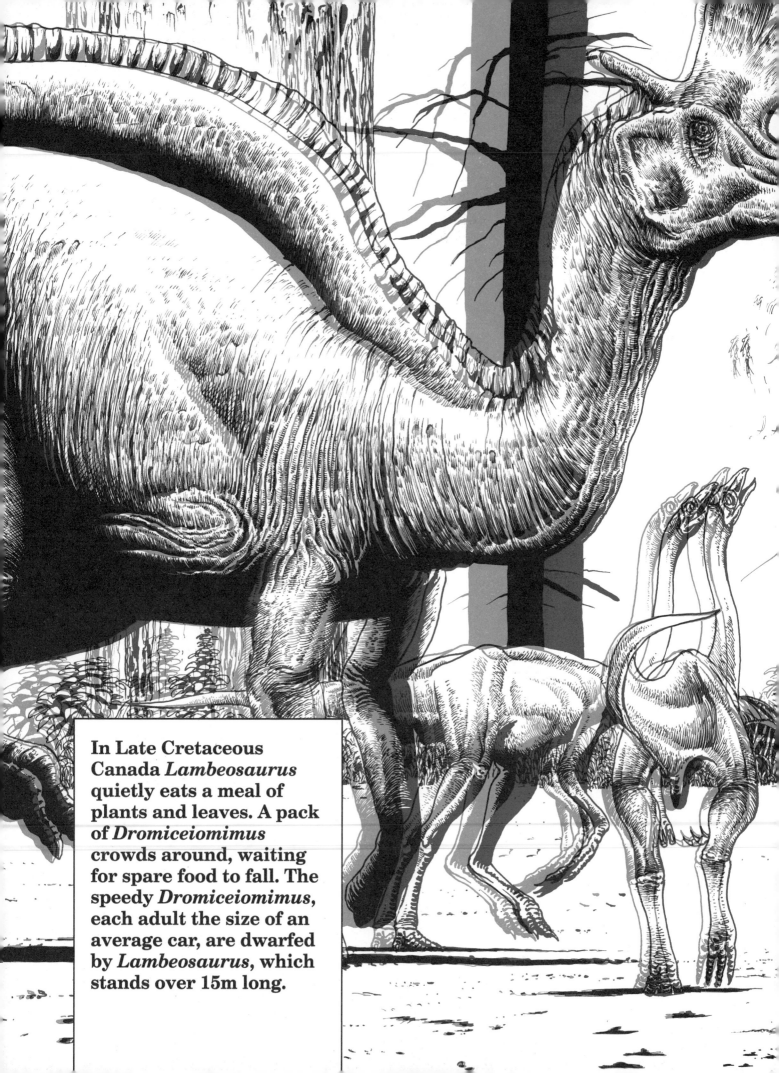

In Late Cretaceous Canada *Lambeosaurus* quietly eats a meal of plants and leaves. A pack of *Dromiceiomimus* crowds around, waiting for spare food to fall. The speedy *Dromiceiomimus*, each adult the size of an average car, are dwarfed by *Lambeosaurus*, which stands over 15m long.

DROMICEIOMIMUS

Lift off!

It is very difficult for an animal that is heavier than air to fly. Flying took millions of years to perfect, and before they could fly, animals had to evolve wings and very light bodies.

All flying creatures have wings of some sort to help them fly. Wings are a special shape. A wing that is flat underneath and curved on top is called an aerofoil. When an animal is airborne, the air flows over the top of the aerofoil faster than it flows beneath it. This difference in the speed of the air lifts the flying animal up and keeps it airborne. The wings of aeroplanes are aerofoils – but nature thought of it first!

Argentavis was the largest bird ever to fly. It lived about six million years ago and soared through the air searching for dead or dying animals on which to feed.

Strong chest muscles for flapping wings

FLAPPING FLYERS
Animals such as pterosaurs, birds and bats learned how to flap their wings to fly (birds and bats are still flapping, of course). Pushing down on the air by flapping the wings also lifts an animal and keeps it up in the air. Flapping flight helps animals to travel long distances in search of food. Some birds today have such strong muscles that they can fly for thousands of kilometres.

Light, hollow bones reduce a bird's weight and make flying easier.

THE GLIDERS AND SOARERS
Some animals do not flap their wings, they glide. Flying mammals and reptiles use flaps of skin which they stretch out so they can glide. These also act as aerofoils when flying. Many flapping flyers glide to give their wings a rest. Pterosaurs and large birds like *Argentavis* probably rode on the air currents like huge kites. When the air hit the edge of the vast aerofoil wing it lifted the animal up.

HOLLOW BONES
Large birds today, such as the albatross, also ride the air currents and can stay in the air for hours without flapping their wings. All flying animals need to be as light as possible. Bones are very heavy so, in order to fly, animals such as pterosaurs and birds needed to have bones that weighed very little. So they evolved hollow bones which were very light.

Today's Blue-footed Booby does not flap its wings to slow down, and often falls over on landing.

Long pointed wings over 7m in length for soaring and gliding

Wings were aerofoils that helped to lift *Argentavis* into the air

Lightweight skeleton is designed for flight

This Jumbo jet weighs many tonnes but can fly using aerofoils, just like a bird.

Long tail feathers for steering

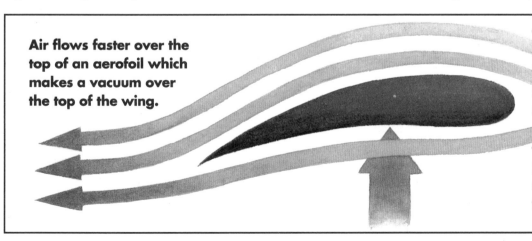

Just before landing, today's macaw spreads its wings to slow down its speed.

LIGHTEN UP

Light bones, together with wings or skin flaps, enabled these animals to get into the air and stay there more easily than an animal with heavy, solid bones. Even the gigantic prehistoric bird *Argentavis* was light enough to fly.

STEERING IN AIR

Once an animal is flying, it may need to change direction. Many birds have long, tail feathers which, like a rudder, help them turn right or left. Some birds steer with their feet too, while other flying animals use their wings to change direction.

Air flows faster over the top of an aerofoil which makes a vacuum over the top of the wing.

The air under the wing is at a higher pressure so it pushes the wing up. This keeps the owner of the wing – bird, bat, pterosaur or aeroplane – in the air.

115

Learning to fly

An animal that can fly can escape from enemies more easily and catch food that land animals cannot reach.

GLIDING INTO FLIGHT

Animals that glide do not flap their wings. They leap from a branch, open their wings or skin flaps, and let the air carry them along until they land again. Gliding may have evolved because animals that lived in trees needed to leap from tree to tree to escape a predator or to reach food.

The earliest flying animals, apart from insects, were the pterosaurs. These flying reptiles first appeared about 190 million years ago. That's 70 million years before the first bird. Experts have different theories of how these reptiles first came to fly. Did they glide or jump? Either or both theories may be correct. Sometimes evolution tries out two ways of doing the same thing.

SKINNY WINGS

Pterosaurs had wings of skin, not feathers. These may have developed from flaps of skin which helped their ancestors to glide from tree to tree.

This reptile may have glided from branch to branch to catch its prey.

ANCIENT AND MODERN GLIDERS

Several living animals, such as the flying lemur, have skin flaps so they can glide from tree to tree. We also know that several ancient reptiles, such as *Coelurosauravus* (a 'flying' lizard), glided in a similar way.

Is it true

that scientists do not really know how flight began?

Yes. Scientists are not yet certain which of these theories explains how pterosaurs, birds or bats evolved wings. Of course the evolution of wings and flight took millions of years. Perhaps one day a palaeontologist will discover a fossil that answers this question.

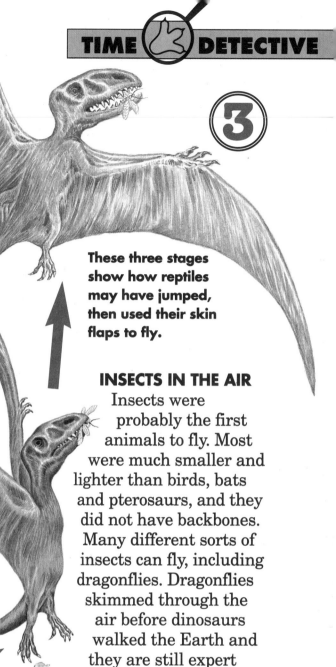

These three stages show how reptiles may have jumped, then used their skin flaps to fly.

JUMPING INTO FLIGHT

Some experts prefer the jumping theory. They say that flapping flight evolved first because animals jumped into the air to catch prey. A small running reptile that hunted insects found that if it jumped into the air it could catch many more flying insects.

FLAPS FOR FLYING

Such a creature may have developed flaps of skin on its arms to scoop up insects. Over a great deal of time, these flaps of skin might have become strong enough to hold the reptile in the air for a few seconds while it caught insects. Eventually they evolved into wings. Of course it was much harder to jump into flight from the ground than it was to fall out of a tree and glide.

INSECTS IN THE AIR

Insects were probably the first animals to fly. Most were much smaller and lighter than birds, bats and pterosaurs, and they did not have backbones. Many different sorts of insects can fly, including dragonflies. Dragonflies skimmed through the air before dinosaurs walked the Earth and they are still expert flyers today.

Dragonflies are insects, and insects were the first animals to fly. They skimmed the air before the Age of Dinosaurs.

117

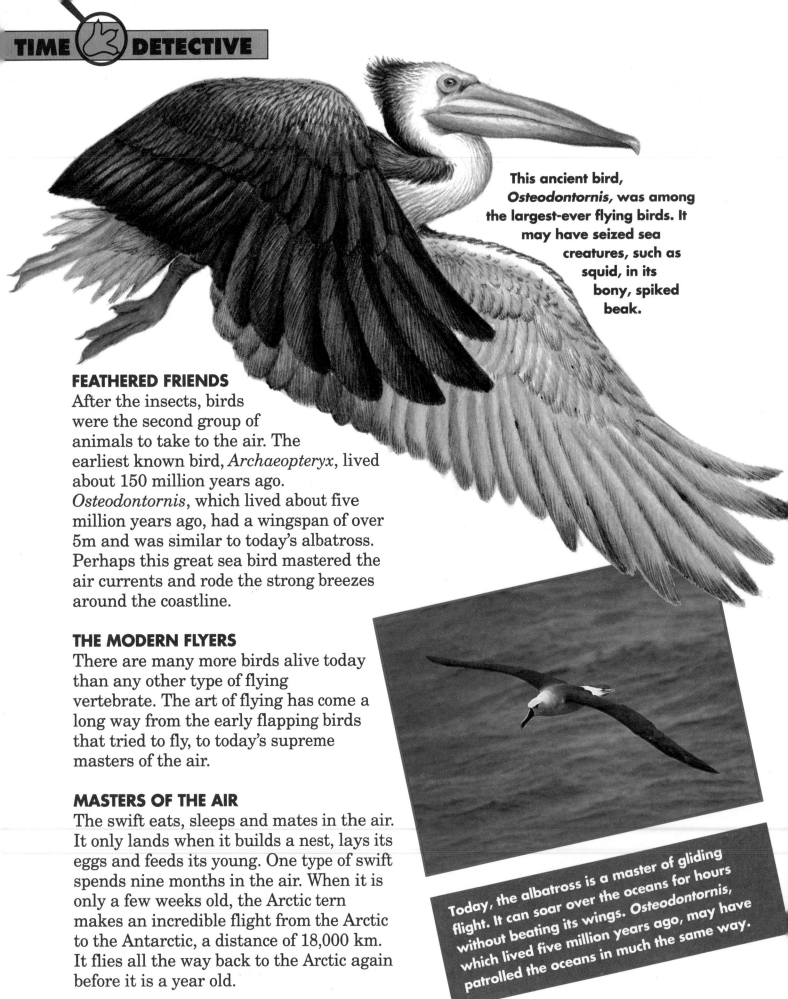

This ancient bird, *Osteodontornis*, was among the largest-ever flying birds. It may have seized sea creatures, such as squid, in its bony, spiked beak.

FEATHERED FRIENDS

After the insects, birds were the second group of animals to take to the air. The earliest known bird, *Archaeopteryx*, lived about 150 million years ago. *Osteodontornis*, which lived about five million years ago, had a wingspan of over 5m and was similar to today's albatross. Perhaps this great sea bird mastered the air currents and rode the strong breezes around the coastline.

THE MODERN FLYERS

There are many more birds alive today than any other type of flying vertebrate. The art of flying has come a long way from the early flapping birds that tried to fly, to today's supreme masters of the air.

MASTERS OF THE AIR

The swift eats, sleeps and mates in the air. It only lands when it builds a nest, lays its eggs and feeds its young. One type of swift spends nine months in the air. When it is only a few weeks old, the Arctic tern makes an incredible flight from the Arctic to the Antarctic, a distance of 18,000 km. It flies all the way back to the Arctic again before it is a year old.

Today, the albatross is a master of gliding flight. It can soar over the oceans for hours without beating its wings. *Osteodontornis*, which lived five million years ago, may have patrolled the oceans in much the same way.

118

GOING BATTY

Bats are the third group of vertebrate flyers. They are flying mammals. The earliest known bat lived about 50 million years ago. *Icaronycteris* was an early bat from North America. Most bats are fairly small and fly at night. No one knows how this mammal developed wings and learned to fly. It probably developed the ability to fly to take advantage of a good source of food from flying insects. Bats can't take off from the ground as many birds do – to get airborne, bats drop off a tree, rock or building.

Like most bats of today, *Icaronycteris* lived on flying insects. It was probably a skilled flyer, capable of catching insects on the wing.

The flying lemur is a mammal which lives in China and Indonesia. It jumps from tree to tree, stretching its legs wide. The flap of skin in between allows it to glide for up to 80m.

IT'S A FACT

AIR SPEED RECORD

One of the fastest animals in the world is a bird. The peregrine falcon can reach speeds of 131km/h when it is diving through the air for prey. It usually preys on other birds.

ODDBALLS

Today there are gliding animals which are not birds or bats. These are the 'flying' lizards, frogs, snakes, fishes, foxes, lemurs and squirrels. None of them has wings. Lizards, foxes, lemurs and squirrels have flaps of skin. Fishes use huge fins to glide over the tops of waves. Frogs use their feet, and the flying snakes their whole bodies.

119

A DAY IN THE LIFE OF PARASAUROLOPHUS

ONE DAY IN THE CRETACEOUS PERIOD, JUST AFTER THE SUN HAS RISEN OVER ALBERTA, A HERD OF PARASAUROLOPHUS IS GRAZING BY THE BANKS OF A RIVER...

...AND ONE YOUNGSTER HAS SPOTTED SOMETHING IT HAS NEVER SEEN BEFORE—AN ARMOURED PALAEOSCINCUS.

LITTLE PARASAUROLOPHUS GETS TOO CLOSE AND CUTS ITS LEG.

THE MOTHER DOES WHAT SHE CAN TO HELP HER BABY TO SAFETY.

THE HORROR STRUCK ADULT GETS TO THE DEEP WATER JUST IN TIME...

ALONE WITH ITS PREY, THE TYRANNOSAURID IS AT LEISURE TO GORGE ITSELF UNTIL IT IS FULL.

BUT IT'S TOO LATE, THE YOUNG PARASAUROLOPHUS CANNOT RUN QUICKLY ENOUGH TO ESCAPE A DREADFUL DEATH.

...A MOMENT LATER AND SHE WOULD HAVE MET A SIMILAR FATE TO HER YOUNGSTER.

THE MOTHER SEES HER BABY IN TROUBLE AND PUSHES IT BACK TOWARDS THE REST OF THE HERD WHO HAVE CARRIED ON MUNCHING, UNAWARE OF THE INCIDENT.

... FOR A PREDATORY TYRANNOSAURID, WHOSE EXPERIENCE TELLS HIM THAT LARGE HERDS SOMETIMES OFFER EASY PREY, HAS SPOTTED THE INJURED BABY PARASAUROLOPHUS.

BUT THE CALM IS ABOUT TO BE SHATTERED...

THE TERRIFIED PARASAUROLOPHUS RUN FOR THE SAFETY OF THE WATER.

AFTER THEIR EXHAUSTING SWIM, SOME OF THE PARASAUROLOPHUS HERD FILL THEIR BELLIES WITH THE PLANTS ON THE FAR BANK.

HEARING THE LOUD BELLOWING THAT BOOMS FROM THE LEADER'S HUGE CREST THE HERD FOLLOW HIM ON THEIR MIGRATION TRAIL...

BUT THE LEADER KNOWS THAT IT IS TIME TO MOVE ON...

... BUT SADLY, THE CURIOSITY FROM WHICH ALL YOUNG ANIMALS LEARN, HAS BEEN RESPONSIBLE FOR THE DEATH OF ONE LITTLE DINOSAUR.

Improve and test your knowledge with...

FACT FILE

Fascinating facts
to read and
10 fun questions
to answer!

1 A *Branchiosaurus* was the size of:
a) an adult human's palm
b) an adult human's foot
c) an adult human's arm

2 Carl Linnaeus invented a system for:
a) catching *T rex*
b) naming animals and plants
c) writing scientific papers

3 Carrots and red algae are red because:
a) they are sunburnt
b) they contain carotenoids
c) they are ready to eat

4 *Archaeopteryx* was a:
a) fish
b) reptile
c) dinosaur

5 Animals learned to fly to:
a) get a better view
b) catch food
c) show off

6 The first plants on Earth lived:
a) in water
b) under the ground
c) on dinosaurs

7 Armoured *Scutosaurus* survived by eating:
a) plants
b) meat
c) berries

8 Which animals were the first to fly?
a) insects
b) pterosaurs
c) birds

9 *Carcharodon* was an enormous:
a) carrot
b) shark
c) tree

A star of ill omen

Every 26 million years or so, there seems to be a mass extinction of animals – big or small. Some scientists think that a currently unknown star comes close to the solar system at this time. They think it disturbs the orbits of the comets, throwing them all over the place. Some of these comets inevitably hit the Earth, causing the extinctions.

Wrong horns

In 1887 the first Triceratops remains to be found were a pair of horn tips. The American palaeontologist Othniel C. Marsh, who discovered them, thought that they were the horns of some kind of bison!

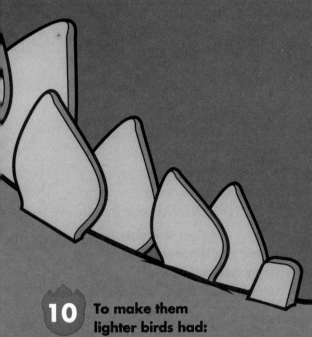

10 To make them lighter birds had:
a) empty tummies
b) small suitcases
c) hollow bones

Absolutely abominable!

The giant ape Gigantopithecus from the Pleistocene Epoch in China must have stood nearly three metres tall. Some people think that it still survives in the Himalayas and that it is the source of the legend of the abominable snowman.

Abominable snowman

Gigantopithecus

Double teeth

Baryonyx had twice as many teeth in its lower jaw than in its upper jaw. Nearly all other dinosaurs had the same number top and bottom.

Dr. David Norman of Cambridge University answers your dinosaur questions

ASK THE EXPERT

If dinosaurs had survived until today, would they look different from the ones of the Mesozoic?

If dinosaurs had survived until today they would be very different from the ones we know from the Mesozoic Era because they would have continued to evolve for a further 66 million years. Mammals, for example, have evolved from small, almost mouse-sized creatures through a bewildering variety of types, from whales and bats to giant rhinoceroses and humans. So goodness knows what dinosaurs might look like if they were alive today. In fact, maybe they are alive, but we do not recognise them because they are so different. Maybe we call them birds!

If Triceratops broke a horn, could it grow a new one?

If *Triceratops* broke its horn, it would not have regrown. The bony core of the horn would have snapped off and then healed over to form a stump, covered in thick, bony callus. The horny covering, however, would have still grown around the stump, to form a rather deformed horn. Probably not a pretty sight!

Did early birds of prey hunt small dinosaurs?

Almost certainly. Birds of prey, or raptors as they are called, are extremely agressive and will attack almost anything that is small enough to be killed and eaten. So small or baby dinosaurs would have been constantly at the mercy of the flying raptors, especially during the Cretaceous Period when birds of prey flourished.

Why does Tyrannosaurus rex have two words in its name?

Carl Linnaeus, the Swedish philosopher, invented a system for naming all living organisms in the 18th century. Since then, people all over the world who study animals and plants have agreed to use his system. This involves the use of two names: the first or generic name (*Tyrannosaurus*) and the second or specific name (*rex*). The first name applies to a group of closely related animals such as the big cats. For instance, the generic name for the large cats is *Panthera* and the lion's full name is *Panthera leo* and the leopard's *Panthera pardus*. *T rex* is not a good example because there is only one *Tyrannosaurus* known at present.

ANOMALOCARIS

The largest animal of its time, Anomalocaris was a real 'monster of the deep'.

 ore than 500 million years ago, the Early Cambrian seas seethed with activity. Some extraordinary creatures lived on the sea bed. Among this community of marine 'oddballs', the largest, *Anomalocaris,* was a nightmare vision.

STRANGE FIND

Anomalocaris was found in the Burgess Shale, a slab of rock from a mountain in British Columbia, Canada, which was once part of the sea bed. At first, experts thought that *Anomalocaris* was actually several different animals. Various parts of its body were mistaken for a worm, a jellyfish, a headless shrimp and even a squashed sea cucumber! Eventually, scientists worked out that all these amazing parts fitted together to form just one bizarre animal.

BURIED DEEP

The fine-grained mud that buried *Anomalocaris* had preserved its remains in wonderful detail. Experts set about the task of putting together the 'jigsaw' of fossils to reveal what *Anomalocaris* actually looked like. The finished result was amazing.

GRASPING CLAWS

Anomalocaris roamed the sea floor like a miniature spacecraft. It was a fearsome predator with great bulging eyes on short stalks, and it had a voracious appetite. It caught its prey with two terrifying, curved claws. Once a victim was in its grasp, *Anomalocaris* drew the unlucky creature down and under its huge, round head.

TERRIBLE TEETH

Inside its ever-open mouth, *Anomalocaris* had layers of sharp teeth and bony plates. These went some of the way down its gullet. Once inside the cavity, the crushed victim was shredded like cheese on a grater.

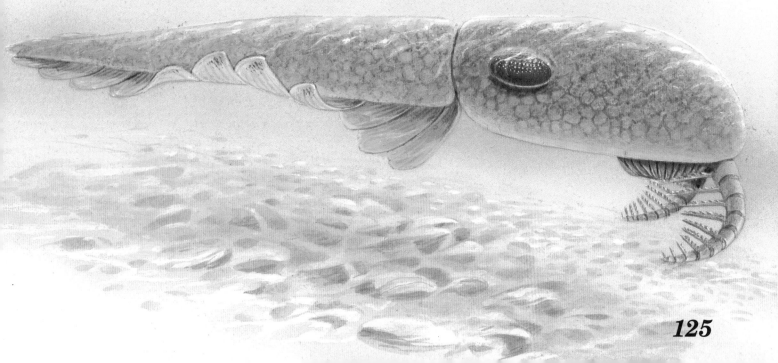

The fossil of *Anomalocaris* was found in the Burgess Shale in Canada. It lived in the seas more than 500 million years ago.

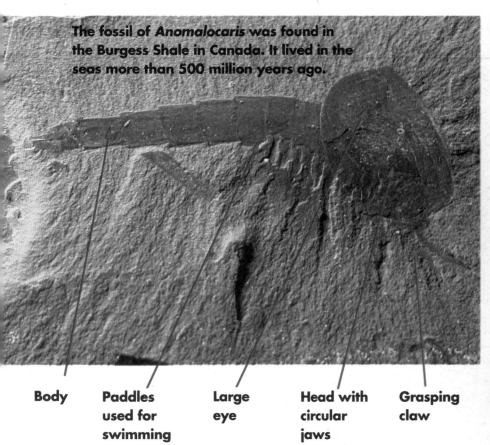

Body

Paddles used for swimming

Large eye

Head with circular jaws

Grasping claw

To move fast through the water, chasing after prey, *Anomalocaris* probably used its side paddles to create wave-like motions.

MONSTER FACTS

- **NAME:** *Anomalocaris* (a-<u>nom</u>-al-oh-<u>kar</u> is) means 'odd shrimp'
- **GROUP:** unknown
- **SIZE:** up to 60cm long
- **FOOD:** all sea creatures of the time
- **LIVED:** about 520 million years ago in the Early Cambrian Period in the seas in many parts of the world

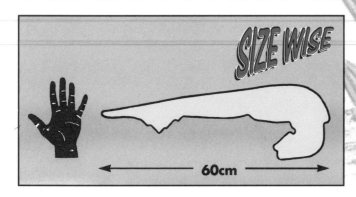

SIZE WISE

← 60cm →

NUTCRACKER JAWS

There was no escape for its victims. *Anomalocaris* had a circular jaw which, when opened, revealed a gaping mouth with a powerful rim. *Anomalocaris* used it like a sinister nutcracker to crunch and destroy its prey. Experts thought at first that the round fossil was just a jellyfish which had a hole in the middle.

STREAMLINED SWIMMER

Anomalocaris was probably a good swimmer because, as it had no limbs, it had no way of crawling or even walking along the sea bed. Its streamlined body and side paddles must have powered *Anomalocaris* through the water with wave-like movements as it chased ferociously after any small prey that crossed its path.

ONE OF A KIND

As most of its companions on the sea bed were not much longer than your fingers, the arm-sized *Anomalocaris* must have seemed like a real giant in the Cambrian seas. This unique sea creature has no known relatives or descendants. Its 'one-off' design has been described by some as a cross between a lobster and a modern stingray. Scientists have had problems classifying it, and are still puzzling today over which of the animal groups it should really be placed in.

The special body shape of *Anomalocaris* has been described as a cross between the modern stingray (above) and the lobster (below).

IT'S A FACT

HIDDEN SPECIMENS

The 65,000 specimens from 120 different kinds of animal which have been found in the Burgess Shale were not all buried at the same time. Scientists have found five distinct animal communities which were buried over several million years. In geological terms this is just a 'blink' in time, and gives us a fascinating snapshot of animal life hundreds of millions of years ago.

SCUTELLOSAURUS

About the size of today's labrador dog, *Scutellosaurus* carried light armour on its back for protection.

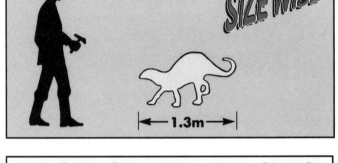

SIZE WISE

← 1.3m →

MONSTER FACTS

- **NAME:** *Scutellosaurus* (skoo-<u>tell</u>-oh-<u>saw</u>-rus) means 'small-scaled reptile'
- **GROUP:** dinosaur
- **SIZE:** 1.3m long
- **FOOD:** low-lying plants
- **LIVED:** about 195 million years ago in the Early Jurassic Period in Arizona, North America

All the way along its low body, *Scutellosaurus* had small, bony studs, or 'scutes', with the largest row along the centre. As it moved among low-growing plants of Jurassic Arizona, *Scutellosaurus'* armoured body made the dinosaur rather 'front-heavy'. Although it ran on two strong hind legs when evading predators, *Scutellosaurus* probably browsed on four legs.

TAIL END
Scutellosaurus had a long tail that took up almost half its total length. When the little dinosaur stood up on its back legs, the heavy tail gave it extra stability.

ON THE RUN
Like its relative, *Lesothosaurus*, this early ornithischian's back legs were longer than its front limbs. It probably ran quite swiftly as it tried to escape carnivores like *Dilophosaurus*.

FOOD AND SHELTER
Scutellosaurus had a small head and long, slender jaws. It probably grasped twigs and small branches with its large, five-fingered hands and held them to its mouth. When it grew tired of walking and feeding in the Jurassic sunshine, *Scutellosaurus* probably found shelter in a shady burrow and laid down to rest.

SCAPHONYX

Scaphonyx was a sturdy reptile, able to eat the toughest food.

 **A**bout as heavy as an average-sized sheep, *Scaphonyx* trundled along on four squat, sprawling legs. It belonged to a family of reptiles called rhynchosaurs, which were named after their 'beaked' heads. These plant-eating animals lived in the Mid-Triassic Period and survived successfully for a short time.

TONGS AND TWIGS

Scaphonyx had a very striking beak which hung down from its face like a pair of tongs. It gathered seeds and twigs in this beak and tucked them inside its mouth with its large tongue.

SIZE WISE

1-2.5m

MONSTER FACTS

- **NAME:** *Scaphonyx* (ska-<u>fon</u>-ix) means 'trough-shaped claw'
- **GROUP:** reptile
- **SIZE:** 1–2.5m long
- **FOOD:** fruits, seeds and roots of plants
- **LIVED:** about 200 million years ago in the Mid-Triassic Period in South Africa and Brazil

SNAPPY JAW

The lower jaw slotted into the groove of the upper jaw like the blades of a modern penknife. Inside the reptile's mouth, rows of flat cheek teeth ground tough stems and roots to a mushy pulp.

BACK TO ROOTS

With its strong, clawed feet, *Scaphonyx* probably scratched at the ground for food. Its curved beak was ideal for raking the ground and pulling out hidden roots.

129

The Australian Ark

Australia has been an island for 60 million years and its animals have evolved in a unique way.

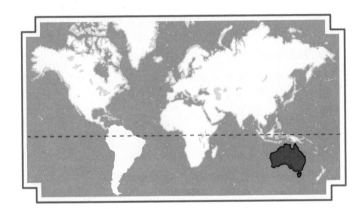

Kangaroos, wallabies, koalas, wombats, possums, platypuses – Australia has all kinds of unique animals that are just not found anywhere else in the world. And if you think that the modern Australian animals are unusual, just wait until you see the truly strange creatures that lived there in prehistoric times!

DOING THEIR OWN THING

Australia gives us a picture of evolution in complete isolation. The continent has now been a separate island for 60 million years, and during this time evolution has gone its own merry way, which has involved no mixing of any other animals from the outside world.

PRIMITIVE EGG-LAYERS

The most primitive Australian animals are the monotremes – mammals which lay eggs. Of these, only the platypus and echidna remain. In the Pleistocene Epoch the giant echidna *Zaglossus* wandered freely and earlier, in Cretaceous times, the platypus *Steropodon* (the oldest known mammal) could be seen.

MARSUPIALS RULE

The most important Australian mammals are the marsupials, or pouched mammals, whose babies are born very tiny. The young are just big enough to crawl into the mother's pouch where they stay until they can fend for themselves.

CONTINENTAL BREAK-UP

Why have the marsupials of Australia survived until today, when they have died out elsewhere? In Cretaceous times, when the marsupials first evolved, Australia, Antarctica and South America were all joined together as one big area. As this continent broke up into individual landmasses, each still had marsupial mammals living on it. But when placental mammals evolved in North America they moved into South America and took over from the marsupials.

DIFFERENT VERSIONS

For example, to live on grasslands an animal needs long legs for running away from enemies, strong teeth and a complex digestive system for eating tough grass. This describes a zebra or an antelope, but also a kangaroo! Over the last 65 million years, Australia has produced marsupial versions of all the existing placental mammals.

The large echidna, *Zaglossus* (above), lived in the Pleistocene Epoch. *Tacyglossus aculeatus*, a close relative (left), still exists today.

The platypus, *Steropodon* (above right), was around in Cretaceous times; the modern duckbilled platypus (right) still lives today.

TOUGH SURVIVORS

Isolated Australia kept on drifting northwards with its cargo of marsupials, which kept adapting continuously to survive the changes in climate and conditions. Unchallenged by any invading placentals from other landmasses, the Australian marsupials remain supreme today. They may look very different from the mammals elsewhere in the world, but they behave in very similar ways.

IT'S A FACT

NOT JUST MAMMALS
Australia has produced strange birds as well as mammals. Some of the biggest that ever existed were ground-dwellers like *Dromornis* (left). This giant bird looked like today's cassowary, was up to 3m tall, and weighed around 300kg.

KILLEROO

Ekaltadeta lurked in the forests of Miocene Queensland. It was a kangaroo with the teeth and temper of a wolf! We know it was a meat-eater because its back teeth were worn from chewing bones.

The ancient kangaroo *Ekaltadeta* (above) was fiercer than this modern kangaroo.

DUMBAT

Many of the large plant-eating marsupials belonged to the group we call the diprotodonts. They were a bit like giant wombats. *Neohelos*, from Pleistocene Queensland, was about the size of a cow, and probably wandered in herds in the leafy forests. Its brain was only the size of a tennis ball, so it was probably not the most intelligent of animals.

GIANT PLANT-EATER

The biggest of the plant-eaters was *Diprotodon*. It was 3m long and stood 2m high at the shoulder. It probably lived very much like a rhinoceros of today, wandering through open woodland on its short legs, and browsing. This creature survived until about 10,000 years ago.

PANDA LOOKALIKE

Hulitherium lived in New Guinea during the Pleistocene Epoch. It chewed young bamboo shoots in the highland forests. It had very much the same sort of lifestyle as some of today's animals such as the spectacled bear in South America, the mountain gorilla in Africa and the giant panda in Asia. It was, in effect, the marsupial giant panda.

The ancient giant marsupial panda, *Hulitherium*, lived on bamboo shoots just like today's giant panda (above left).

MARSUPIAL KING

Big Pleistocene beasts were eaten by the lion-sized marsupial hunter *Thylacoleo* whose name means 'pouched lion'. Unlike other hunters, *Thylacoleo* used its front teeth to kill its prey. When this creature was first discovered, scientists thought it gnawed large fruit! But on closer study, the teeth showed wear from chewing meat.

A fierce *Thylacoleo* lioness prepares to attack plant-eating *Diprotodon*, in defence of her cubs.

GIANTS OF THE PAST

ANOMALOCARIS

Many strange-looking creatures roam the Early Cambrian seas and the biggest and fiercest is *Anomalocaris*. All the other sea creatures are dinner to this hungry predator. *Opabinia* is the unlucky victim this time, and its body is fast disappearing into the predator's ever-open mouth. It will quickly be shredded by *Anomalocaris'* layers of teeth. *Opabinia's* five eyes and terminal claw have proved little protection in this uneven contest.

CHASMOSAURUS

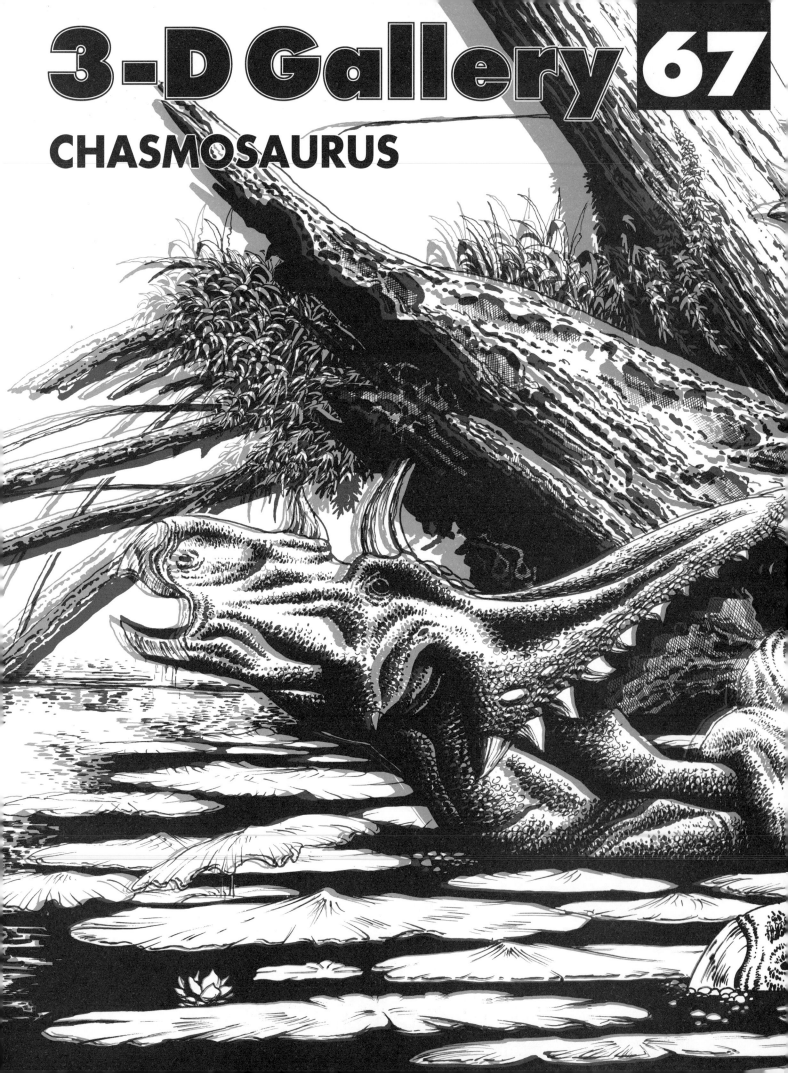

In the heat of the day in Late Cretaceous New Mexico, a herd of *Chasmosaurus* wallows in the cool waters of a lily pond. Despite their great size and sharp, hooked beaks, these ceratopsid are known to have been plant-eaters.

STOP PRESS...

Read all about the latest dinosaur theories!

New theories about dinosaurs are being put forward almost every day. New facts are discovered and new research reported all the time.

BACK TO THE DRAWING-BOARD

Sculptor and palaeontologist Stephen Czerkas has noticed an interesting similarity between the s-shaped bones found in the necks of prehistoric hadrosaurs and those found in modern horses. He thinks that experts may have missed something. Hadrosaurs are usually shown with elegant swan-shaped necks. But if horses and hadrosaurs possess the same shaped neck bones, the Cretaceous plant-eaters

probably had shorter, thicker necks. So it may be back to the drawing board for dinosaur illustrators! Some experts say, however, that because horses are mammals, and dinosaurs are reptiles, comparing them is not a good idea.

PEE-HISTORIC

US researcher Dr Milton R. Grillingham believes that "every drop of water on Earth used to be urine and 99.9 per cent came from dinosaurs". He estimates that a large sauropod took up to 50 minutes to empty its bladder and that the contents would probably fill a small swimming pool. However, most experts think that this is fantasy because they think that, like most reptiles, dinosaurs did not pee.

IT'S A SMALL WONDER

The smallest sauropod ever discovered has been found in Thailand. As yet unnamed, this plant-eater lived in the Late Jurassic Period.

JURASSIC PARK FOR REAL ?

Mary Schweitzer, who worked with Jurassic Park's dinosaur expert Jack Horner, has isolated the red blood cells in a T rex leg bone. Researchers in the US are trying to extract DNA from the cells – something that has never been done before.

Great-granddad ankylosaur

The earliest known ankylosaur has been found in Utah, USA. This armoured dinosaur from the Late Jurassic was as long as a lion and it is still waiting for a name. It may have looked like this *Silvasaurus*, which was found close by in Kansas.

A DINOSAUR IN THEIR OWN BACKYARD

Experts from the Museum of Natural Sciences in Argentina did not realise until recently what treasures were hidden in their own backyard. The 70 million-year-old remains of a dog-sized carnivore were buried right under their noses. It has been named *Alvarezsaurus*.

A SURPRISE FOR THE EGGSPERTS

Only two skeletons of *Compsognathus* have been found so far. The remains of one had some strange-shaped globules preserved near its skeleton. Scientists have found these a puzzle, but now one has suggested they are fossils of this little dinosaur's eggs.

BORN TO KILL

The most ferocious of all flesh-eaters has been discovered in North America. *Utahraptor*'s clawed hands were big enough to fit around a human head. One expert described this predator, which lived over 130 million years ago, as a "night-mare cross between Freddy (in the film 'A Nightmare on Elm Street') and Bruce Lee".

The little bird-hip

Small dinosaurs darted across the hot, dry plains 200 million years ago. These early plant-eaters were the bird-hipped dinosaurs.

Heterodontosaurus

The three dinosaurs pictured here were some of the best known of the bird-hipped dinosaurs. They belonged to a major group, called the ornithischians. They all had backward-pointing, bird-like hips. All three also had similar backbones and their lower jaws all ended in a beak-like bony tip.

WHO WERE THEY?

Lesothosaurus, meaning 'Lesotho's lizard', was an early armoured fabrosaurid. Named the 'small-shield lizard', because of the bony studs down its back, *Scutellosaurus* was a scutellosaurid dinosaur. *Heterodontosaurus*, meaning 'mixed tooth reptile', belonged to the heterodontosaurid family.

DOG-SIZED

Lesothosaurus, *Scutellosaurus* and *Heterodontosaurus* were each no taller than a large dog. And like a dog they were all fleet footed.

These successful plant-eaters flourished in early Jurassic times.

140

ped plant-eaters

LONG AND LOW

Scutellosaurus grew up to 134cm long and half of its length was its tail. *Heterodontosaurus* was slightly shorter at 120cm. *Lesothosaurus* was just 90cm long – about the same size as a skateboard.

EARLY STARTERS

Scutellosaurus and *Lesothosaurus* were first on the scene. They appeared early in the Jurassic Period, about 200 million years ago. *Heterodontosaurus* arrived about 10 million years later.

Lesothosaurus

Scutellosaurus

IT'S A FACT

NAME CHANGE

When experts dug up an almost complete fabrosaurid skeleton in the 1970s, they called it *Fabrosaurus*. But later the name was changed to *Lesothosaurus* because scientists decided that there was not enough evidence to link this new find with the only remains of *Fabrosaurus* previously discovered, which was a bit of jaw with teeth.

DISAPPEARED

These bird-hips were successful plant-eaters and flourished throughout the northern hemisphere. But they had all died out by 180 million years ago.

ALL IN THE FAMILY

These three dinosaurs are known from quite well preserved skeletons. But experts have discovered scattered fossil fragments belonging to further members of these families. A single broken jaw with teeth is all that exists of *Fabrosaurus*. A few jaws with teeth of *Echinodon,* and tooth fragments of *Alocodon,* have also been found. Experts have identified more heterodontosaurids too. They have excavated a skull belonging to *Abrictosaurus* and small pieces of the jaws of *Geranosaurus* and *Lycorhinus*.

CHECK LIST

- ATE PLANTS
- RAN ON TWO LEGS
- SMALL
- BIRD-LIKE HIPS

1 ONE IN THREE

Heterodontosaurus was so called because, unlike most other dinosaurs and reptiles, it had three kinds of teeth. This small plant-eater had sharp cutting teeth at the front. It had tusk-like fangs behind and broad, ridged teeth at the back. Each type of tooth did a different job. The pointed teeth on its upper front jaw worked with its lower 'beak' to nip off leaves. Its sharp fangs could shred tough vegetation, which was then ground up with its back teeth.

CHOPPING...

Fabrosaurids simply chopped their food up. But heterodontosaurids were able to chew the vegetation they ate. That meant they could digest it more quickly. *Lesothosaurus* had slender, leaf-like teeth which it used to shred shoots. It swallowed the bits and digested them slowly in its large stomach.

...AND CHEWING

Heterodontosaurus was a much more efficient eater. It used its special cheek teeth to chew plants. This dinosaur could hold the bits in its fleshy cheek pouches so they didn't drop out of its mouth while it chewed.

TUSKERS

Heterodontosaurids are remarkable for their tusk-like front teeth. They may have used them, like modern warthogs do, to defend themselves against attack as well as to eat.

2 BALANCING TAIL

The early plant-eaters were easy prey for hungry meat-eating dinosaurs. The plant-eaters relied on their long, powerful hind legs to outrun their slower attackers. *Lesothosaurus* had hollow bones, like a bird, so it had a light body. It used its long tail to counterbalance its body so that it could stand and run swiftly on its hind legs.

CHECK LIST
- BEAK-LIKE LOWER JAWS
- LONG, SLENDER HIND LEGS
- LONG, STIFF TAILS

3 UP AND DOWN

Heterodontosaurus and *Lesothosaurus* had long, slender foot bones. These bones did not need to be very strong because both dinosaurs were small and light. The shape of their hind feet shows that both were speedy runners. *Scutellosaurus* probably sprinted along on its hind legs, too. But it had longer arms, so experts think it might have fed and rested on all-fours.

DEEP SLEEP

Experts believe these early plant-eaters might have slept, or aestivated, during the dry season. A pair of *Lesothosaurus* skeletons was found curled up and surrounded by worn teeth. The skulls contained a full set of teeth. Scientists think the dinosaurs might have slept away the hottest, driest months, just as many modern creatures do. They could have shed their teeth and grown new ones as they slept. Heterodontosaurids may have aestivated, too. But some experts think there is not enough evidence to prove it.

4 SHELL SHOCK

Scutellosaurus was unusual because it was covered in bony plates, rather like a modern crocodile. If it was cornered, the dinosaur could have used its body armour as a means of defence.

HIS AND HERS

Scientists were puzzled when they found a heterodontosaurid called *Abrictosaurus* which had no tusks. They now think it may have been a female *Heterodontosaurus*. Today's male musk deer have tusks but the females have none. *Heterodontosaurus* and *Abrictosaurus* may have been the male and female of the same species.

Is it true that heterodontosaurids fed on very tough plants?

Yes, probably. Heterodontosaurid teeth have been found which are very worn down. Experts say this could have happened as a result of the dinosaurs eating hard, spiky shoots and leaves.

HE WAS SO GOOD AT HIS JOB THAT HE WAS QUICKLY PROMOTED...

WHAT'S IN THE LETTER, CHARLES?

THEY'VE ASKED ME TO BE DIRECTOR OF THE SURVEY!

WALCOTT WAS A BRILLIANT ADMINISTRATOR, BUT HE LOVED BEING OUT IN THE FIELD. WITH HIS WIFE AND FAMILY HE OFTEN HOLIDAYED IN THE CANADIAN ROCKIES.

IT'S FREEZING, FATHER!

WE'LL SOON BE BACK AT CAMP, SIDNEY!

GOSH! I'VE NEVER SEEN SO MANY FOSSIL IMPRINTS!

BUT IT WAS TOO LATE IN THE SEASON TO DO ANY DIGGING. NOT UNTIL 1910 COULD THEY RETURN TO THE AREA....

HAVE YOU FOUND SOMETHING CHARLES?

YOU BET I HAVE! I THOUGHT THAT SLAB WE FOUND LAST YEAR MUST HAVE BROKEN OFF FROM A LARGER SLAB—AND I WAS RIGHT!

MANY OF THE FOSSILS WERE SENT BACK EAST TO FORM ONE OF THE MOST IMPORTANT COLLECTIONS IN THE WORLD....

IT'S A TREASURE CHEST—A VERITABLE TREASURE CHEST!

WALCOTT CONTINUED TRAVELLING TO THE SITE, CALLED "BURGESS SHALE" FOR MANY YEARS. HIS DISCOVERIES TELL US ABOUT ANIMALS THAT LIVED OVER 500 MILLION YEARS AGO— MOST ARE NOW EXTINCT, BUT ONE SURVIVOR WAS THE ANCESTOR OF MAN!

Improve and test your knowledge with...

FACT FILE

Ichthyosaurus holds all the answers. See how you score in the quiz.

It's mine

Icarosaurus was a little flying lizard from the Triassic rocks of New Jersey. The only fossil was found by a schoolboy, who gave it to a museum. Forty years later, he realised that it was legally his property, so he claimed it back. Now it has disappeared into his private collection, never to be seen by the public again.

1 Where was *Anomalocaris* first found?
a) in the Gobi desert
b) in the backyard
c) in the Burgess Shale

2 Round globules found near *Compsognathus* are thought to be:
a) its eggs
b) its teeth
c) its toys

3 *Scaphonyx* was about as heavy as an average:
a) dog
b) sheep
c) cow

4 Which dinosaur was found buried in the backyard of the Argentinian Museum of Natural Sciences?
a) *Buriedosaurus*
b) *Alvarezsaurus*
c) *Argintosaurus*

5 Where were dinosaur footprints mistaken for human ones?
a) in Texas
b) in a museum
c) under the sea

6 What took up half of *Scutellosaurus'* body?
a) its tail
b) its neck
c) its head

7 Was *Cladoselache*:
a) a beaver?
b) a living fossil?
c) a 'cutting shark'?

8 How much did *Dromornis* weigh?
a) around 50kg
b) around 1kg
c) around 300kg

Crocofish

Some sea crocodiles at the time of the dinosaurs were so well adapted to sea life that they had paddles for limbs, and fish tails.

146

Beefy bison stew

In 1984 the Swedish palaeontologist Bjorn Kurten made stew from the flesh of a 30,000-year-old frozen bison. He found it "agreeable...with an unmistakable beefy aroma".

Hands down

Hadrosaurs had broad 'hands' which were padded underneath to protect the foot as the dinosaur walked. These pads left a smooth, curved print which once misled scientists into thinking that hadrosaurs, such as Edmontosaurus, had webbed fingers.

9 *Hulitherium's* diet consisted of:
a) bamboo shoots
b) rice
c) berries

10 The brain of *Neohelos* was the size of:
a) a football
b) a tennis ball
c) a balloon

Mammoth funeral

The first mammoth bones to have been found in France were thought to have been the bones of giants – and they were given Christian burials!

Oldest living things

A frozen mastodon discovered in Ohio, USA, had frozen – but still living – bacteria in its gut. At 11,000 years old, these bacteria are the oldest living things known.

Answers to the questions on inside back cover

ASK THE EXPERT

Dr. David Norman of Cambridge University answers your dinosaur questions

If there were dinosaurs in Alaska and Antarctica, how did they survive the cold?

Curiously enough, it was not as cold as you might think in Antarctica, or inside the Arctic Circle. At the time of the dinosaurs there was no ice covering either the North or the South Pole. The trees that grew at the time in these areas were deciduous, which means they shed their leaves each year, and this suggests a climate with warm summers. Dinosaurs were probably summer migrants that went there to eat the abundant plant growth and then moved away in the dark winters.

In Texas there is supposed to be a rock that has human footprints beside dinosaur footprints. Is this true?

This is a very old story which has been used by people known as 'creationists' who do not believe in evolution, or the history of life on Earth based on fossil records. The claim that human footprints are found among dinosaur footprints comes from the incorrect identification of weathered carnivorous dinosaur footprints that resemble human footprints.

Were there more volcanoes in dinosaur times?

Dinosaurs lived for such a long period of time (about 160 million years) that it is very unwise to make general statements about things like dinosaurs and volcanoes. There were times when dinosaurs lived when there were not many volcanoes, and other times – particularly near the end of the Age of Dinosaurs – when there were some enormous volcanic eruptions which were far greater than anything we see today.

Did dinosaurs ever eat insects?

It seems likely that the smaller dinosaurs, such as *Compsognathus*, ate insects as part of their regular diet for at least part of the time. However, it also seems very likely that baby dinosaurs would have eaten insects regularly. Today, insects certainly feature in the diets of young crocodiles and are actually a very nourishing source of food.

MUTTABURRASAURUS

Muttaburrasaurus was a rare Australian dinosaur with a strange bump on its nose.

So far, very few dinosaurs have been found in Australia, although experts believe that many once lived in that part of the world. Speedy *Leaellynasaura* and armoured *Minmi* lived on the eastern side of Australia at about the same time as *Muttaburrasaurus* lived in the Northwest. And hundreds of dinosaur tracks have been found in southern Queensland.

MOST COMPLETE
Of all the dinosaur skeletons discovered in Australia so far, *Muttaburrasaurus* is the most complete.

IMPORTANT FIND
Experts think that it was a relative of the ornithopods, *Iguanodon* and *Camptosaurus*. It was an important find because it showed that such dinosaurs lived in southern as well as northern parts of the world.

WALKING WATCH-TOWER
Twice the height of an adult human and as long as an elephant, *Muttaburrasaurus* strode about the plains of Cretaceous Australia searching for lush vegetation on which to feed. By rearing up to its full height, the plant-eater could see for a long way and could probably spot an enemy in plenty of time to run away.

FLAT HEAD
Like its relative *Iguanodon*, *Muttaburrasaurus* had a large, rather flat head. But it also had an unusual feature of its own.

149

MONSTER FACTS

- **NAME:** *Muttaburrasaurus* (<u>mut</u>-a-<u>bur</u>-a-<u>saw</u>-rus) means 'Muttaburra reptile' after the place in Australia, where it was found
- **GROUP:** dinosaur
- **SIZE:** up to 7m long
- **FOOD:** plants
- **LIVED:** about 105 million years ago in the Mid-Cretaceous Period at Muttaburra, Queensland, Australia

STRIKING PROFILE

Above its snout was a hollow, arched dome rather like those found on some hadrosaurs such as *Kritosaurus*. This gave the dinosaur a striking profile which may have helped other dinosaurs to recognise it.

THUMBS UP

Muttaburrasaurus' fossil did not include a complete hand. But, as it is like *Iguanodon* in so many ways, experts think it also shared another feature. *Iguanodon* had a thumb spike on each hand for raking down branches or for defence. It is very likely that *Muttaburrasaurus* also had spiky thumbs which it used to slash or stab at predators.

CUT AND SLICED

Muttaburrasaurus had a toothless beak for nipping off shoots. It had teeth at the sides of its mouth, which were better suited to cutting and slicing plants than were *Iguanodon*'s grinding teeth. It is possible that *Muttaburrasaurus* had to cope with different types of vegetation than its more northerly relations. Some experts have even suggested that *Muttaburrasaurus* ate meat.

SIZE WISE

7m

150

UP AND DOWN

Muttaburrasaurus usually walked on two powerful legs with its long, tapering tail held out above the ground. But when it came across a particularly tempting cluster of ferns or horsetails, *Muttaburrasaurus* probably flopped forwards on to all fours and bent its head low to browse among the ground-covering plants.

The skeleton of *Muttaburrasaurus*, the most complete dinosaur found in Australia, is on show at the Queensland Museum in Brisbane.

A model of *Muttaburrasaurus*.

Is it true that dinosaurs also lived in New Zealand?

Yes. One dinosaur has been found in New Zealand and there are probably many others still to be found. A vertebra of a theropod was found on New Zealand's North Island by Ralph Molnar in 1980.

151

LYSTROSAURUS

Like the hippopotamus of today, *Lystrosaurus* may have wallowed in muddy water.

Lystrosaurus was a member of a family of mammal-like reptiles called the dicynodonts. These plant-eaters lived all over the world before the dinosaurs began their reign. These unusual reptiles had barrel-shaped bodies, short tails and short, sturdy legs.

SOME LIKE IT WET

Dicynodont means 'two dog-like teeth' and *Lystrosaurus* had a pair of fangs which hung from its upper jaw like Dracula's. They could be seen even when its jaws were closed. The rest of its jaw was toothless. *Lystrosaurus* probably lived on land and waded along the edge of rivers and lakes, and tugged at tough vegetation with the help of its hard beak. It may have used its tusks for digging up roots to eat.

MONSTER FACTS

- **NAME:** *Lystrosaurus* (ly-stro-saw-rus) means 'shovel reptile'
- **GROUP:** mammal-like reptile
- **SIZE:** up to 1.5m long
- **FOOD:** plants
- **LIVED:** about 240 million years ago in the Early Triassic Period in Antarctica, South Africa, India and China

SIZE WISE

1.5m

WELL-TRAVELLED

Lystrosaurus has given scientists yet more proof that land masses were once joined together. Its remains have been found in places as far apart as China, South Africa, India and even Antarctica.

SALTOPUS

One of the oldest of all dinosaurs, *Saltopus* was only about the size of a cat.

A tiny skeleton was found in very poor condition in a sandstone quarry in Scotland at the beginning of this century. In some places, only hollows remained in the rocks to show where the bones had been. So experts used the same technique that we use when making jelly in a mould, and made casts from the shape of the hollows. When they were turned out, the casts revealed what *Saltopus'* bones looked like.

RUNNING AND JUMPING

Saltopus was a light, speedy, agile dinosaur that weighed less than a bag of sugar. It looked like a featherless chicken, and some experts think that *Saltopus* may even have been able to jump. It probably ran quickly, and took long, leaping strides as it speeded along.

SMALL SNACKS

Like its relative, *Coelophysis*, *Saltopus* used speed to catch its dinner. Small, nifty mammals and lizards were snatched up in its narrow jaws, and even flying insects were pursued by this tiny predator. It probably used its five-fingered hands to keep prey firmly in its grasp.

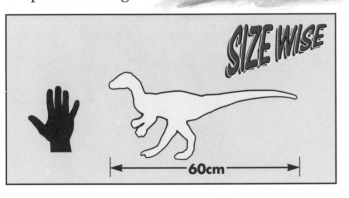

SIZE WISE

60cm

MONSTER FACTS

- **NAME:** *Saltopus* (salt-oh-pus) means 'leaping foot'
- **GROUP:** dinosaur
- **SIZE:** 60cm long
- **FOOD:** small animals and insects
- **LIVED:** about 250 million years ago in the Late Triassic Period in Scotland

Grasslands and grazers

It is difficult to imagine a world without grass. Yet the world was completely without any kinds of grass until about 40 million years ago.

Grass is a familiar plant that covers lawns and meadows. It is one member of a group called the grasses. Grasses make your breakfast, because oats and corn are grasses called cereal crops. Your hamburger bun is baked with flour from wheat, another cereal grass. Even the burger meat comes from cattle which eat grass. Millions of people and animals depend on grasses for food.

NEW FOOD FOR NEW ANIMALS

Grasses were a new food source, and had a huge impact on animal evolution. Before grasses, many animals were browsers, which means they ate the leaves of bushes and trees. The new grasses brought in a new range of different animals. These were the grazers, which ate grasses and lived in the new grassland habitats.

Zebras and wildebeest are modern grassland grazers. They thrive on the abundant grass available in areas such as the Ngorongoro Crater in Tanzania pictured here. Just as the early grazers had to watch out for predators like *Megantereon*, so today's grazers keep a look-out for lions and other predators.

EARLY GRAZERS

Dinosaurs did not eat grass. Not because they didn't like it, but because there wasn't any in the Age of the Dinosaurs. Grasses probably appeared in the Eocene Epoch, about 40 million years ago. In South America, many fossils have been found that were possibly early grass-eaters. *Rhynchippus,* from early Oligocene times, was horse-shaped and 1m long. *Macrauchenia* from the Pleistocene was around 3m long. Llama-like *Theosodon*, from the early Miocene, was 2m long.

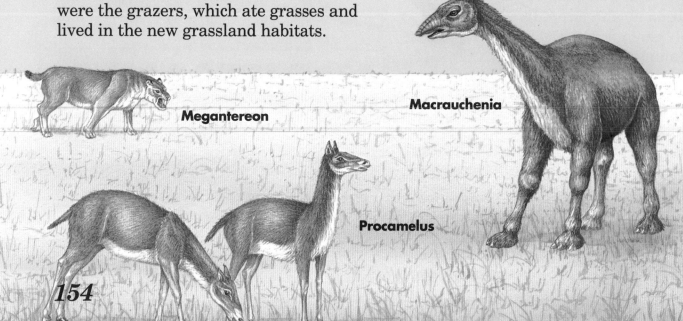

Megantereon

Macrauchenia

Procamelus

154

The feathery shoots that are standing upright on this Tufted Hair Grass are its flowers. The plant's short stems are not so easy to see as they are lying on the ground.

CAMELS AND CATTLE

Procamelus lived in North America in the late Miocene Epoch. It was a small member of the camel family, about 1.5m long. Unlike today's camels, it didn't have a prominent hump, but like them it did have strong grass-grinding cheek teeth. *Pelorovis* was a grazer from Africa that lived during the Pleistocene Epoch around two million years ago. It was about 3m long and was related to the buffaloes of today, with a large, muscular body and huge, down-curved horns.

What is GRASS?

Grass is a member of the Gramineae, or grasses, family. It is part of the large group called Angiosperms, or flowering plants. All grasses 'lie on their sides'. The green bits that stick up are the leaves. The stems are short and lie on the ground. They also have underground stems and bunches of thin roots. The flowers, called spikelets, grow on tall stems and are usually fluffy or feathery. Because grasses lie on their sides, they can survive repeated eating by grazing animals.

Pelorovis

Rhynchippus

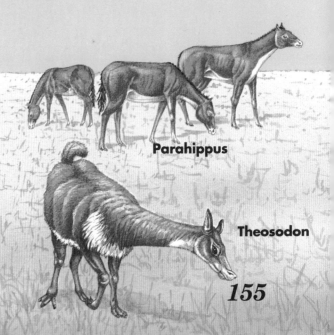

Parahippus

Theosodon

DROUGHT AND FIRE

During Miocene times, it seems that the trees which covered much of the land died away, and grasses took their place. Why? The main reason was the changing climate. Much of the world became cooler and drier. Trees cannot survive long, dry periods, but grasses can. Grasses have stems on the ground and roots underneath which stay alive during a drought. Grasses can even survive bush fires and will send up new green shoots from the roots.

GRAZED GRASS GROWS AGAIN

Another reason for the success of grass is its 'lying-on-its-side' design. If an animal nibbles a normal upright plant, it eats the growing tips of the main stem. So the plant may die. If an animal nibbles a grass, it eats only the ends of the leaves. The leaf bases and stems on the ground keep growing. So grass can be grazed many times, yet keep growing. This is why it is such a good food plant for animals.

These fossilized teeth of *Parahippus* were worn down by eating grass.

THE ULTIMATE GRAZERS

In North America and Asia, the spread of grasslands produced very efficient grazing animals – horses, zebras and asses. One early horse shows how animals adapted to the new grasslands habitats. This is the 2m-long *Parahippus* from early Miocene times, which came out of the woodlands to eat grass instead of its usual diet of leaves.

CHANGING TEETH

How do we know these animals ate grass? As usual, fossil teeth give good clues. Grass leaves contain a hard chemical called silica, the same substance that forms sand. So eating grass wears teeth down. The new grazers evolved hard cheek teeth to resist wear, and high crowns to mash up the grass and get out the juicy goodness.

Wheat is one of the most successful crops that is grown worldwide.

Grass and leaves are tough and difficult to digest. So plant-eaters such as antelopes, deer and cows partly chew their food and then swallow it into the rumen, for early digestion. They then bring up, or regurgitate, the semi-digested food to chew it once more. It is then swallowed again for further digestion in the other stomach chambers.

Highland cow

Is it true that grasses are the most successful plants?

Yes, especially since people started growing crops. Three-quarters of all farmland grows cereals and other grasses. There are between 7,500 and 10,000 kinds of grasses around the world, including:

- lawn and meadow grasses
- weeds such as couch grass and fescue
- all cereal crops, such as wheat, oats, barley, rye, rice, corn, maize and sorghum
- marram grass on sand dunes
- the millet you give to pet budgies
- fluffy white pampas grass
- tall, juicy sugarcane
- woody-stemmed bamboos

Many grazers, such as *Parahippus* (right), developed powerful shoulder and hip muscles, and long, slim legs to run away from predators. They also evolved sharp senses: big all-round eyes, swivelling ears and long noses.

GRASSLANDS TODAY

PLACE	GRASSLAND NAME
East Africa	Savanna
Southern Africa	Veldt
North America	Prairie
South America	Pampas

HOOVES

Running fast would damage claws or nails. So many grazers evolved light and strong hooves. Hoofed mammals, or ungulates, include cattle, pigs, giraffes, horses, rhinos and deer.

GRASS – THE LIFE-GIVER

So you can see how much the evolution of grasses affected animal life. Remember this, next time you sit on it for a picnic!

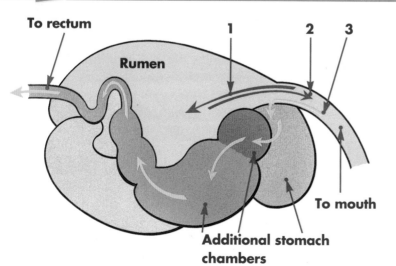

To rectum

Rumen

1 2 3

Additional stomach chambers

To mouth

CHEWING THE CUD

When grazers eat grass, they eat it twice! The first time around, the grass is swallowed quickly and taken down to the first stomach, or rumen, where it is partially digested (1). All this food is then sent back (2) to the mouth in pellets, where it is chewed again. This is called 'chewing the cud' and is done when the animal is at rest in a safe place. Chewing the cud can take several hours. The chewed cud is swallowed once again (3) and sent into further stomach chambers for digestion.

GIANTS OF THE PAST

On the flat marshes in Mid-Cretaceous Queensland, Australia, a group of *Muttaburrasaurus* is feeding peacefully on horsetails and ferns. Nearby, some *Ornithochierus* are catching fish to feed to their hungry young.

MUTTABURRASAURUS

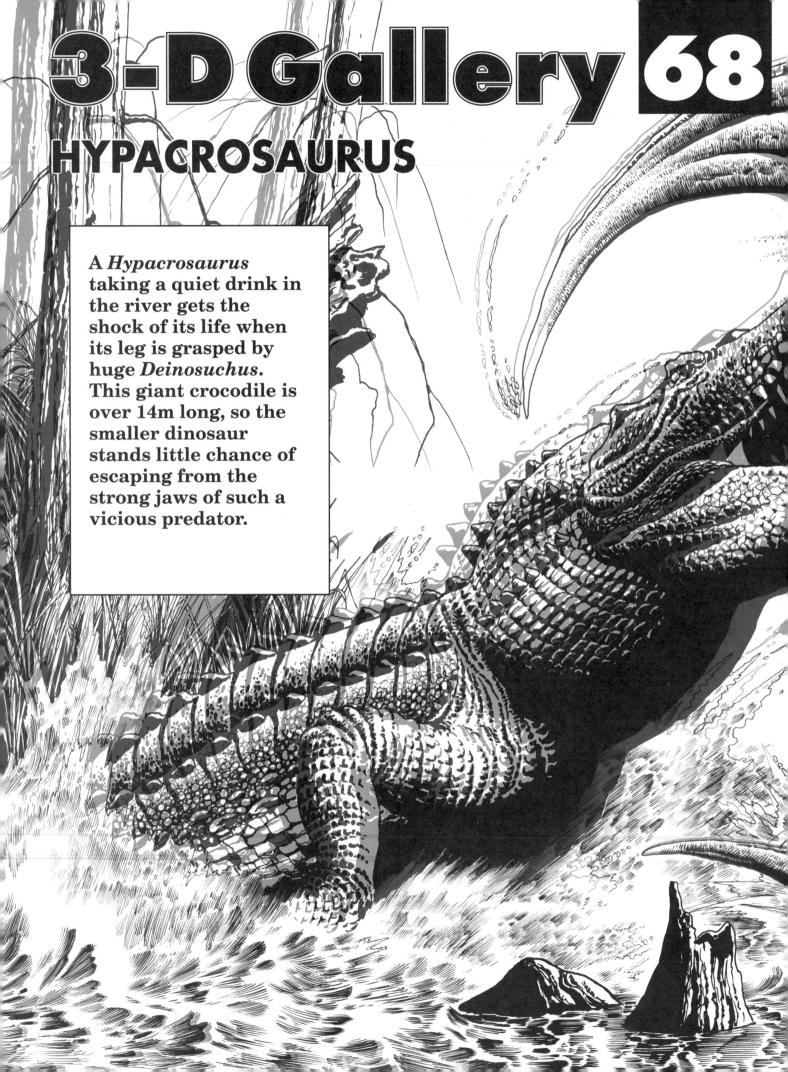

HYPACROSAURUS

A *Hypacrosaurus* taking a quiet drink in the river gets the shock of its life when its leg is grasped by huge *Deinosuchus*. This giant crocodile is over 14m long, so the smaller dinosaur stands little chance of escaping from the strong jaws of such a vicious predator.

STOP PRESS 2...

MORE LATE NEWS FROM THE MESOZOIC!

Sauropods with spikes, new dinosaurs from Britain, and yet another 'big bang' are some of the latest dinosaur news. Experts take a long time to make their ideas public because they have to check out all the facts scientifically before they can publish them.

A COMPLETE CLIFFHANGER!

Geologist Steve Hutt has made history by unearthing the most complete dinosaur skeleton ever found in Britain. More than 100 bones from a brachiosaurid as long as two elephants were found buried in a

cliff on the Isle of Wight in 1992. He also found two huge teeth of a predator, probably a megalosaur. Experts think that the dinosaurs had a battle and the big plant-eater lost.

SAUROPODS GET A NEW IMAGE

A sculptor and palaeontologist from Utah has challenged the view that sauropods had smooth, streamlined body shapes. Stephen Czerkas examined the remains of a *Diplodocus*-like dinosaur found in Wyoming, North America, and concluded that at least part of its whiplash tail had spikes running along the centre. How far these spikes extended along the dinosaur's back is a mystery. But it seems that sauropods may never look the same again.

FROZEN IN TIME

It is only in the last few years that dinosaur remains have been found in Antarctica. Hidden by the ice and snow, fossilized remains have been hard to find. Among the new discoveries are an ankylosaur (as yet unnamed), an ornithopod and a meat-eater with some strange horns.

Is this Jurassic Park?

A huge tooth and some vertebrae, found deep in the Cotswold Hills in western England by Kevin Gardner and his young daughter, have unlocked the door to a wonderful discovery. The bones found belonged to two dinosaurs, *Megalosaurus* and *Cetiosaurus* from the Jurassic. Six years and several tonnes of clay later, more than 30,000 bones and teeth have been revealed. Experts believe up to four different dinosaurs lived in this small area as well as some mysterious bird-like creatures.

The dawn of the dinosaur age

In the foothills of the Andes Mountains, South America, an Argentinian student picked up an unusual rock. Inside lay two tiny teeth of what is probably the world's oldest known dinosaur. Recently named Eoraptor or 'dawn stealer', this flesh-eater lived 225 million years ago. A fierce predator, Eoraptor has been called the 'most primitive dinosaur ever found'.

The day the Earth went bang

Experts think they have a new clue as to why dinosaurs disappeared 66 million years ago. New evidence shows that a collision took place in the solar system. A huge crater, about 300km wide and 24km deep, found in the Yucatan Peninsula, Mexico, was probably caused by an asteroid which may have wiped out the dinosaurs.

163

Mass extinctions

Although the mass extinction that killed off the dinosaurs was spectacular, it was not the only one in the Earth's long history.

When all sorts of animals die at the same time we call it a mass extinction. What a terrible-sounding disaster!

ANIMALS – NO MORE...

Extinction means dying out completely. Can you imagine that? If, for instance, all the whales in the world suddenly died, we would only know them as pictures in books. There would be no more whales, ever.

THE SUCCESS OF THE SURVIVORS

But species dying out is all part of evolution. The dinosaurs died out 66 million years ago and look what happened after that. Because they disappeared from the Earth, the mammals were able to take over and develop into the great variety of mammal life we see around us today. All because of the great dinosaur extinction.

ALL GO TOGETHER

So let us take a close look at what happened 66 million years ago at the end of the Cretaceous Period. It was not only the dinosaurs that became extinct. Many other animals did as well. The pterosaurs died out, as did the great sea reptiles such as the plesiosaurs and the mosasaurs.

T rex

Mosasaurus

164

SEA DEATHS

And it was not just the large beasts that became extinct. Most of the microscopic creatures that floated in the sea died out too, as did the ammonites that were so common in the oceans.

Elasmosaurus

Ammonite

Triceratops

THE BIG QUESTIONS

Why did this happen? And why were the mammals spared? Why did the birds survive? Why was there no effect on the modern types of fishes? Why did the crocodiles live on while their relatives, the dinosaurs, did not? There are no simple answers. We just don't know for sure.

WITH A BANG

There are lots of possible explanations. Maybe something from space crashed into the Earth – something like a mountain of rock, which is called a meteorite, or a mass of ice, which is called a comet. The damage such a collision would have done to the environment could have killed off many types of animals. There seems to be some evidence for this theory in the Cretaceous rocks.

WITH A WHIMPER

On the other hand, these extinctions may have happened slowly. Dinosaurs could have spread diseases as they migrated to new territories. Temperatures may have changed, becoming very hot or very cold, and the big animals may have been unable to adapt quickly enough. There is evidence for this too. Fossils of plants from Cretaceous times show that the vegetation, and hence the climate, did change towards the end of the Cretaceous Period.

WITH A WHIMPER-BANG?

Perhaps the dinosaurs were dying off anyway, when along came a meteorite and finished them off! Certainly there were fewer different dinosaur types towards the end of the Cretaceous Period, with species dying out at a greater rate than new ones evolved. The truth is, we just do not know.

165

FIRST WIPE-OUT

More than half of the world's animals died out at the end of the Ordovician Period, about 440 million years ago. It was the first major mass extinction.

ALL CHANGE AT SEA

In the seas, the trilobites were almost wiped out. They survived, but there were nowhere near as many as there had been before. Just after this period of extinction, the fishes began to evolve to rule the seas.

REEF WRECK

The next mass extinction occurred during the Devonian Period, about 370 million years ago. Many creatures, including some reef-building corals, died out. With few reef-builders, reefs vanished from the shallow seas. Some scientists think that this was due to water, with less oxygen in, sweeping from the deep oceans into the shallow seas. The amphibians, with their ability to breathe outside the water, began to evolve shortly afterwards.

AN ALMOST EMPTY SEA

The biggest mass extinction of them all came at the end of the Permian Period, about 245 million years ago. A staggering 96 per cent of species of sea-living animals died out at this time. This probably occurred because all the continents moved together forming the single supercontinent of Pangaea. As a result, many of the shallow seas were squeezed out from between the merging continents.

TRIASSIC CHANGE

Then, about 210 million years ago, came the mass extinction that brought the Triassic Period to a halt.

245 MYA

370 MYA

440 MYA

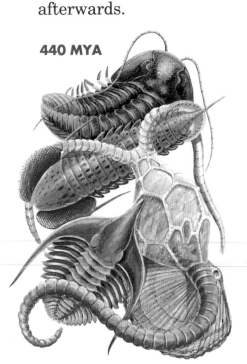

Late Ordovician – 50% of species, including some brachiopods, die out.

Late Devonian – 50% of species, including some fish, corals and trilobites, die out.

Late Permic
living thing

WELCOME, DINOSAURS

Again the sea animals living during the Triassic Period were hit particularly badly, about half of them disappearing for ever. At about this time the dinosaurs really became the masters of the Earth.

BYE BYE, DINOSAURS

The final extinction, at the end of the Cretaceous Period, is the one we know most about. But still we do not know for sure the cause of it.

HISTORY REPEATS ITSELF?

And what of today? Are we living through another mass extinction? Recently we have lost dodos, moas, passenger pigeons, steller's sea cows, marsupial wolves (maybe), and all sorts of other creatures.

Is it true that many amphibians and reptiles died out at the end of the Permian Period?

Yes. About 75 per cent of all the amphibian and reptile families on Earth died out in the biggest mass extinction of life on Earth – so far.

NEW WHALES?

In the far future the fossils in the rocks formed at this time will mark the end of these creatures, and so count as a mass extinction. And if more creatures, such as the whales, die out? It will be very sad for us, and our children, and their children. But, as we have seen, something else will eventually, after millions of years, evolve to take their place. What kind of beast will it be?

66 MYA

210 MYA

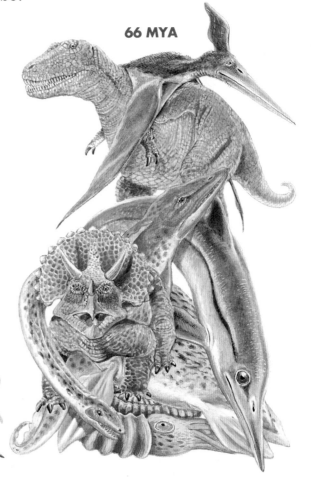

ver 95% of all
ie out.

End of the Triassic – many animals, including most of the land vertebrates, die out.
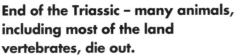

End of the Cretaceous – 50% of species die out, including the dinosaurs.

A DAY IN THE LIFE OF SMILODON

12,000 YEARS AGO A MOTHER SMILODON KEEPS A WATCHFUL EYE ON HER CUBS AS THEY ENJOY A LIVELY ROMP IN THE EARLY MORNING SUNSHINE.

THE PLAINS OF WESTERN AMERICA OFFER PLENTY OF PREY FOR A SKILLED HUNTER LIKE SMILODON.

SOON IT WILL BE TIME FOR THEM TO LEARN TO HUNT...

... THEY ATTACK, CLAWS UNSHEATHED AND SABRE-TEETH READY TO PIERCE THROUGH THE THICK SKIN OF THE GREAT MAMMOTH.

THE MAMMOTH CHARGES ANGRILY TOWARDS ITS ATTACKERS, DOING WHAT IT CAN TO FEND OFF THE VICIOUS ATTACK.

BUT THE MAMMOTH FIGHTS BACK.

SUDDENLY, ONE OF THE CATS STOPS AND STANDS ALMOST PERFECTLY STILL, SNIFFING THE AIR AROUND HER.
CONSTANTLY ON THE ALERT, THE SMILODON HAS CAUGHT A WHIFF OF LIKELY PREY.

THE BIG CATS KNOW EXACTLY WHAT TO DO...

THE YOUNG CUBS WATCH INTENTLY AS THE ADULT SMILODONS MOVE IN.

WHEN THE ADULT SMILODONS ARE AS CLOSE AS THEY CAN BE..

MEANWHILE...

DESPERATE TO FEND OFF THE SNARLING SMILODONS, THE GREAT MAMMOTH FORGETS ABOUT ITS YOUNG JUST LONG ENOUGH FOR THE OTHER SMILODONS TO SPRING THE ATTACK.

THE YOUNG MAMMOTH IS NO MATCH FOR THE KILLING CATS.

THE ADULT SMILODONS MOVE IN FOR THE FEED.

AND ONLY WHEN THEY HAVE HAD THEIR FILL...

... ARE THE LITTLE CUBS ALLOWED TO FEED. BY WATCHING THE ADULTS HUNT, THEY LEARN THE SKILLS THEY WILL SHORTLY NEED WHEN THEY HAVE TO TAKE THEIR PLACE IN THE PACK.

Improve and test your knowledge with...

FACT FILE

Dimetrodon holds all the answers. See how you score in the quiz.

Picking bones

The biggest and most complete Tyrannosaurus skeleton ever found has been confiscated by the American government. Nobody can agree as to who owns it, and until this is sorted out, no research can be done on it.

Half way to whales

An animal mid-way between a land-living creature and a swimming whale has now been found. It is called Ambulocetus and lived in the Eocene in Pakistan. It must have looked like a long-headed, long-tailed sea lion.

5 Mammoths used their tusks for:
a) stabbing carnivores
b) pushing away snow
c) building snowmen

4 Grazers wore down their teeth by:
a) chewing gum
b) chewing grass
c) biting their nails

3 *Deinosuchus* is a giant:
a) bird
b) dinosaur
c) crocodile

2 *Muttaburrasaurus* was as long as:
a) an elephant
b) a horse
c) a kangaroo

1 Dinosaurs did not eat grass because:
a) they didn't like it
b) there was no grass
c) they used it for bedding

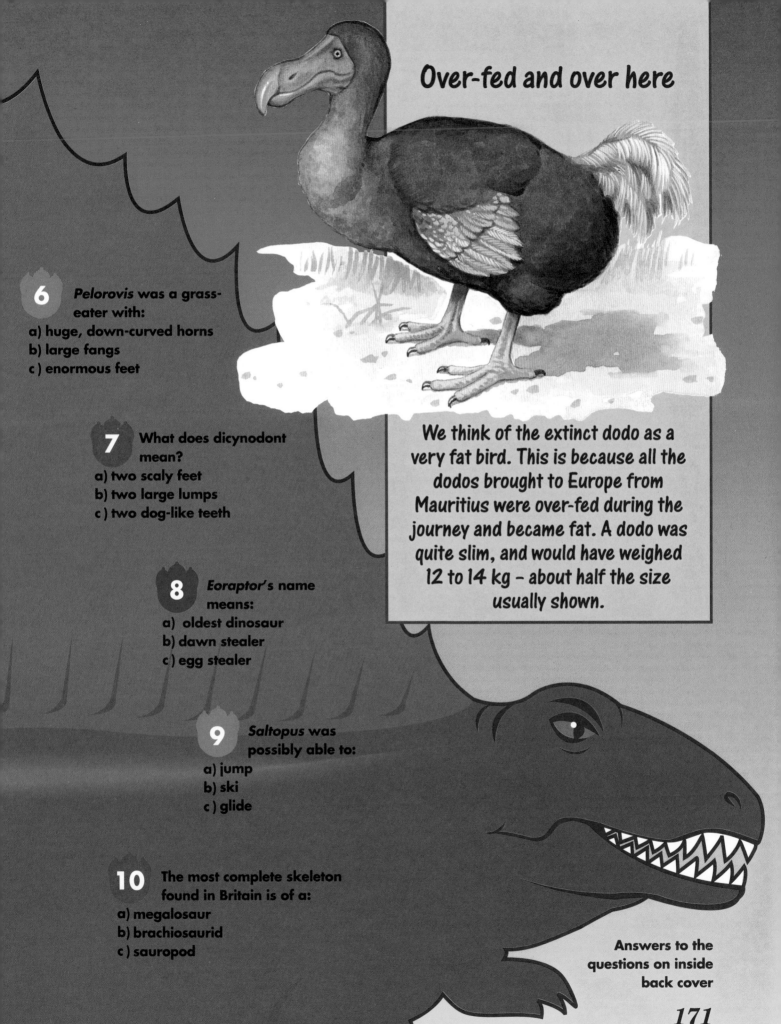

Over-fed and over here

6 *Pelorovis* was a grass-eater with:
a) huge, down-curved horns
b) large fangs
c) enormous feet

7 What does dicynodont mean?
a) two scaly feet
b) two large lumps
c) two dog-like teeth

8 *Eoraptor's* name means:
a) oldest dinosaur
b) dawn stealer
c) egg stealer

9 *Saltopus* was possibly able to:
a) jump
b) ski
c) glide

10 The most complete skeleton found in Britain is of a:
a) megalosaur
b) brachiosaurid
c) sauropod

We think of the extinct dodo as a very fat bird. This is because all the dodos brought to Europe from Mauritius were over-fed during the journey and became fat. A dodo was quite slim, and would have weighed 12 to 14 kg – about half the size usually shown.

Answers to the questions on inside back cover

ASK THE EXPERT

Dr David Norman of Cambridge University answers your dinosaur questions

Can we tell what kind of dinosaurs made a particular footprint?

In general terms, it is possible to tell the difference between the footprints of different dinosaurs. For example, sauropod prints are very large and rounded; ornithopods have quite broad, three-toed prints; theropods have three-toed prints too, but their toes tend to be long and sharply pointed. However, it is not possible to be precise about dinosaur footprints. We cannot yet analyse footprints, like the mythical detective Sherlock Holmes, and say who made them.

What did a mammoth use its big tusks for?

A mammoth's tusks were huge and bow-ended and were almost certainly used as snow ploughs to push away the snow so it could feed on the vegetation below. Its tusks would also have been good weapons for fending off large carnivores (but would have only been useful for pushing animals aside rather than for stabbing). They might also have played a role in attracting a partner during the mating season.

Why is palaeontologist sometimes spelt paleontologist?

The difference in spelling is just a national preference. Palaeontologist comes from palaeontology which was invented in the 1830s in Britain and follows classical spelling. This word has been 'Americanised' and is spelled paleontology by removing the 'a' after the first 'l'. As an Englishman, I prefer the traditional spelling of palaeontology.

If humans had lived with the dinosaurs, could we have trained them to work for us?

I think it is unlikely that dinosaurs could have been trained by humans. It is true that some birds can be trained, and they are closest to the dinosaurs. But dinosaurs were mostly too big and too dangerous. Some more intelligent, non-predatory dinosaurs could well have been trained. But who knows?

DIMETRODON

Sail-backed *Dimetrodon* was as long as a modern hippopotamus and heavier than a tiger.

Dimetrodon had the varied teeth of a mammal, and the scaly skin of a reptile. It belonged to the group of mammal-like reptiles that were the ancestors of true mammals. *Dimetrodon* was a pelycosaur (sail-shaped reptile), a type of animal that appeared about 280 million years ago and died out 30 million years later. It lived before the dinosaurs.

MEAL MACHINE
As its name suggests, *Dimetrodon* had two sorts of teeth. It was a fierce predator with teeth like steak knives. It used two pairs of sharp, pointed canine teeth to rip the skin of its victims. Further back in its jaws, *Dimetrodon* had smaller cutting teeth to slice its food into digestible chunks.

OPEN WIDE!
With its jaws closed, *Dimetrodon* almost looked as if it was grinning. But when it opened its powerful jaws and showed its wide, gaping mouth, its appearance was far from friendly. Because its jaws were so huge, *Dimetrodon* was probably capable of eating animals of its own size.

SPECTACULAR SAIL
Dimetrodon's most dominant feature was the huge sail that rose steeply along its back. The sail of skin was supported by fan-shaped spines like a kite. The sail may have been brightly coloured.

The skeleton of the sail-shaped *Dimetrodon* which lived about 280 million years ago.

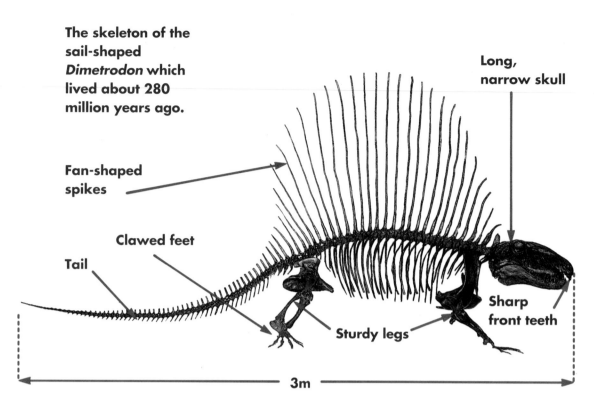

Long, narrow skull

Fan-shaped spikes

Clawed feet

Tail

Sturdy legs

Sharp front teeth

3m

Dimetrodon were carnivores and they often used their razor-sharp front teeth to catch smaller lizards such as *Araeoscelis*.

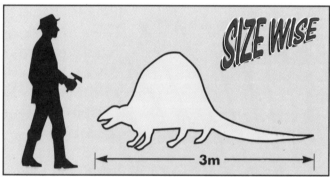

SIZE WISE

3m

IT'S A FACT

HOTTING UP

Dimetrodon's sail meant that its body temperature rose in half the time that it took a sail-less creature to get warm. Experts have worked out that an average-sized animal could raise its body heat by 8°C in two hours. A reptile without a sail needed double the amount of time to reach the same temperature.

EARLY MOVER

Experts think that *Dimetrodon's* sail helped it to be an efficient hunter. Athletes know how important it is to 'warm up' before a race. When a body is cold, it moves more slowly. As it stood in the warmth of the morning sun, *Dimetrodon's* sail absorbed the heat and its body temperature rose. This meant that *Dimetrodon* was active earlier than its cold-blooded, slow-moving prey.

CHILL OUT

Dimetrodon also cooled down quickly by moving to a shady spot where its sail gave out excess heat. This ability to control its body temperature quickly was a great advantage. It was like having a radiator built into its body.

HELD DOWN

Like the huge-headed carnosaurs of the dinosaur age, *Dimetrodon*'s skull was very big compared to the rest of its body. The animal's weight was supported by four sprawling legs with clawed feet. As *Dimetrodon* crawled along, its claws gripped the ground beneath for extra stability. They were also effective weapons. Small creatures were easily caught and held down as *Dimetrodon*'s ferocious jaws loomed towards them.

MONSTER FACTS

- **NAME:** *Dimetrodon* (die-<u>met</u>-ro-don) means 'two long teeth'
- **GROUP:** mammal-like reptile (MLR)
- **SIZE:** 3m long
- **FOOD:** meat
- **LIVED:** about 280 million years ago in Early Permian Period in Texas and Oklahoma, USA

175

THERIZINOSAURUS

On each hand *Therizinosaurus* had a gigantic claw which was about as long as a child's arm.

uring an expedition to the Gobi Desert, Mongolia, in 1948, scientists discovered some large, bony claws. Later, a bit of another claw, an arm, legs and a tooth were found. They belonged to *Therizinosaurus*, a dinosaur that could easily tear open flesh.

LONG REACH

Therizinosaurus was long enough to reach both ends of a tennis net at once. It walked on two strong legs, holding its long tail out behind. Its arms were as long as a small car.

CURVED CLAWS

But this dinosaur's most amazing feature was its curved claws. To get an idea of the actual size of its biggest claws, hold out your arm and curve it round slightly. *Therizinosaurus'* largest claws were roughly the length from your neck to your wrist.

SIZE WISE

12m

MONSTER FACTS

- **NAME:** *Therizinosaurus* (<u>ther</u>-ih-zin-<u>oh</u>-saw-rus) means 'scythe reptile'
- **GROUP:** dinosaur
- **SIZE:** up to 12m long
- **FOOD:** meat, insects, plants
- **LIVED:** about 75 million years ago in the Late Cretaceous Period in Mongolia

LETTING RIP

So what did *Therizinosaurus* use its great claws for ? Like other fierce predators, it probably used the talons as weapons to tear its victim's flesh. Some experts have even suggested that *Therizinosaurus* ripped open anthills with its claw. But it surely must have taken a great many ants to satisfy the hunger of this huge animal!

LAGOSUCHUS

The rabbit-sized *Lagosuchus* was probably an ancestor of the dinosaurs.

Scurrying along on its two skinny legs, *Lagosuchus* looked just like a miniature dinosaur. Experts think that *Lagosuchus*' legs and hips were too primitive for it to be a real dinosaur. But it did also share many of the same features as small, two-legged dinosaurs.

TWICE AS LONG

Many animals that run fast have legs of a similar shape. The dinosaur *Velociraptor* had long legs with muscular thighs and slender shins. It could take long strides and move at great speed. *Lagosuchus* had shins which were twice the length of its thighs. So, like *Velociraptor*, it must have been a good sprinter. *Lagosuchus* was also more like a dinosaur than a reptile as it could run with its hind legs held under its body and not sprawled out on either side.

CLOSE ANCESTORS

Some experts think *Lagosuchus* was related to pterosaurs and crocodiles.

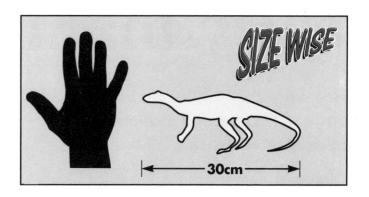

SIZE WISE

30cm

MONSTER FACTS

- **NAME:** *Lagosuchus* (lag-oh-sook-us) means 'rabbit crocodile'
- **GROUP:** reptile
- **SIZE:** about 30 cm long
- **FOOD:** meat
- **LIVED:** about 220 million years ago in the Mid-Triassic Period in Argentina.

SOMETHING IN COMMON

Lagosuchus had a long, thin tail like a dinosaur, which helped to balance its head and neck as it ran along after prey. Its light frame made it a very agile hunter. It had a narrow head, slender jaws and a pointed snout.

Condylarths – the early mammals

Not long after all the dinosaurs died out, the first hoofed mammals appeared on Earth.

Picture an animal as big as a sheep, with a leg at each corner, a tail at one end, five toes on each foot and 44 teeth in its jaws. It doesn't sound very special does it? Just another animal with no distinctive features and one which had not particularly adapted to a special way of life. This animal is called *Ectoconus* and it lived in the Early Palaeocene Epoch in North America.

EVOLUTION'S RAW MATERIAL

Ectoconus is the kind of animal that evolution likes to work on, to produce more specialised animals that can live in different habitats.

The tiny *Hyopsodus*, a condylarth, came from Wyoming in the USA.

SPECIAL GROUP

Ectoconus is a member of a mammal group called the condylarths (<u>con</u>-dee-larths) which developed at the very beginning of the Age of Mammals. It was the basic model from which more complex animals evolved. It seems likely that all the ungulates (the hoofed mammals), the elephants and even the whales came from these beasts.

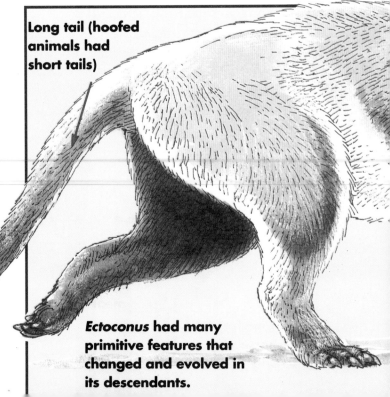

Long tail (hoofed animals had short tails)

Ectoconus had many primitive features that changed and evolved in its descendants.

Is it true

that there is a living condylarth?

The animal alive today that is most closely related to the condylarths could well be the aardvark of Africa (right). The problem is that it is so specialised as a termite-eater that it is difficult to see a connection with its primitive ancestors.

Andrewsarchus were gigantic meat-eating condylarths.

SOME EARLY TRIES

However, while they all existed together as a group, the condylarths developed into a number of different forms. One early form displayed claws instead of hoofs or nails.

THE MEAT-EATERS

Another form of condylarth became meat-eaters, hunting the creodonts and the modern carnivores. *Andrewsarchus* was a gigantic meat-eating condylarth. Whales probably evolved from these meat-eaters.

HOOFS ARRIVE

Yet another form developed hoofs on its toes. *Phenacodus* was the earliest of the hoofed animals. It may have evolved into the odd-toed ungulates (animals like horses), the even-toed ungulates (animals like deer and antelope) or the strange extinct ungulates that once lived in South America.

ALL GONE

As a group, the condylarths existed until the Oligocene Epoch. Their descendants became so specialised, as running animals, as swimming animals, or as ant-eating animals, that we cannot see any resemblance between them and the primitive creatures that existed in the earliest Palaeocene times.

Flat cheek teeth like a plant-eater

Long, canine teeth like a meat-eater

Five-toed feet (the horse has only one)

Amblypods

One early development from the condylarth line was a special group that we call the amblypods – the 'slow feet'.

Amblypods were all large plant-eaters. They wandered the Palaeocene and Eocene forests of North America and Europe in the same way as today's rhinos and hippos. To support their weight, their feet grew stout and their nails developed into hoofs.

ROOTERS

The earliest amblypods date from the Mid-Palaeocene. These were the pantodonts which were about the size of dogs. Later types developed into pony-sized animals such as *Barylamda,* and hippopotamus-sized animals such as *Coryphodon.* They probably looked a little like bears, with their heavy bodies and flat feet, but their mouths often had very large teeth for dealing with their plant food. They probably scraped about in the ground for roots and tubers like pigs do today.

What is ? AN ARSINOITHERE

We are not quite sure. It looked a bit like a uintathere, with its rhinoceros-like body, but it had a pair of enormous hollow (yes, hollow) horns on its head. It was not related to the uintatheres, nor to anything else we know. It lived in the forests of Africa in Oligocene times.

Barylamda

180

Uintatherium

Coryphodon

HORNED BEASTS

The most spectacular of the amblypods belonged to a group called the uintatheres (<u>oo</u>-in-ta-theers). These looked a bit like rhinoceroses but their heads had a set of six horns. The first pair may have been sheathed in horn, but the other two pairs were probably covered in skin like those of a giraffe. Not content with these, the uintatheres had huge tusks in the upper jaw, probably used for defence, or for slashing bark off trees. *Uintatherium* was the largest of the uintatheres.

COME AND GONE

The amblypods were not a very intelligent line of beasts; none of them had much of a brain. They had all died out by the Oligocene, by which time their places had then been taken by other heavy-footed, hoofed mammals that had evolved from the original condylarths.

Arsinoitherium had two enormous horns that were hollow.

Some early amblypods looked like today's two-horned black rhino.

181

GIANTS OF THE PAST

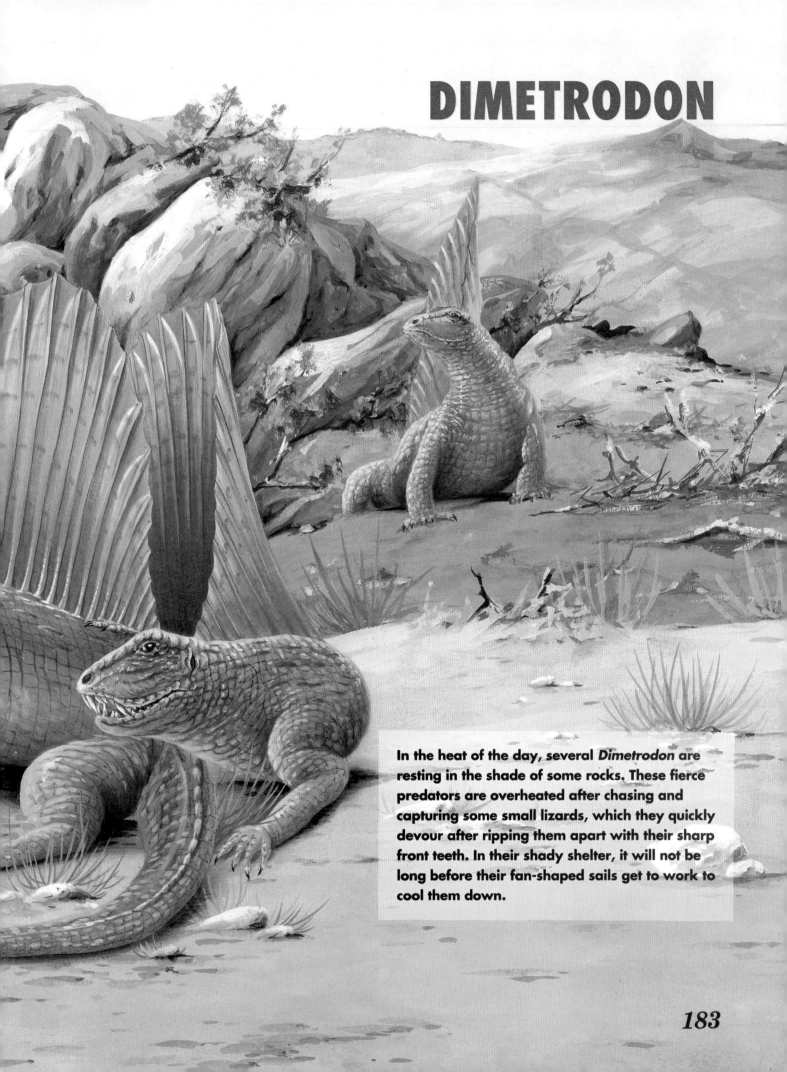

DIMETRODON

In the heat of the day, several *Dimetrodon* are resting in the shade of some rocks. These fierce predators are overheated after chasing and capturing some small lizards, which they quickly devour after ripping them apart with their sharp front teeth. In their shady shelter, it will not be long before their fan-shaped sails get to work to cool them down.

SPINOSAURUS

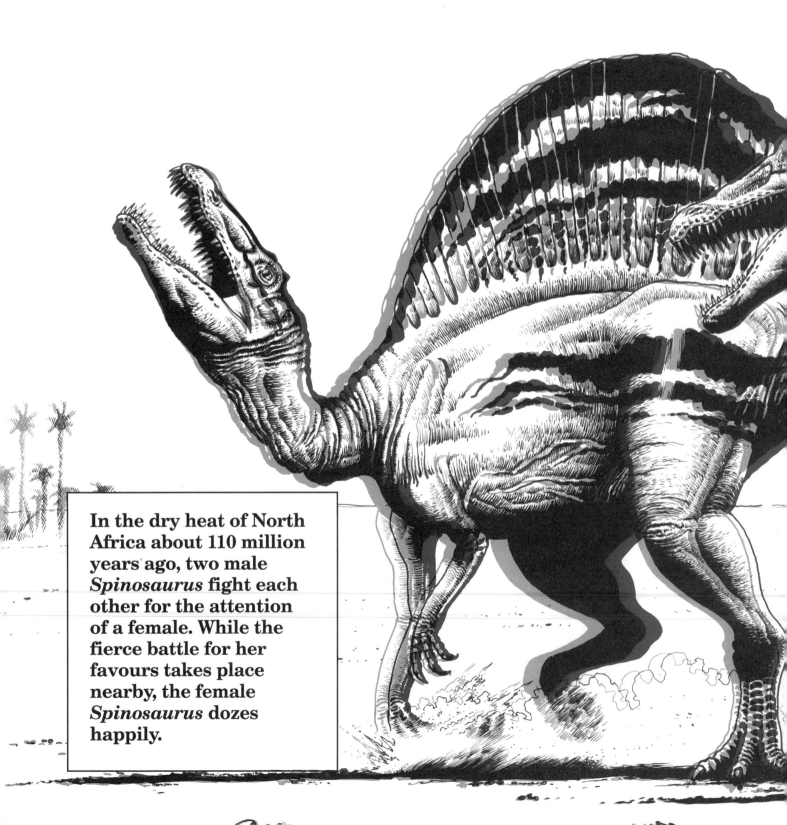

In the dry heat of North Africa about 110 million years ago, two male *Spinosaurus* fight each other for the attention of a female. While the fierce battle for her favours takes place nearby, the female *Spinosaurus* dozes happily.

Stories in the bones

The skeleton of a prehistoric animal can tell experts what it ate and how it moved, as well as its size and shape.

n animal's shape is usually well suited to the life it leads. Here you can see how varied skeletons can be and what they can show us about their owners.

HARD FACTS

Just like humans, prehistoric animals needed a skeleton in order to support their muscles. The skeleton protected the heart, brain and other soft parts of the animal. Most skeletons are very hard, so they fossilize easily.

SIMILAR SKELETONS

If a prehistoric animal is like a modern animal, it is much easier to restore its skeleton. The Columbian mammoth, for example, looked very like a modern elephant.

Ichthyosaurus skeleton

Front flippers for steering   Streamlined shape for swimming   Strong tail

LIKE A DOLPHIN

The skeleton of the reptile *Ichthyosaurus* is very similar to that of today's dolphin. *Icthyosaurus'* body was streamlined for fast swimming. It swam by swishing its tail from side to side. Its front flippers were used for steering through the water.

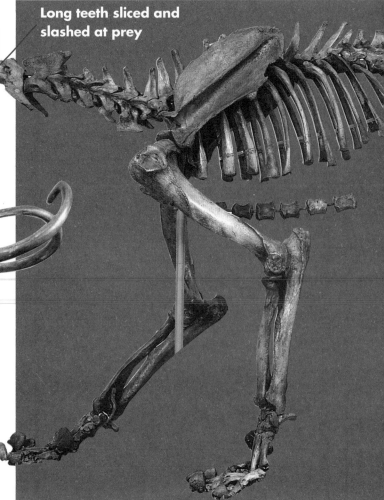

Long teeth sliced and slashed at prey

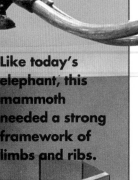

Like today's elephant, this mammoth needed a strong framework of limbs and ribs.

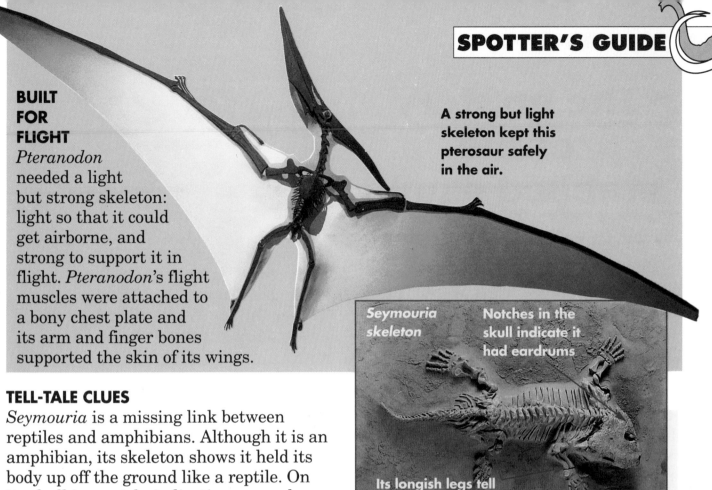

BUILT FOR FLIGHT

Pteranodon needed a light but strong skeleton: light so that it could get airborne, and strong to support it in flight. *Pteranodon*'s flight muscles were attached to a bony chest plate and its arm and finger bones supported the skin of its wings.

A strong but light skeleton kept this pterosaur safely in the air.

TELL-TALE CLUES

Seymouria is a missing link between reptiles and amphibians. Although it is an amphibian, its skeleton shows it held its body up off the ground like a reptile. On its skull is a notch, indicating an eardrum, so it could hear on land. It lived 260 million years ago in the Permian period.

Seymouria skeleton

Notches in the skull indicate it had eardrums

Its longish legs tell us it could lift its body and walk

SMILODON – SHORT LEGS, LONG TEETH

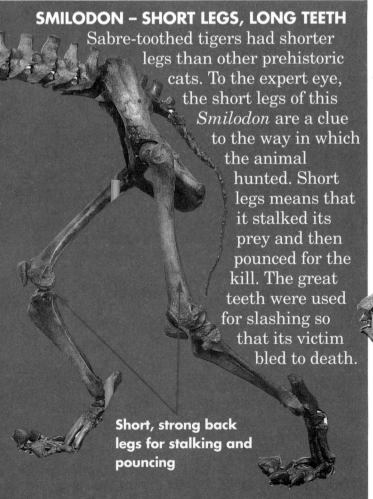

Sabre-toothed tigers had shorter legs than other prehistoric cats. To the expert eye, the short legs of this *Smilodon* are a clue to the way in which the animal hunted. Short legs means that it stalked its prey and then pounced for the kill. The great teeth were used for slashing so that its victim bled to death.

Short, strong back legs for stalking and pouncing

INSIDE AND OUT

Glyptodon was a member of the only mammal group to have a skeleton both inside and outside its body. Its huge shell protected both the outside of its body and the second skeleton inside. This 'mammal tortoise' was related to today's armadillos.

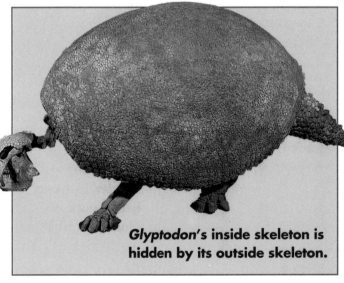

Glyptodon's inside skeleton is hidden by its outside skeleton.

187

The mystery of the stabbed skull!

A gaping skull wound made 35 million years ago set time detectives on the track of the solution to an unsolved mystery.

**W**hat had scarred the fossil skull so badly? When scientists solved this puzzle, they discovered they had also found the answer to a far more important question. Follow the clues to find out how they did it.

CLUE 1

The fossilized skull was found in North America more than 40 years ago. Experts were excited to discover that it belonged to a new species of prehistoric biting cat. They called it *Nimravus bumpensis*.

CLUE

Nimravus was called a biting cat because it killed its prey by biting it on the neck and breaking the backbone. It was a powerful hunter with few enemies. But this *Nimravus* had clearly been the victim of a savage attack. What creature would have dared to pounce on it?

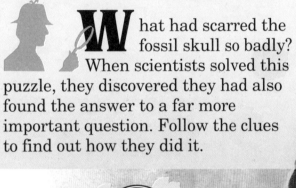

188

CLUE

A deep scar in the skull showed that *Nimravus* had been dealt a violent, stabbing blow. How had its attacker inflicted such a gaping wound?

CLUE

The size and shape of the wound showed that it must have been made by a slashing, tusk-like tooth. So scientists asked themselves: what other hunter living at the same time as *Nimravus* was armed with such a fearful weapon?

GOT IT!

Experts have agreed that the mystery attacker must have been a sabre-toothed tiger. The only creature alive at the time that was capable of striking such a savage blow was *Eusmilus*. It must have lashed out with its huge, blade-like front teeth and pierced *Nimravus* through the skull. *Nimravus* escaped being gored by both *Eusmilus'* sabre teeth because it had a narrow head. So, while one tusk-like tooth struck home, the other sliced empty air.

IT'S A FACT

STAB WOUND

A sabre-tooth killed by stabbing its prey with its blade-like front teeth. It normally aimed for its victim's neck arteries and waited for the creature to bleed to death before feeding.

189

SAVED
Eusmilus stabbed *Nimravus* in the head and not the neck, and *Nimravus* survived the blow. Experts noticed that the gash in the biting cat's skull had a bumpy ring around it. This was the scar the wound left when it healed. So *Nimravus* obviously lived long enough to recover from the attack.

RARE FIND
The discovery of a wound in the *Nimravus* skull was very exciting. It was the first clear proof scientists had found of how a sabre-tooth attacked. Experts had guessed that *Eusmilus* must have stabbed its victims with its tusk-like front teeth. Now they had the evidence to prove it.

SAVAGE STRUGGLE
Why did *Eusmilus* strike? Perhaps *Nimravus* was trying to steal its kill. The sabre-tooth could have lashed out ferociously to drive the biting cat away.

TERRIBLE TUSKS
Eusmilus had some of the longest front teeth of any sabre-tooth. They were so long it must have been quite difficult to lash out with them. Experts have calculated that *Eusmilus* had to open its lower jaw as wide as 90° before it could stab its prey effectively.

BORN TO RUN
Nimravus was probably pinned down by *Eusmilus*. But somehow it managed to struggle free. The biting cat was built for speed. Scientists believe it could have run as fast as a modern cheetah. Once *Nimravus* broke loose, it could have sprinted away. The slower-moving sabre-tooth would have been unable to catch it.

Is it true
that *Eusmilus* could have died in the fight?

No fossil evidence has been found to show what happened to the *Eusmilus* that attacked *Nimravus*. But it is possible that the sabre-tooth could have been fatally injured in the struggle. If *Nimravus* had bitten *Eusmilus*, it would have hung on until it killed the sabre-tooth. That was how it hunted.

MYSTERY SOLVED

So, from one fossilized skull, scientists have been able to work out that a terrible fight between two prehistoric cats took place over 35 million years ago. And that one of them survived a savage wound. From one skull, a wealth of fascinating information has been revealed!

These leopards (above) are only play fighting but, as they play, they are practising survival skills.

Eusmilus

Nimravus

191

A DAY IN THE LIFE OF TOROSAURUS

SO MANY OF THE HUGE ANIMALS ARE MOVING FORWARDS THAT THE TOROSAURS ON THE RIVER BANK LOSE THEIR BALANCE AND TUMBLE INTO THE ROARING WATERS BELOW.

NORTH AMERICA, 65 MILLION YEARS AGO, AND A HERD OF MIGRATING TOROSAURS IS ON THE MOVE...

...BUT THE RAINS HAVE TURNED A STREAM INTO A RAGING TORRENT. THE LEADERS STOP, BUT THE ANIMALS AT THE BACK OF THE HUGE COLUMN TRUNDLE ON.

THE ANIMALS AT THE BACK PUSH ON AND ON...

SOME OF THE ANIMALS AT THE FRONT FIND THE STRENGTH TO FORCE THEIR WAY THROUGH THE WATER AND CLAMBER UP THE BANKS TO SAFETY.

WEAKENED BY THEIR STRUGGLE, YOUNG TOROSAURS ARE EASY PREY FOR PREDATORY CROCODILIANS.

FOR THOSE IN THE WATER, ANOTHER DANGER LOOMS.

OTHERS ARE LUCKIER, OR SO IT SEEMS, BUT AS THEY REACH THE SAFETY OF THE FAR BANK...

...FORCING MORE AND MORE ANIMALS INTO THE WATER.

BUT OTHERS ARE NOT SO LUCKY.

THE LEADERS ARE TALL ENOUGH TO FORCE THEIR WAY THROUGH THE SWIRLING WATERS.

UNABLE TO KEEP THEIR BALANCE IN THE WATER, YOUNG CALVES TOPPLE OVER AND DROWN.

...THE GROUND BEGINS TO SLIDE INTO THE RIVER,

HUNDREDS OF THE PANIC-STRICKEN TOROSAURS ARE FORCED UNDERWATER BY THEIR COMPANIONS FALLING ON TOP OF THEM.

THE SURVIVORS HEAD ONWARDS, THE RIVER BEHIND THEM IS FULL OF THEIR DEAD AND DYING.

SOME ESCAPE TO DRY LAND, BUT OTHERS TUMBLE BACK INTO THE WATER.

SEVERAL HOURS AFTER THE FIRST TOROSAUR TUMBLED INTO THE WATER, SOME OF THE BEASTS AT THE BACK OF THE COLUMN MANAGE TO REACH THE FAR BANK.

SOON SCAVENGERS WILL GATHER TO GORGE THEMSELVES ON THE REMAINS OF THE TOROSAURS.

Improve and test your knowledge with...

FACT FILE

Follow the footprints to complete the quiz and get to the bottom of the question!

Using nature's workers

In the 1880s, John Bell Hatcher discovered hundreds of teeth from little Cretaceous mammals in Wyoming, USA. He found these tiny teeth in anthills. The ants had carried them to the surface.

1 Dimetrodon was a:
a) sail-shaped pterosaur
b) long-tailed dinosaur
c) sail-backed reptile

2 Therizinosaurus' arms were as long as a:
a) small car
b) racing bike
c) large truck

3 What did amblypod mean?
a) big ears
b) slow feet
c) long nose

4 Ichthyosaurus' skeleton was like that of:
a) today's elephant
b) today's dolphin
c) yesterday's dog

5 How did Dinilysia kill its victims?
a) with a knife
b) with poison
c) by suffocation

6 Seymouria is the missing link between:
a) plants and animals
b) fish and dinosaurs
c) reptiles and amphibians

7 Ectoconus lived in the Palaeocene Epoch in:
a) North Africa
b) North America
c) North Pole

8 Diprotodon was an ancestor of
a) the wombat
b) the kangaroo
c) the koala

9 Nimravus was a:
a) biting cat
b) spitting cat
c) pussy cat

10 Uintatheres had:
a) two horns
b) six horns
c) three horns

Light dinosaur

One of the biggest dinosaur balloons ever built was over 18 metres long and eight metres high. It was a sauropod built for New York's Thanksgiving Day parade in 1963. Called 'Dino', it was made from almost 300 square metres of neoprene-coated nylon and was inflated with 200 cubic metres of helium.

Big moles

When people in the Ukraine found buried frozen mammoths, they thought that they were huge burrowing animals that died when they smelt fresh air.

Hear, hear!

The earliest fossil bats, Icaronycteris and Palaeochiropteryx, lived during the Eocene Epoch in Wyoming in the USA and in Germany. They were quite primitive, but they already had the echolocation radar system that today's bats use for hunting.

Answers to the questions on inside back cover

ASK THE EXPERT

Dr David Norman of Cambridge University answers your dinosaur questions

Why are some reptiles called dinosaurs and others aren't?

All the dinosaurs were reptiles and, like all reptiles, they had scaly skins and laid shelled eggs. However, unlike other reptiles, dinosaurs tucked their legs beneath their bodies and could lift their bodies high off the ground. Living reptiles don't walk like this. Their legs stick out from the sides of their bodies. Because of this difference dinosaurs were given their special name.

Can we tell what sort of noises dinosaurs made?

There are very few dinosaurs that give any clues about the noises they made. A plastic model of *Parasaurolophus'* tubular crest has been made by one expert. This vibrates and produces a sound in response to other noises made near it. Generally, I would imagine that big dinosaurs probably had big roars, while smaller ones just twittered.

Why have sharks not changed since the Age of the Dinosaurs?

Sharks have changed quite a lot actually, but outwardly the differences are masked by their streamlined bodies. These have remained as they were because these animals swim in water. And in water, that is simply the best shape to be.

Are mammoths the only Ice Age animals to be found frozen or have there been others?

No, mammoths are not the only creatures which have been found frozen in the ice. Woolly rhinos have been found, as well as deer, musk oxen, wolverines, squirrels and many others. And an early human hunter was found recently in the Alps.

DINOSAURS!
DISCOVER THE GIANTS OF THE PREHISTORIC WORLD

PARKSOSAURUS

Parksosaurus was one of the best sprinters in the dinosaur world.

Parksosaurus was one of the last survivors of a family of agile little dinosaurs called hypsilophodontidae. This family included *Hypsilophodon* and *Leaellynasaura*. Built to run fast, these two-legged dinosaurs have been found all over the world and are often compared to the elegant gazelles of today. *Parksosaurus* lived about 50 million years later than *Hypsilophodon* and was found in the dinosaur-rich rocks of Alberta, Canada.

LIVING WITH GIANTS

In the warm, sub-tropical climate of Cretaceous Canada, *Parksosaurus* lived with much larger neighbours such as the plant-eating hadrosaur, *Lambeosaurus*, and ferocious *Albertosaurus*. *Parksosaurus* was about as long as a small car and came up to the waist of an average adult human. It managed to survive among the giants that shared its territory because it was so agile and fast-moving.

HALF A HEAD

When it was found, all that remained of *Parksosaurus* was an incomplete skull. The skull was buried in sand on its left side, so that part of it was quite well preserved. Unfortunately, the right side of the skull was more exposed and these parts had become damaged and broken.

FAST LEG SWING

A light-weight dinosaur, *Parksosaurus* ran with the easy, gliding style of an athlete. Its feet and shin bones were long, and the strong upper bones of its legs helped *Parksosaurus* to swing its legs backwards and forwards at great speed. It could accelerate fast to run away from enemies.

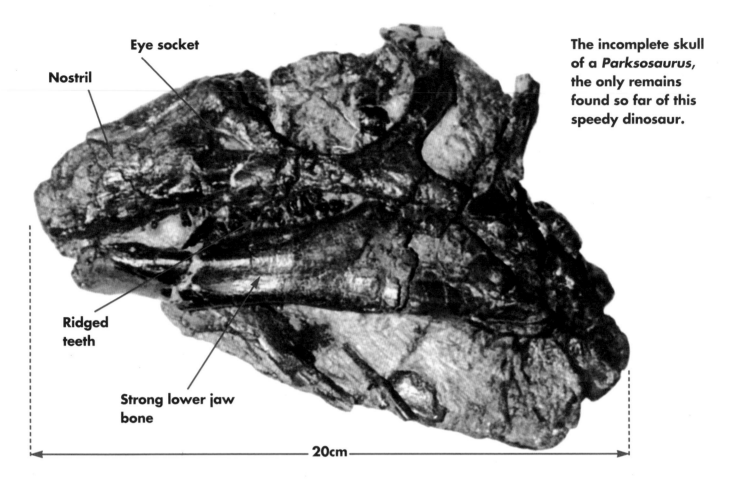

Nostril

Eye socket

Ridged teeth

Strong lower jaw bone

20cm

The incomplete skull of a *Parksosaurus*, the only remains found so far of this speedy dinosaur.

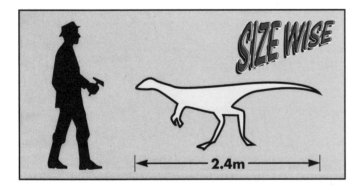

SIZE WISE

2.4m

MONSTER FACTS

- **NAME:** *Parksosaurus* (parx-oh-saw-rus) is named after a Canadian palaeontologist, William Parks.
- **GROUP:** dinosaur
- **SIZE:** 2.4m long
- **FOOD:** plants
- **LIVED:** about 70 million years ago in the Late Cretaceous Period in Alberta, Canada

FINGERS AND TOES

Like *Hypsilophodon*, *Parksosaurus* probably had long, slender feet with sharp claws on each of its four toes to grip the ground when it ran. Its arms were short and its five-fingered hands probably had small claws to help it tear leaves from branches.

SHARP FOCUS

Speed alone was not always enough to save a small plant-eater from harm. *Parksosaurus* also needed sharp eyes so that it could spot signs of danger. All around its large eyeball, *Parksosaurus* had a ring of small bones. These supported the eye and eyelid, and experts think that this may have given the dinosaur good sight.

WELL CHEWED

Chewing food slowly and thoroughly helps break it down and this helps to prevent stomach ache! *Parksosaurus* developed a good system of chewing. It had strong jaw muscles and cheeks. As it munched plants and leaves, they were crushed by an overlapping line of ridged teeth at the sides of its mouth.

BACK AND FORTH

The food was constantly pushed back on to the teeth by the dinosaur's pouch-like cheeks so it could be chewed over and over again. Only when it was ground to a pulp was the food finally digested in the stomach.

Is it true that hypsilophodonts lived on Earth longer than any other ornithopod dinosaurs?

Yes. Hypsilophodonts lived from the middle of the Jurassic Period to the end of the Cretaceous, spanning some 100 million years. These successful, agile plant-eaters have been found in Asia, Antarctica, Australia and Europe.

Although *Parksosaurus* was much smaller than many other dinosaurs, it managed to survive successfully because of its speed and agility.

NOTHOSAURUS

Even the most slippery fish were not safe from the sharp teeth of *Nothosaurus*.

Nothosaurus swam in Triassic seas alongside the early ichthyosaurs, but they did not have such streamlined bodies. *Nothosaurus* had wide, flat limbs that it probably used to drive its body through the water in a sort of doggy-paddle style.

DASH AND GRAB
Nothosaurus had long, sharp teeth. The reptile would snatch a fish in its jaws, piercing through the flesh. The helpless fish was held in the secure grasp of these interlocking jaws until the struggle was over and *Nothosaurus* swallowed its supper.

HOLE IN THE HEAD
Nothosaurus belonged to a group of reptiles called euryapsids (yoo-ree-ap-sids) that had a hole in the front of their skulls. Most of them had disappeared by the end of the Triassic.

SIZE WISE

3m

MONSTER FACTS

- **NAME:** *Nothosaurus* (no-thoh-saw-rus) means 'spurious reptile'
- **GROUP:** reptile
- **SIZE:** up to 3m long
- **FOOD:** fish and sea creatures
- **LIVED:** about 215 million years ago in Mid-Triassic Germany and South Africa

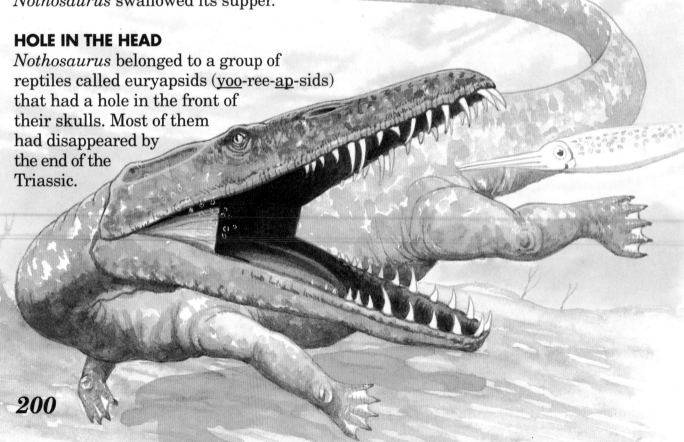

DRAVIDOSAURUS

Dravidosaurus is the only stegosaur known to have lived in India.

*ravidosaurus* lived millions of years after its stegosaur relatives roamed the Earth. The African stegosaur, *Kentrosaurus,* lived in the Jurassic Period more than 70 million years before *Dravidosaurus* appeared. The Indian dinosaur seems to have been the last of the stegosaurs.

NIP AND MUNCH

Dravidosaurus was named in 1979 from the remains of a skull but other fossils have been found since then. It was about as long as a small car with a tiny, low-slung head. As it ambled along on four short, sturdy legs, *Dravidosaurus* stooped to munch at plants and shoots that grew within its reach. It nipped off leaves with its toothless beak and then crushed them with its ridged teeth.

SIZE WISE

3m

MONSTER FACTS

- **NAME:** *Dravidosaurus* (dra-<u>vid</u>-oh-<u>saw</u>-rus) means 'reptile from southern India'
- **GROUP:** dinosaur
- **SIZE:** up to 3m long
- **FOOD:** plants
- **LIVED:** about 65 million years ago in the Late Cretaceous Period in southern India

KEEP OFF

Like other stegosaurs, *Dravidosaurus* had armour plates along its back to deter meat-eating predators from attacking it.

Giants and thunder

Millions of years ago, giant mammals, relatives of today's rhinos, hippos and tapirs, thundered across the land.

E lephants are big! Have you seen a live one? A big male is the largest living land animal. It weighs 6 tonnes and stands 3.5m tall at the shoulder. But if you had been in Asia about 30 million years ago, you might have seen the biggest land mammal that ever lived; it was called *Indricotherium*.

BIGGER THAN BIG?

Indricotherium was more than 8m long, and weighed up to 20 tonnes. It was 5.5m high at the shoulder. Its massive body was supported on four pillar-like legs. With its long, thick neck, it could stretch up to eat leaves nearly 8m above the ground!

RHINO WITHOUT A HORN

Indricotherium was not a giant elephant, or a massive giraffe. It was a rhino. Like many prehistoric rhinos, it had no horns. The rhino group was larger in prehistoric times; today, it has only five species. Rhinos belong to the mammal group called the odd-toed ungulates.

ONE OF THE FIRST

One of the first rhinos was *Hyrachyus*, which lived about 40 million years ago. Its remains have been found in China, France and Wyoming in North America.

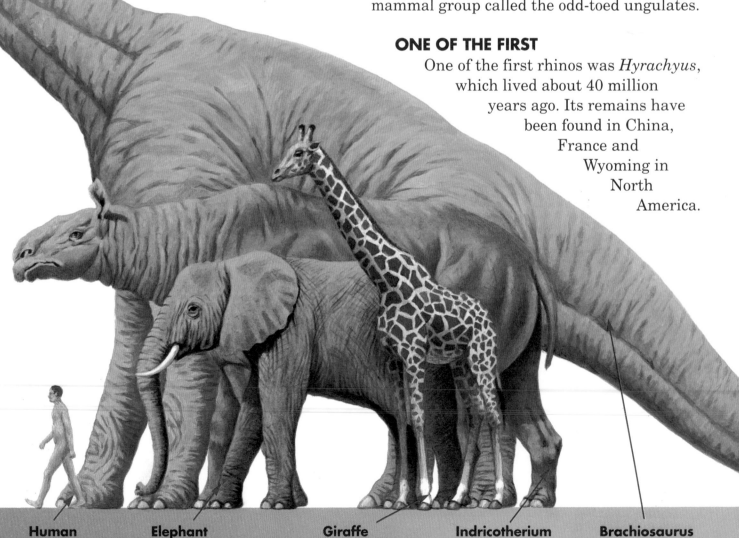

Human   Elephant   Giraffe   Indricotherium   Brachiosaurus

beasts

Looking like a cross between a tapir and a primitive rhino, *Hyrachyus* lived in North America during the Eocene Epoch.

RHINOS GALORE

Hyrachyus had three small hoofs on each foot, and was about the size of a pig. In fact, it was very similar to the pig-like tapirs, another group of odd-toed ungulates. Some prehistoric rhinos looked more like hippos. One was *Teleoceras*. It lived 10 million years ago in central North America. It had a barrel-shaped body and stumpy legs, and was 4m long. Some prehistoric rhinos had nose horns; one was *Elasmotherium*. It roamed Europe and Asia about a million years ago. It was the size of an elephant with a horn on its nose that measured up to 2m long!

Indricotherium was the largest land mammal. It would have been dwarfed by a *Brachiosaurus* but was bigger than today's elephant.

What is ? AN ODD-TOED UNGULATE

Ungulates are mammals with hoofs on their feet, instead of claws or nails. There are two main groups today:

● Odd-toed ungulates. On each foot they have three hoofs, like rhinos and tapirs. Or one hoof per foot, like horses and zebras.

● Even-toed ungulates. On each foot they have four or two hoofs. This group includes camels, pigs, hippos, giraffes, deer, antelope, sheep, goats and cattle.

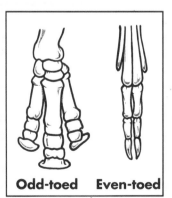

Odd-toed   **Even-toed**

PIGS OF THE FOREST

Tapirs are pig-shaped, odd-toed ungulates. They live in the forests of Central and South America and South-East Asia. There are four species living today. But, like rhinos, there were many more tapirs in prehistoric times.

THE TAPIR'S 'TRUNK'

Heptodon was a small, early tapir that lived 50 million years ago in North America. Later on there was *Helaletes* which lived about 40 million years ago. This tapir had the beginnings of a long, fleshy snout, like a small elephant trunk, which tapirs still have today. A tapir uses it for sniffing and probing, and pulling food into its mouth. *Miotapirus*, another tapir from North America, lived 20 million years ago. The tapir group is one of the most ancient of mammal groups.

Heptodon was an early tapir. It looked rather different from today's tapir pictured on the right.

Brontotherium (left), from North America, and *Embolotherium*, from Mongolia, were 'thunder beasts' that lived 40 million years ago.

Tapir

BIG-NOSED 'THUNDER BEASTS'

The rhinos and tapirs had some really weird odd-toed cousins, the brontotheres ('thunder beasts') and the chalicotheres. These were massive-bodied plant-eaters, too. But they have all died out.

MASSIVE LUMBERERS

One of the first big brontotheres, which lived 40 million years ago, was *Brontops*. It was about the size of today's female elephant. It had two odd horns on its nose. These 'horns' were growths of bone covered by thick skin. Later came *Embolotherium* of Mongolia, and *Brontotherium* of North America – both massive beasts 2.5m high.

Is it true

that chalicotheres still survive today?

Er ... possibly. There are stories from the icy wastes of Siberia of huge, horse-like creatures with long front legs and big claws. They are pictured on stone tombs from over 2,000 years ago, and there are still many rumours today. There are also tales of a creature, very like chalicotheres, that lives in the dense forests of Africa. It is called the 'nandi bear'. But, like the Loch Ness Monster, in Scotland, the existence of such animals is probably wishful thinking rather than serious science.

BATTLING AND DEFENDING

Why did some rhinos and brontotheres have such huge, strange nose-horns? Perhaps they were used for defence against attacking meat-eaters of their time, such as the creodonts. Or perhaps the horns were a sign of size and strength. These animals charged and pushed and battled with rivals of their own kind to become leaders of the herd, or to win mates at breeding time.

HOOFS TO CLAWS

A close relation to *Embolotherium* and *Brontotherium* was the 3m-long chalicothere *Moropus*, from 15 million years ago. Its fossils come from North America. *Moropus* had a long neck and front legs, and a body that sloped down at the back. Its hoofs had become shaped like claws. It may have walked on the soles of its feet, or on its curled-over knuckles, like a gorilla!

The chalicotheres were strange browsers. They had very short hind legs and walked on the knuckles of their front feet.

GIANTS OF THE PAST

A small herd of *Parksosaurus* flees in panic across the sub-tropical landscape of Late Cretaceous Canada. Will their natural speed and agility enable them to escape from the large and hungry *Albertosaurus* that has surprised them as they feed? Or will one of the small plant-eaters meet its doom today?

PARKSOSAURUS

207

NANOTYRANNUS

On the mud flats in Montana during the Late Cretaceous, some *Nanotyrannus* are quietly feeding on an *Edmontosaurus* they have just killed. The *Nanotyrannus* look up startled as they hear the roar of a *T rex* that has come to steal a share of their kill.

Ambush!

How did prehistoric animals hunt for their food?

When we are hungry it is easy to find food. We can buy a hamburger, or some fish and chips. But suppose we were wild animals having to hunt for our food, which was usually trying to run away? Meat-eating animals have survived up to now because they have evolved a number of different ways to catch the food they need.

BY SURPRISE

Ambush is one of these ways. It takes great patience, but not a great deal of energy. The hunting animal first lies hidden, then it leaps out on its victim, catching it by surprise. The cats, like lions, lynxes, and even the domestic tabby, are great masters of this type of hunting.

Modern lions in the Serengeti ambush their victims by surprise, just like *T rex*.

A FROZEN CLUE

The lions and their relatives hunted by ambush in ancient times too. In 1979, gold miners found the 36,000-year-old mummified body of an extinct bison in the frozen ground of Alaska.

CLUES IN THE ICE

The bison was partially eaten and the nostrils had been crushed. Lions had done this. The lions had lain in wait for the bison herd to come by, and pounced.

TOO HEAVY

Some of the big dinosaurs hunted by using the ambush technique too. *Tyrannosaurus* was probably too big and heavy to do much chasing about.

TYRANNOSAURUS KILL

T rex probably laid in wait in thickets for duckbilled dinosaurs to pass by. Then it burst out on them, bringing down one of the herd with a snap of its mighty jaws.

In the same way as today's fisherman, *Baryonyx* used to wait patiently for a suitable fish to catch.

COME FISHING

Watch someone fishing. He hunts in the same way, standing motionless until a fish comes close enough to be hooked and trapped.

FISH-EATER

Baryonyx probably fished in much the same way. It had a big claw on its hand, and long jaws full of teeth – just like a fish-eating crocodile. Experts think that it waited by a stream for a fish to swim by. It then hooked the fish out with its claw, and grabbed it with its jaws. Fish bones were found in a *Baryonyx'* stomach, so fish must have been its last meal.

211

'Dinosaur gazelles'

These hypsilophodonts were so fast on their feet that they were nicknamed the 'dinosaur gazelles'.

These three successful hypsilophodont dinosaurs were plant-eaters. They first appeared in the Late Jurassic Period.

The hypsilophodonts were one of the most successful dinosaur groups that ever lived.

Tenontosaurus

Hypsilophodon

LONG LIFE
These medium-sized plant-eaters flourished for about 100 million years. And they spread to almost every continent in the world.

IN AT THE END
The first hypsilophodonts appeared in the Late Jurassic Period, about 150 million years ago. New family members started to arrive in Cretaceous times. *Thescelosaurus* was the last hypsilophodont to roam the Earth. It appeared 70 million years ago and was finally wiped out in the mass extinction of all the dinosaurs that occurred some 4 million years later.

CHECK LIST
- MEDIUM SIZED
- ATE PLANTS
- RAN ON TWO LEGS

LITTLE . . .

The three dinosaurs shown here are some of the best known hypsilophodonts. The family was named after *Hypsilophodon*, which means 'high ridge tooth'. This plant-eater was shorter than a man and about 2m long.

Dryosaurus

. . . AND LARGE

Dryosaurus was almost twice as big as *Hypsilophodon*. *Tenontosaurus* was the real giant of the family. It was about the size of a modern tank and actually grew to more than 6m long.

WHEN AND WHERE

Dryosaurus was one of the earliest hypsilophodonts. It spread all over the world. Fossil remains have been found as far afield as North America and East Africa. *Hypsilophodon* appeared in the Early Cretaceous Period, almost 120 million years later. All the skeletons found so far have come from the Isle of Wight. *Tenontosaurus* arrived a few million years later and died out about 108 million years ago. It was discovered in North America.

FAMILY LIKENESS

Hypsilophodonts changed very little in appearance over a period of 100 million years. *Hypsilophodon* looked very much the same as *Thescelosaurus*, although there were, in fact, 40 million years between them. *Dryosaurus* and *Thescelosaurus* both looked like small iguanodonts. Scientists think that because of the close resemblance, iguanodonts and duckbilled dinosaurs may have evolved from the family of hypsilophodonts.

1 FLAT OUT

Hypsilophodonts were called 'dinosaur gazelles' because they could run so fast. When danger threatened they sprinted off at top speed. They were built to move quickly. The hind legs of *Hypsilophodon* were very similar to those of today's Thomson's Gazelle. They were made to swing backwards and forwards very quickly to help the dinosaur build up speed. The hypsilophodonts could dash along much more quickly than most other plant-eaters.

2 OUT OF ITS TREE

Early experts believed *Hypsilophodon* lived in trees because it had long fingers and toes. For almost 100 years, artists drew the dinosaur perched like a bird on a branch. It was not until 1974 that Professor Peter Gallow changed their minds. He proved that there was no evidence to show that *Hypsilophodon* was a tree dweller. In fact it was well adapted to live on the ground.

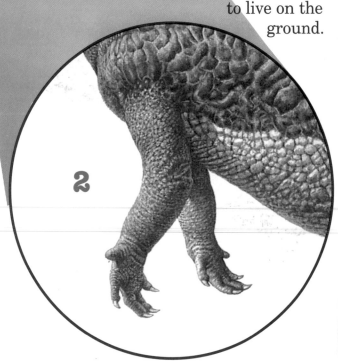

3 EAT UP

The hypsilophodonts were more efficient eaters than many earlier dinosaurs. And that was why the family survived for so long. *Hypsilophodon*, or 'high ridge tooth', was named because of its cheek teeth. When it ate, the upper and lower teeth locked together to form a flat surface for chewing its food. It also had powerful jaws to help it cope with tough plants.

4 TOOTH TRUTH

Tenontosaurus might have looked more like a small *Iguanodon*. But the way its teeth were arranged showed it was really a hypsilophodont. This dinosaur had a long, deep head to allow it to take in lots of food. There was also plenty of room for its huge, powerful jaw muscles.

ALL FOURS

Tenontosaurus was much bigger than most hypsilophodonts. It weighed up to one tonne and had an enormous tail. The dinosaur also had longer, thicker arms than other members of the family. Because of these differences, it probably moved in a different way. *Tenontosaurus* ran along on its hind legs like other hypsilophodonts, but it might have walked on all four legs.

SUCKED UNDER

Experts think that *Hypsilophodon* must have lived in herds. They have discovered more than 20 skeletons in the same part of a cliff on the Isle of Wight. The herd could have been trapped in quicksand. The dinosaurs must have been buried very quickly because their skeletons were so well preserved.

Is it true that a skeleton of *Tenontosaurus* was found surrounded by other dinosaur skeletons?

Yes. Experts made a remarkable discovery in Montana, USA. They found a *Tenontosaurus* skeleton that was surrounded by the skeletons of five *Deinonychus*. These meat-eating dinosaurs were ferocious hunters with blade-like teeth and clawed toes. We do not know what really happened, but perhaps the *Deinonychus* attacked *Tenontosaurus* and were killed during the death struggles of the plant-eating giant.

CHECK LIST

- FAST RUNNER
- POWERFUL HIND LEGS
- LONG, STIFF TAIL

215

A DAY IN THE LIFE OF BRACHIOSAURUS

THE JURASSIC PERIOD, 160 MILLION YEARS AGO IN WHAT IS NOW NORTH AMERICA. A HERD OF BRACHIOSAURUS IS PEACEFULLY FEEDING.

NONE OF THEM EATS THE LOWEST LEAVES AS THE DINOSAURS FIND IT DIFFICULT TO LOWER THEIR LONG, LONG NECKS FAR ENOUGH DOWN TO REACH THEM.

THE YOUNG STAY CLOSE TO THEIR MOTHERS...

... FOR DANGER IS NEVER FAR AWAY.

ALLOSAURUS RELEASES THE DYING BABY AND LASHES OUT AT THE ANGRY MOTHER. BUT BRACHIOSAURUS BRINGS ITS ENORMOUS WEIGHT INTO PLAY AND SLAMS HER FOOT DOWN ON ALLOSAURUS' TAIL.

THE HUGE BULK OF AN ADULT BRACHIOSAURUS IS ENOUGH TO DETER AN ATTACK FROM ALL BUT THE MOST DESPERATE PREDATOR..

SEIZING ITS CHANCE, ALLOSAURUS DARTS ACROSS THE DUSTY GROUND, ITS CLAWS POISED TO SLASH OUT AT THE YOUNG HERBIVORE.

... BUT A YOUNG ONE IS NO THREAT, ESPECIALLY IF ITS MOTHER IS BUSY FEEDING.

THE BABY BRACHIOSAURUS CAN DO LITTLE TO PROTECT ITSELF FROM THE ASSAILANT'S DEADLY CLAWS. BUT ITS HEART-RENDING SQUEALS ALERT ITS MOTHER.

NOTHING CAN SAVE THE YOUNG BRACHIOSAURUS, BUT ITS MOTHER INSTINCTIVELY TRIES TO RESCUE HER BABY.

SHE WHIPS THE TRAPPED ALLOSAURUS WITH HER LONG TAIL, AGAIN AND AGAIN, AND THE GREAT CARNIVORE CRASHES TO THE GROUND.

BUT IT IS TOO LATE TO SAVE HER BABY...

... AND SHE SHUFFLES OFF TO JOIN THE REST OF HER HERD AS IT MOVES ON TO A NEW FEEDING GROUND.

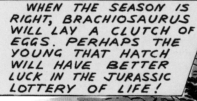

WHEN THE SEASON IS RIGHT, BRACHIOSAURUS WILL LAY A CLUTCH OF EGGS. PERHAPS THE YOUNG THAT HATCH WILL HAVE BETTER LUCK IN THE JURASSIC LOTTERY OF LIFE!

Improve and test your knowledge with...

FACT FILE

Fascinating facts
to read and
10 fun questions
to answer!

Cold feet

Iguanodon footprints have been found on rock surfaces in the cold wastes of Spitzbergen. The climate within the Arctic Circle must have been much less harsh in Cretaceous times.

1 Skeletons of *Deinonychus* were found surrounding:
a) *Tenontosaurus*
b) *Parksosaurus*
c) *Dravidosaurus*

2 *Nothosaurus* was:
a) a reptile
b) a dinosaur
c) a shark

3 Early experts believed that *Hypsilophodon*:
a) flew like a pterosaur
b) swam underwater
c) lived in trees

4 *Parksosaurus* is often compared to today's:
a) cheetah
b) gazelle
c) sprinter

5 *T Rex* caught its prey by:
a) lying in ambush
b) running after it
c) jumping out of trees

6 *Edaphosaurus* may have been able to:
a) swallow plants whole
b) eat fish
c) crunch up mollusc shells

7 Trilobites are probably all:
a) extinct
b) in hiding
c) on holiday

8 *Hyrachyus* was one of the first:
a) rhinos
b) tapirs
c) pigs

9 *Baryonyx* had jaws like a:
a) meat-eating lion
b) fish-eating crocodile
c) plant-eating sheep

218

Is it a bird? Is it a dinosaur?

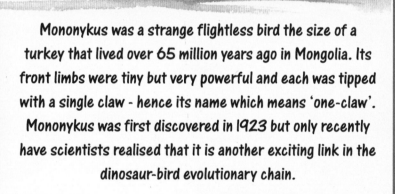

Palaeontologists rule OK?

The central European palaeontologist Franz von Nopcsa, famous for his reconstruction of Polacanthus and his work on Archaeopteryx, tried to raise an army and set himself up as king of Albania just before the First World War.

Bird bones

Most bird fossils that have been found are of sea birds. This is because animals that die in the sea have a better chance of becoming fossils.

Mononykus was a strange flightless bird the size of a turkey that lived over 65 million years ago in Mongolia. Its front limbs were tiny but very powerful and each was tipped with a single claw - hence its name which means 'one-claw'. Mononykus was first discovered in 1923 but only recently have scientists realised that it is another exciting link in the dinosaur-bird evolutionary chain.

A chink in the armour

Ankylosaurus, the biggest armoured dinosaur we know, is only known from an incomplete skeleton.

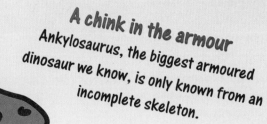

10 Odd-toed ungulates have:
a) lost one of their toes
b) one or three hoofs per foot
c) one or two hoofs per leg

ASK THE EXPERT

Dr David Norman of Cambridge University answers your dinosaur questions

Are all the trilobites extinct?

No trace of any trilobites has been found since the very rare ones of the Late Permian Period. Although we cannot say that every bit of the present sea bed has been scoured to prove that there are no living trilobites, the odds seem to be against there being any.

Did the duckbilled dinosaurs really have webbed fingers?

No, I do not think so. The four fingers of their hands are quite well preserved, and the first two end in broad, flattened hoofs. This is characteristic of animals that walk on firm ground rather than move by swimming. A few mummified skeletons from North America seem to show skin linking the fingers, as if they were webbed, but I think it is much more likely that this skin is the flattened toe pads. These have probably spread sideways as the animal was compressed and then fossilized.

Why do dinosaurs have such big names?

Mainly because we do not have a common name for dinosaurs. Most living animals have common names, but their scientific names are just as long as those of dinosaurs: a poodle is *Canis domesticus* and a human is *Homo sapiens*. So the real problem is that we have not given dinosaurs common names.

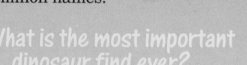

What is the most important dinosaur find ever?

One of the most important finds was the discovery of the earliest dinosaur – the bones of *Megalosaurus* – in about 1817. In the 1960s the discovery of *Deinonychus* made us realise that birds and dinosaurs are related, and the finding of dinosaur nests was important too. So, the choice is yours.

DINOSAURS!
DISCOVER THE GIANTS OF THE PREHISTORIC WORLD

DIPROTODON

The gentle, plodding, giant wombat, *Diprotodon*, was one of the biggest marsupial mammals ever known.

As long as a rhinoceros, *Diprotodon* was a chunky, slow-moving animal. It looked very different from the small, furry wombats that live in Australia today. In prehistoric times marsupials (mammals with pouches) were more widespread than they are today. But it was in Australia that they survived most successfully.

LAND OF THE GIANTS

On the large island continent of Australia, marsupials did not have to live in competition with other mammals and so they thrived. Plant-eating *Diprotodon* lived at the same time as other huge marsupials such as the giant kangaroo, *Sthenurus*.

FURRY 'HIPPO'

Imagine the body of a hippopotamus covered with fur, with a huge head at one end and a short, skinny tail at the other. In spite of its size, *Diprotodon* was a peaceful plant-eating creature which browsed on leaves from small bushes.

STICKY END

Experts think that *Diprotodon* probably moved around in herds. Fossils have been found at Lake Callabonna in south-east Australia. The *Diprotodons* appear to have drowned when the dried, crusty surface of the lake gave way under their weight and they fell into the mud below.

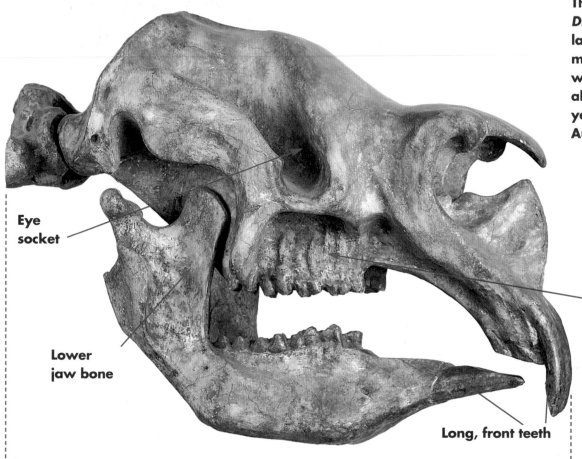

Eye socket

Lower jaw bone

The skull of *Diprotodon*, the largest known marsupial, which lived about 10,000 years ago in Australia.

Broad, flat cheek teeth

Long, front teeth

50cm

SIZE WISE

3m

MONSTER FACTS

- **NAME:** *Diprotodon* (<u>dye</u>-pro-toe-don) means 'two first teeth'
- **GROUP:** mammal
- **SIZE:** 3m long
- **FOOD:** plants
- **LIVED:** about 10,000 years ago in the Pleistocene Epoch in Australia

USEFUL TEETH

Diprotodon was well-equipped to eat a diet of plants. Its long front teeth stuck out like chisels and were ideal for cropping leaves and digging into the ground to pull out plants. At the back of its jaw, *Diprotodon* had broad, flat cheek teeth for grinding up tough shoots into an easily digested pulp.

CLAW COMB

Diprotodon's four stout legs were powerfully built. Its feet were broad and sturdy with clawed toes. These claws were used to keep *Diprotodon* clean. It probably groomed its fur by running its claws through its fur like a comb.

DIPROTODON DISAPPEARS

Diprotodon was not a natural athlete and could not rely on speed to keep safe. It was a large and easy target for the bone-tipped weapons of prehistoric people. Some experts believe that this is the main reason why animals such as *Diprotodon* became extinct. Others scientists think that changes in climate led to its subsequent disappearance.

Today's wombat is smaller than a *Diprotodon*, but its head is a similar shape.

Diprotodon probably cleaned its own fur, and the fur of its young, with its broad, clawed feet.

223

PROCOMPSOGNATHUS

Procompsognathus preyed on fast-running mammals, small lizards and flying insects.

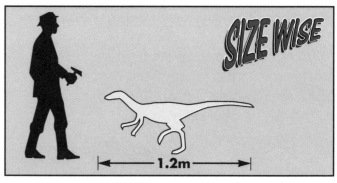
SIZE WISE
1.2m

This tiny predator had keen senses and fast reactions. As a lizard or small mammal shot into the open, *Procompsognathus* leapt into action with its head stretched forward and its tail up. It probably hunted in small packs on the dry plains of Triassic Germany.

DAINTY BUT DEADLY

Once caught, it was important for *Procompsognathus* to hold on to its wriggling prey. It grasped the helpless victim with tiny five-fingered hands and tore at the flesh with pointed, curved teeth.

WIDE EYED

A dinosaur as small as *Procompsognathus* needed to stay alert even when feeding. Although its head was small enough to fit into the palm of your hand, its eyes were huge. With small darting movements of its head, *Procompsognathus* resembled a garden bird on the look-out for a cat.

MONSTER FACTS

- **NAME:** *Procompsognathus* (pro-comp-sog-nay-thus) means 'before Pretty Jaw'
- **GROUP:** dinosaur
- **SIZE:** 1.2m long
- **FOOD:** small animals and insects
- **LIVED:** about 215 million years ago in the Late Triassic Period in southern Germany

FAMILY MATTERS

Procompsognathus was related to other predators such as *Syntarsus* and *Coelophysis*.

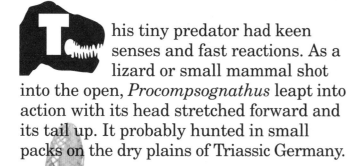

MELANOROSAURUS

With its elephantine legs and long tail, *Melanorosaurus* was one of the largest of the early dinosaurs.

s long as three cars, *Melanorosaurus* was a huge, plant-eating dinosaur related to *Camelotia* from England and *Riojasaurus* from South America. An ancestor of the great sauropods that lived during the Jurassic and Cretaceous Periods, *Melanorosaurus* had a massive, heavy body, long tail and it walked on four straight limbs, like those of an elephant.

SIZE WISE

12m

MONSTER FACTS

- **NAME:** *Melanorosaurus* (mel-an-oro-saw-rus) means 'Black Mountain reptile'
- **GROUP:** dinosaur
- **SIZE:** up to 12m long
- **FOOD:** plants
- **LIVED:** about 210 million years ago in the Late Triassic Period in South Africa

BROWSER

Melanorosaurus probably browsed on plants and leaves within the reach of its little head. Unlike *Plateosaurus*, experts do not think it reared up on its hind legs to reach the top of tall trees.

HEADLESS REMAINS

Although *Melanorosaurus'* skull has not been found, it is probable that its head was small compared to the size of its large body. It cropped leaves with spoon-shaped teeth and swallowed gastroliths (small stones) to help it digest its tough food.

225

Cloven Hoofs

Archaeotherium

Meet the fascinating ancestors of today's sheep, cattle, pigs, camels, giraffes, hippopotamuses and deer.

I n almost any farmyard you will find even-toed ungulates (ETUs). You know them better as sheep, goats, cattle and pigs. They are called ETUs because they are ungulates (hoofed mammals) and have an even number of hoofs (toes), on each foot. Most ETUs have two hoofs per foot, but some have four. ETUs are also known as 'cloven-hoofed' animals. Cloven means split or divided.

ETUS EVERYWHERE

As well as finding ETUs in the farmyard, you will find them in many other habitats. The deer in the woods are ETUs. So are the camels in the deserts. ETUs on the North American prairies include bison and pronghorn antelopes. In Africa, they include hippos, giraffes and gazelles. Fossils show that ETUs appeared more than 50 million years ago, not long after the last dinosaurs died out. They are a very successful group of animals.

Metridiochoerus lived in Africa 3 million years ago and used its impressive fangs for fighting.

The hippos of today (above) closely resemble their ancestors *Hippopotamus gorgops* (right) from the Pleistocene Epoch.

PIGS AND PRE-PIGS

Some early ETUs looked like pigs, but they were not true pigs. One was *Archaeotherium*, a pig-sized creature with bony bumps on its cheeks and lower jaw. It roamed eastern Asia and North America 30 million years ago, grubbing up roots with its tough teeth. *Dinohyus* lived in North America around 15 million years ago. It looked and lived like a pig, but was in fact bigger than a cow! *Metridiochoerus* was a true pig that lived 3 million years ago in Africa. It had four fearsome fangs that it used for fighting and feeding.

HIPPOS THROUGH THE AGES

Hippopotamuses are ETUs too. They have had the same shape for millions of years. *Hippopotamus gorgops* lived in Africa over a million years ago. Its eyes were on bony 'stalks' so it could keep watch while the rest of its head was under the water.

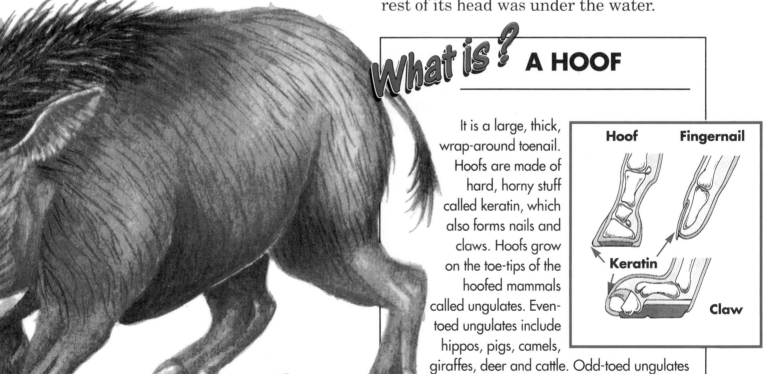

What is? A HOOF

It is a large, thick, wrap-around toenail. Hoofs are made of hard, horny stuff called keratin, which also forms nails and claws. Hoofs grow on the toe-tips of the hoofed mammals called ungulates. Even-toed ungulates include hippos, pigs, camels, giraffes, deer and cattle. Odd-toed ungulates include horses, zebras, tapirs and rhinos.

Hoof   Fingernail

Keratin

Claw

227

Camels today mainly live in the desert, unlike their ancestors *Alticamelus* (right) which roamed in woods and swamps.

GIRAFFE-LIKE CAMELS

The camel group appeared around 40 million years ago in North America. Modern camels are best suited to desert life, but prehistoric camels lived in all types of habitats, such as woods and swamps. *Protylopus* was a very early camel from south-west North America. It was a combination of rabbit and deer. One metre tall *Stenomylus* lived 20 million years ago and looked more like a gazelle. Some camels evolved enormously long necks, like giraffes, for reaching succulent leaves. *Alticamelus*, also known as *Aepycamelus*, from 10 million years ago, could reach 3m high. *Titanotylopus*, from 2 million years ago, was even loftier, and could reach up to 5m.

DEER-LIKE GIRAFFES

Unlike prehistoric camels, prehistoric giraffes did not have very long necks. *Prolibytherium*, from 20 million years ago, resembled a deer, with bony outgrowths that looked like leaf-shaped antlers. *Sivatherium* was another deer-like giraffe from North Africa and India, which lived less than 5 million years ago.

Is it true **that ETUs are the most numerous large mammals in the world?**

Almost. There are many millions of wild deer, antelopes and gazelles. There are millions of camels, llamas, alpacas and their cousins. And in addition to these wild ETUs there are also:
- 1,200 million cattle
- 1,200 million sheep
- 500 million goats
- 800 million pigs
- 130 million water buffalo

But there are well over 5,000 million of a single species of large mammal – it is a type of ape. It's the human.

The highland cow (left) is a descendant of *Bos primigenius* (right).

DEER-LIKE, BUT NOT DEER

Many prehistoric ETUs looked like deer, but they were not true deer. Some were 'first horns', from North America. *Protoceras* had three pairs of bony knobs on its face and lived 25 million years ago. Much later, 5 million years ago, came the 2m-long *Synthetoceras*. Its strange-looking nose horn was Y-shaped.

TRUE DEER

The true deer group only evolved recently. The males have antlers that fall off and grow again each year. *Eucladoceros*, for example, had antlers up to 1.7m across. It browsed in the woods of Italy, 3 million years ago.

Sivatherium was a deer-like giraffe that lived in North Africa and India during the Pleistocene Epoch.

ANTELOPE-LIKE PRONGHORNS

The living pronghorn of North America is the only survivor of one ETU group called the antilocaprids. But in North America 25 million years ago there were many animals in this group. *Ilingoceros* was an antilocaprid with twisted antlers. *Hayoceros* was another and had two sets of antlers.

COWS, THEN AND NOW

Another big group of ETUs includes the antelopes, gazelles, cattle, sheep and goats. *Gazella*, from 20 million years ago, was one of the earliest. The cattle you see in the fields today were mostly bred from wild cows called aurochs. *Bos primigenius* was a huge auroch, more than 3m long, which lived in Europe, Asia and North Africa for a million years. The last ones died less than 400 years ago.

229

GIANTS OF THE PAST

In the heat of Pleistocene south-east Australia, some *Diprotodon* are grazing on the salt flats of Lake Callabonna. Their contentment is soon shattered as the dry, crusty surface gives way beneath their weight, thrusting them into the mud below. Unable to escape from the sticky slime, the helpless animals give up the struggle and sink below the surface.

PACHYRHINOSAURUS

On the plains of Alberta, Canada, over 75 million years ago, a *Pachyrhinosaurus* mother and her two calves are startled by a *Saurolophus*. The high-spirited calves have nothing to fear from this peaceful plant-eater, and charge off to take a closer look.

The packs

On the great plains of Africa, jackals and vultures feed on the remains of a gnu after the bigger predators have eaten their fill.

If animals hunt together in packs, can it make it easier for them to catch and kill prey?

Imagine if you had to hunt for your own food. It would not be very easy because most animals can run faster than you can. You could get together with some of your friends and plan the hunt together. Some of you could start the chase, others could head the animal off, or divert it, and yet others could lie in wait to make the actual kill.

GETTING THE ACT TOGETHER

This is how some animals hunt. Dogs, such as the wolves and the Cape hunting dogs, are the masters of co-operative hunting. In the past, people have made use of the pack-hunting ability of dogs to catch deer and other animals. Even today packs of hounds are kept for hunting.

CO-OPERATIVE DINOSAURS

Experts think that some dinosaurs hunted in groups. When *Deinonychus* was first discovered in the late 1960s, several skeletons were found around the remains of the big plant-eater *Tenontosaurus*. It could be that a pack of *Deinonychus* attacked one animal, and some of them were killed in the attempt.

234

SOMEONE ELSE'S LEFTOVERS

Another way for a carnivore to find meat is to dine on the leftovers of another creature's kill. This is called scavenging. Today, after a pride of lions has made a kill, hyenas, jackals and vultures will gather to eat what is left.

Allosaurus

ANCIENT EVIDENCE

There is plenty of evidence that scavenging took place during the Age of the Dinosaurs. At one site, in Wyoming, USA, the remains of a *Camarasaurus*, torn apart by its killers, has been found. And there are also teeth, and the teethmarks, of three different types of meat-eaters scattered around the site.

FOSSIL THIEVES

What probably happened was that the *Camarasaurus* was killed by a big *Allosaurus*. This ate its fill and moved on. A group of smaller *Ceratosaurus* came along, and ate what they needed. Tiny *Ornitholestes* darted in and out taking what food they could. Maggots and beetles would also have enjoyed a meal.

Ceratosaurus

Deinonychus probaby hunted in packs and they would have been able to kill big Tenontosaurus.

Camarasaurus

Ornitholestes

Evidence has been found in an incomplete *Camarasaurus* skeleton that it was partly eaten, probably by an *Allosaurus*. Other scavengers, such as *Ceratosaurus* and *Ornitholestes*, also came for a share.

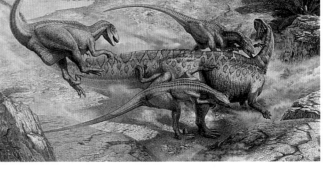

Introducing the lizard-teeth!

A new type of plant-eating dinosaur, as big as a truck, appeared about 150 million years ago and soon spread throughout the world.

The lizard-teeth dinosaurs, or iguanodontids, took over from the long-necked sauropods. They were not as big, but they were very successful. By the middle of the Cretaceous Period, large numbers of lizard-teeth dinosaurs roamed the land.

LOOK-ALIKE

Iguanodontids were named after *Iguanodon*. When *Iguanodon* was first discovered, scientists did not know very much about dinosaurs. They thought it was probably a giant iguana lizard. It was only later that experts realised it was a plant-eating dinosaur. Remains of *Iguanodon* have been found in what would have been marshy areas of Europe. Evidence now indicates that *Iguanodon* probably lived in herds, feeding together on the rich vegetation to be found in Cretaceous times, such as horsetails, ferns and cycads.

Muttaburrasaurus

Iguanodon

Camptosaurus

Is it true that *Iguanodon* could swim?

Some scientists believe *Iguanodon* must have been able to swim because it travelled so far. In those days, Europe had many large islands separated by shallow seas. *Iguanodon* could have swum across the narrowest channels.

Ouranosaurus

The iguanodontids lived during the Late Jurassic and Cretaceous Periods. These dinosaurs were all large, heavy animals with broad feet. Their strong hands had fingers ending in flat, hoof-like nails for walking on all-fours.

IGUANODONTID CHECKLIST

- LARGE HORSE-LIKE HEAD
- HEAVY BODY
- LONG TAIL

ALL IN THE FAMILY

Since *Iguanodon* was named, many more similar-looking dinosaurs have been found. These dinosaurs are all members of the same iguanodontid family.

FIRST AND LAST

Camptosaurus was the first iguanodontid. It appeared just under 150 million years ago at the end of the Jurassic Period. *Iguanodon* arrived in the Early Cretaceous Period and was still around 20 million years later. It was the most successful of the lizard-teeth. *Ouranosaurus*, *Probactrosaurus* and *Muttaburrasaurus* flourished in the Mid Cretaceous Period.

BIGGEST AND BEST

Iguanodon was the giant of the family. It is also one of the best known dinosaurs. The mighty plant-eater was over 9m long and 5m high – as big as a double-decker bus.

HEAVY-WEIGHTS

Muttaburrasaurus, *Ouranosaurus* and *Camptosaurus* were just as heavily built as *Iguanodon*. But they were about 2m shorter.

FAR AND WIDE

Lizard-teeth dinosaurs are mainly found in the northern continents but remains have been discovered right across the world. *Iguanodon* probably evolved in western Europe. It then spread to Asia and as far north as Norway. *Camptosaurus* has been found in North America, as well as in Europe. *Ouranosaurus* was dug out of the sands of the Sahara Desert in West Africa. *Muttaburrasaurus* is the only iguanodontid to have been found in Australia.

1 THUMBS UP

Lizard-teeth possessed a lethal weapon. It was a spur-like claw on the first finger of each hand. The bulky plant-eaters needed some way of defending themselves. They were too big to outrun speedy meat-eaters. But if they were cornered, they could strike out with their fearsome thumb spikes. Experts believe that *Iguanodon* must have been more than a match for most predators. It could have caused terrible injuries to the eyes, face and neck of its attacker with a well-aimed spike.

CROPPING AND GRINDING

Why were the iguanodontids so successful? Experts believe that it might have been because they could use their broad beaks to crop foliage quickly and efficiently. And the iguanodontid dinosaurs had a large number of cheek teeth, which meant they could grind up a great deal of food at once.

MORE SUCCESSFUL

Iguanodontids were more efficient feeders than the long-necked sauropods. Towering giant sauropods, such as *Diplodocus*, had to grind their food down in their huge stomachs. So it took them much longer to digest the tough plants they ate.

2 ODD ONE OUT

Not all the iguanodontids could defend themselves with a vicious stab. The earliest family member, *Camptosaurus*, did not have a fully developed thumb spike. It was more primitive than the later lizard-teeth in other ways, too. It was smaller than the other iguanodontids and had four toes on each foot rather than three like *Iguanodon*. Like the others, however, it had small hoofs on both its fingers and toes to help it walk on all fours.

3 SAILING ALONG

Ouranosaurus was related to *Iguanodon*. But it looked very different. A spectacular skin 'sail' ran down its back, supported by a 'fence' of bony spines. Scientists think the tall crest probably helped to keep the dinosaur's body at the right temperature. If it was too hot, *Ouranosaurus* could lose heat through its sail. If the weather was too cold, it could angle its crest to take as much heat as possible from the sun.

4 DOWN UNDER

Muttaburrasaurus was an important find because so few dinosaurs have been discovered in Australia. Unlike *Iguanodon* it had a large bump on its nose. The size of its nose has puzzled experts. Perhaps it helped *Muttaburrasaurus* to have an extra good sense of smell. Or maybe it distinguished a male from a female.

IT'S A FACT

MULTI-PURPOSE

Iguanodontids had very special hands that could be used in many different ways. Their thumb spikes may have been used as defensive weapons. The dinosaurs probably walked on their middle fingers when they were on all fours. These fingers were strong and hoof-like.

IGUANODONTID CHECKLIST

- SPIKED THUMB
- ATE PLANTS
- BROAD, HORNY BEAKS

THE PAINTER AND FOSSIL HUNTER

OUT OF SCHOOL, LAKES AND A FRIEND SPENT MOST OF THEIR TIME SEARCHING FOR FOSSILS IN THE FOOTHILLS OF DAKOTA.

NOT MUCH LUCK TODAY ARTHUR!

NO, LET'S GO. HEY—, WAIT! WHAT'S THAT?

ARTHUR DUG AROUND THE BONE HE'D SPOTTED, AND VERY SOON UNEARTHED THE VERTEBRAE OF A HUGE ANIMAL ...

WHAT ARE YOU DOING, ARTHUR?

SKETCHING IT! I DON'T KNOW WHAT IT IS, SO I'LL SEND THE DRAWING TO AN EXPERT.

HE DUG DEEPER—SO DEEP THAT THE WALLS OF HIS TRENCHES HAD TO BE PROPPED UP TO STOP THEM CAVING IN—THEN ONE DAY HE HIT AN UNDERGROUND SPRING.

AAARGH!

BY SUMMER 1881, FOSSIL HUNTING WAS AT FEVER PITCH, WITH EXPEDITIONS THROUGHOUT THE AREA. LAKES WAS A KEEN PAINTER. HERE IS A SMALL VERSION OF HIS PAINTING OF DIGGINGS AT COMO BLUFF, WYOMING, WITH AN EARLY UNION PACIFIC LOCOMOTIVE IN THE DISTANCE.

BUT THE DIGGING SEASON WAS SHORT. HE COULD NOT WASTE TIME. HE BALED OUT WITH ONE HAND AND DUG FOSSILS WITH THE OTHER.

THANKS TO THE DOGGED HARD WORK, IN ALL WEATHERS, OF ARTHUR LAKES AND HIS FRIENDS, FOSSIL BONES WERE SENT BACK EAST BY THE TONNE!

HE ALSO PRODUCED INVALUABLE NOTES, AND MANY PAINTINGS, THAT TELL US WHAT IT WAS LIKE TO HUNT FOR FOSSILS IN THE RUGGED OLD AMERICAN WEST. THIS WATERCOLOUR SELF PORTRAIT HE CALLED—IRONICALLY—**THE PLEASURES OF SCIENCE!**

Improve and test your knowledge with...

FACT FILE

Ichthyosaurus holds all the answers. See how you score in the quiz.

Mastodon for dinner

Scientists have looked at the marks on mastodon bones and have worked out how early people butchered these great beasts. They drove wedges of wood between the bones to dismember the huge mastodon carcasses. It must have been a messy and back-breaking job!

1 Hoofs are made of:

a) skin
b) keratin
c) leather

2 *Iguanodon's* lethal weapon was:

a) a finger hoof
b) a horny beak
c) a thumb spike

3 *Diprotodon* was one of the biggest known:

a) marsupial mammals
b) furry hippopotamuses
c) kangaroos

4 Whose name means 'red reptile'?

a) *Erythrosuchus*
b) *Epigaulis*
c) *Eomanis*

5 Early camels lived in:

a) deserts
b) woods and swamps
c) caves

6 *Deinonychus* probably hunted:

a) alone
b) in packs
c) with bigger dinosaurs

7 The little dinosaur, *Procompsognathus*, ate:

a) water plants
b) small animals and insects
c) other dinosaurs

8 Living off meat killed by another animal is called:

a) scrounging
b) scavenging
c) co-operative hunting

Old frog

Recently a frog from the Eocene Epoch was found preserved in amber in the Dominican Republic.

242

Famous fossil

You probably know that each American state has its own state flag. Well, the state of Colorado in the USA has its own state fossil - Stegosaurus!

Sauropod with a fin!

Amargasaurus is a 9m long plant-eater from late Cretaceous Argentina. It has a very unusual sail-like ridge on its neck and back. Experts have yet to discover the purpose of this strange-shaped fin.

 9 Even-toed ungulates have:
a) lots of toes the same length
b) an even number of toes
c) toes on both feet

 10 Metridiochoerus lived 3 million years ago in:
a) Africa
b) Mongolia
c) Europe

Little octopus

The oldest true octopus so far discovered is Proteroctopus found in the Jurassic rocks of southern France. It is only 14cm long and its longest tentacle is 3.6cm long.

ASK THE EXPERT

Dr David Norman of Cambridge University answers your dinosaur questions

Did people kill off the big Ice Age mammals?

There is no doubt that early human hunters killed Ice Age mammals. However, whether humans actually caused the extinction of these creatures is not certain. I think it is suspicious that the rise and spread of early humans around the world coincides roughly with the extinction of many of the large Ice Age mammals. So my general feeling is that the answer is yes!

Which was the most far-ranging dinosaur?

Iguanodon has been found as far away as North America, Europe and Mongolia. *Brachiosaurus* has been found in North and South America. But which one spread the furthest? I can't be sure.

Do dinosaur experts ever meet and exchange ideas and theories?

Yes, they do, although perhaps not as often as some of us would like. But every year there are meetings of scientific societies in various countries around the world, where some dinosaur experts meet and discuss their latest discoveries or new ideas.

If 'theropod' means 'mammal footed', what is so mammal-like about a theropod's foot?

Theropod actually means 'beast foot'. The name 'beast' is often used when naming fossils and living mammals. Similarly, 'saurus' has been used for reptiles. In the case of theropod, the name refers to the 'beastly' nature of the foot, which was designed for walking and killing, with its big curved claws.

ANKYLOSAURUS

Ankylosaurus was one of the last and largest of the armoured dinosaurs.

s it ambled through the Cretaceous forests of North America, gigantic *Ankylosaurus* was almost as well protected as a military tank. It grew to be longer than a double-decker bus and only the biggest and fiercest carnivores like *Tyrannosaurus rex* would have threatened this plant-eater.

REPEL ALL BOARDERS!

Ankylosaurus had several kinds of armour to protect its body from the teeth and claws of predators. Bony plates shielded the upper part of its bulky body from attack. These were divided into flexible bands which allowed *Ankylosaurus* to move quite easily. As an extra defence, sharp triangular spikes pointed outwards to repel the dinosaur's enemies.

245

Is it true

that all ankylosaurids lived in North America?

No. There are only two well-known ankylosaurids that came from North America: *Euoplocephalus* and *Ankylosaurus*. Several more, including *Shamosaurus*, *Pinacosaurus* and *Saichania*, have been found in Asia. All these ankylosaurids have been found in rocks dating from the Cretaceous Period.

HARD HEADED

A blow to the head can be fatal but *Ankylosaurus*' skull was very well protected. Its head was almost as wide as it was long and was covered in bony plates which ran along the top and sides. On either side of its head, a pair of spikes added to *Ankylosaurus*' armoury. Its wide, toothless beak acted like a shovel and helped it to scoop up plants and branches.

LIFE-SAVER

Like other ankylosaurids, such as *Euoplocephalus* and *Saichania*, *Ankylosaurus* had a weapon at the end of its long tail.

WELL CLUBBED

A heavy mass of bone grew out on either side of its tail bone to form a massive club as big as a large suitcase. This boulder-like growth was not for decoration. When attacked, it could save *Ankylosaurus*' life.

SWINGING ALONG

Strong muscles around its hips and along its tail helped *Ankylosaurus* to lift the club into the air and swing it at an enemy with great force. If a huge, two-legged predator received a leg-breaking blow from the tail club, the result was dramatic. The crippled creature toppled over and lay helplessly at the mercy of other carnivores while *Ankylosaurus* plodded off unharmed.

SIDE-STEP

In spite of its squat and heavy body, *Ankylosaurus* was quite an agile dinosaur. It was able to side-step a bigger enemy and attack it, if necessary.

A palaeontologist digs out the skull and skeleton of a *Saichania*, an ankylosaurid from Asia.

SIZE WISE

10m

MONSTER FACTS

- **NAME:** *Ankylosaurus* (an-<u>ky</u>-low-<u>saw</u>-rus) means 'fused reptile'
- **GROUP:** dinosaur
- **SIZE:** 10m long
- **FOOD:** plants
- **LIVED:** about 80 million years ago in the Late Cretaceous Period in North America

NOT SPEEDY

Although *Ankylosaurus* could defend itself and was quite agile, it could not rely on its short, stocky legs for speed to outrun its enemies.

FLIPPING OVER

Ankylosaurus had another weak spot. Its armour was incomplete. By flipping *Ankylosaurus* on to its back, an enemy could attack its soft underbelly. The problem was how to do it!

The bony plates and sharp spikes on the back of *Ankylosaurus* helped protect it against fierce predators.

DIPLOCAULUS

Diplocaulus was an amphibian with an extraordinary-looking head, shaped rather like a boomerang.

Found in the ponds and swamps of North America, _Diplocaulus_ lived 270 million years ago. It was an amphibian and grew to be as long as a badger. It featured the same sprawled legs as those of a modern salamander or newt. But its head really set it apart – it was unlike that of any other known animal. On its head it had extraordinary wing-shaped bones that stuck out just like a huge boomerang. These grew out from what would have been _Diplocaulus'_ cheekbones. As the head increased in size, so did these bones.

MONSTER FACTS

- **NAME:** _Diplocaulus_ (di-plo-<u>kawl</u>-us) means 'two fold stem'
- **GROUP:** amphibian
- **SIZE:** 80cm long
- **FOOD:** fish
- **LIVED:** about 270 million years ago in the Early Permian Period in Texas, USA

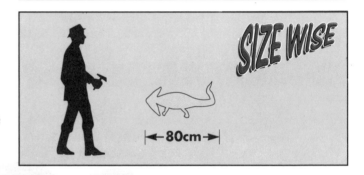

SIZE WISE

|←80cm→|

WHAT A MOUTHFUL!
A big head would possibly have protected _Diplocaulus_ from predators. An enemy needed a very wide mouth to swallow _Diplocaulus_. Many must have given up and looked for easier prey.

UP AND UNDER
Experts were puzzled by this 'boomerang' head. What was it for? Several suggestions have been made. Some scientists think that it acted like wings to lift _Diplocaulus_ quickly through the water. It could then attack unsuspecting fish near the surface.

PTERANODON

Although weighing only the same as a small child, *Pteranodon* had a wider wingspan than any known bird.

ith a wingspan that would have stretched from the trunk to the tail of an elephant, *Pteranodon* must have cast a great shadow over its prey. It swooped down to catch fish, rather as an albatross does today.

DAINTY BONES

In spite of its immense size, *Pteranodon* was only about as heavy as a small child. This was because it had light, hollow bones. The arrangement of its joints and muscles meant that *Pteranodon* could flap its wings as it flew.

TOP CREST

Pteranodon had a narrow, bony crest at the back of its head, and a long, toothless beak at the front.

SIZE WISE

7m

FLIGHT PATH

Some experts think that the crest helped *Pteranodon* change direction as it flew. Inside its horny beak and between its lower jaws, there was a pouch of skin. When it scooped up its prey from the sea, *Pteranodon* may have saved the fish to eat later, by storing it in this handy pouch, just as today's pelican does.

MONSTER FACTS

- **NAME:** *Pteranodon* (<u>ter</u>-an-<u>o</u>-<u>don</u>) means 'winged and toothless'
- **GROUP:** pterosaur (flying reptile)
- **SIZE:** wingspan 7m wide
- **FOOD:** fish
- **LIVED:** about 70 million years ago in the Late Cretaceous Period in Wyoming, USA

249

Steaming into life

The Precambrian is the earliest period. It makes up 88 per cent of the Earth's history! Yet we know little about it.

The sky is dark, lightning flashes and the rain lashes down. The rocks are hot under foot – so hot that the rain evaporates to form steam as soon as it hits them.

WHERE ARE WE?

The air is thick with steam, and with deadly gases which seep and gasp from the volcanoes. Nothing can possibly live here. Where are we? Venus? Mars? No. This is our own planet Earth – 4,800 million years ago.

IN THE BEGINNING...

Scientists think that about 4,600 million years ago, the Earth formed from cold dust. The mass of dust began to heat up as it was crushed together by gravity. Then the dust began to melt and turned to rock.

These sulphur-rich hot springs are in Iceland. The first living things on Earth probably developed in conditions as harsh as these.

THE FIRST ATMOSPHERE

The gases that formed the first atmosphere were mainly poisonous – methane and hydrogen. More gases, including carbon dioxide and water vapour, seeped to the surface through volcanoes, and, as the Earth cooled, the water vapour turned back to water.

WATERY HOME

When the surface was cool enough, the water began to gather in hollows which enlarged to form the first oceans. We think that life began as soon as the surface was cool enough to hold water.

FIRST LIVING THINGS

The first living things would have been tiny molecules, tinier than the eye can see. These molecules could produce copies of themselves. They were the first life, although nothing like the animals we know today.

Life began with single cells like this.

Fossil stromatolites in Australia show that single-celled creatures lived over 3,000 million years ago.

These 600 million-year-old soft-bodied creatures, like sea-pens and jellyfishes, are called the *Ediacara* animals, after the area in Australia where they were first discovered.

IT'S A FACT

A NEW NAME
Scientists used to call the single-celled stromatolite-builders 'blue green algae' but the more modern name is 'cyanobacteria'.

LITTLE PACKETS OF LIFE
As time went on, these molecules became more and more complex, and eventually the first cells developed. A cell is the basic building brick of all living things. It contains all the living material and all the molecules, and it can copy itself. A cell is encased in a tiny sack. Some living things consist of only one cell, but most, including ourselves, contain millions and millions.

TRAPPED IN MUD
Scientists have found what seem to be the fossils of single cells in ancient rocks in Western Australia, dating from over 3,000 million years ago. These single-celled creatures are called stromatolites.

A DEVELOPING ZOO
The earliest many-celled animals do not seem to have appeared until about 700 million years ago. Then, from rocks around the world, we can find fossils of soft-bodied animals, such as jellyfish, worms and sea-pens. All this was happening in the sea. But what lived on land at this time? Nothing.

251

Shells arrive

In the Cambrian Period, animals in the sea developed hard shells. But there were no plants, and no life on land at all.

In the Cambrian Period something strange happened. All sorts of animals suddenly developed hard shells. We are not sure why. Perhaps the salts in the sea water enabled animals to absorb chemicals and lay down hard layers in their skin.

THE START OF THE FOSSIL RECORD

Hard shells fossilize better than soft bodies, so rocks from this time are full of fossils. This event – 570 million years ago – marks the beginning of the geological time we call the Cambrian Period.

A DIFFERENT WORLD

If we looked at our world from space during the Cambrian Period we would not be able to recognise very much. There would be the vast blue of the ocean, and a few fluffy white clouds. But the continents would have been a totally different shape, with no green on them – they would have been just naked, brown rock.

In Cambrian times the world's continents were spread out along the Equator. There were many shallow seas at the continents' edges and most of the fossils that we know are preserved on the shallow-water deposits formed here.

Vauxia

Pikaia

Trilobite

Brachiopods

LOTS OF STRANGE ANIMALS

The animal life during the Cambrian Period was amazingly varied. The Burgess Shale, which was once beneath the oceans and now forms part of the Canadian Rockies, shows us what life was like. Here thousands of strange little animals – both soft-bodied and hard-shelled – were engulfed by a mud-slide which preserved them perfectly.

ALL OVER THE WORLD

In the Cambrian rocks we can see that many of the groups of animals that are alive today had begun to appear. There were the shelled molluscs with tentacles, which evolved into today's clams and winkles, and the joint-legged arthropods, which evolved into today's crabs and lobsters. The spiny starfishes and sea urchins, the corals, sponges and worm-like creatures, also appeared at this time.

THE NAME

Cambrian rocks were first studied in Wales. They took their name from 'Cambria' – the ancient name for Wales.

Is it true that there were no land-living animals in the Cambrian Period?

Not really. Nothing lived full-time on land but there are fossils of tracks laid down on a beach. These fossils are called *Climactichnides* and look like motorcycle tyre tracks. They would have been made by some shallow-sea animal that dragged itself out of the water for a while. *Climactichnides*, shown here, would have been about 30cm long.

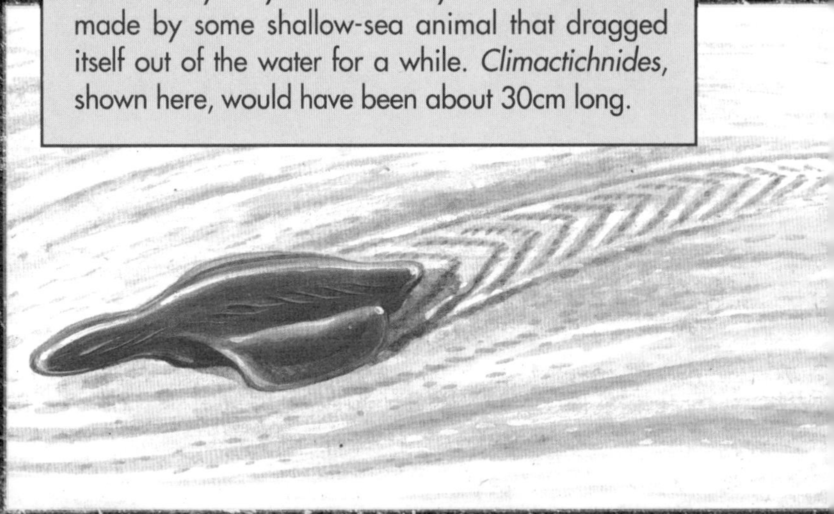

An important type of shellfish was a creature called a brachiopod. Brachiopods developed a hard shell, just like today's shelled molluscs, because they had the same way of life – sitting on the sea floor and filtering food out of the water. Fossilized brachiopods are shown in the background picture on this page.

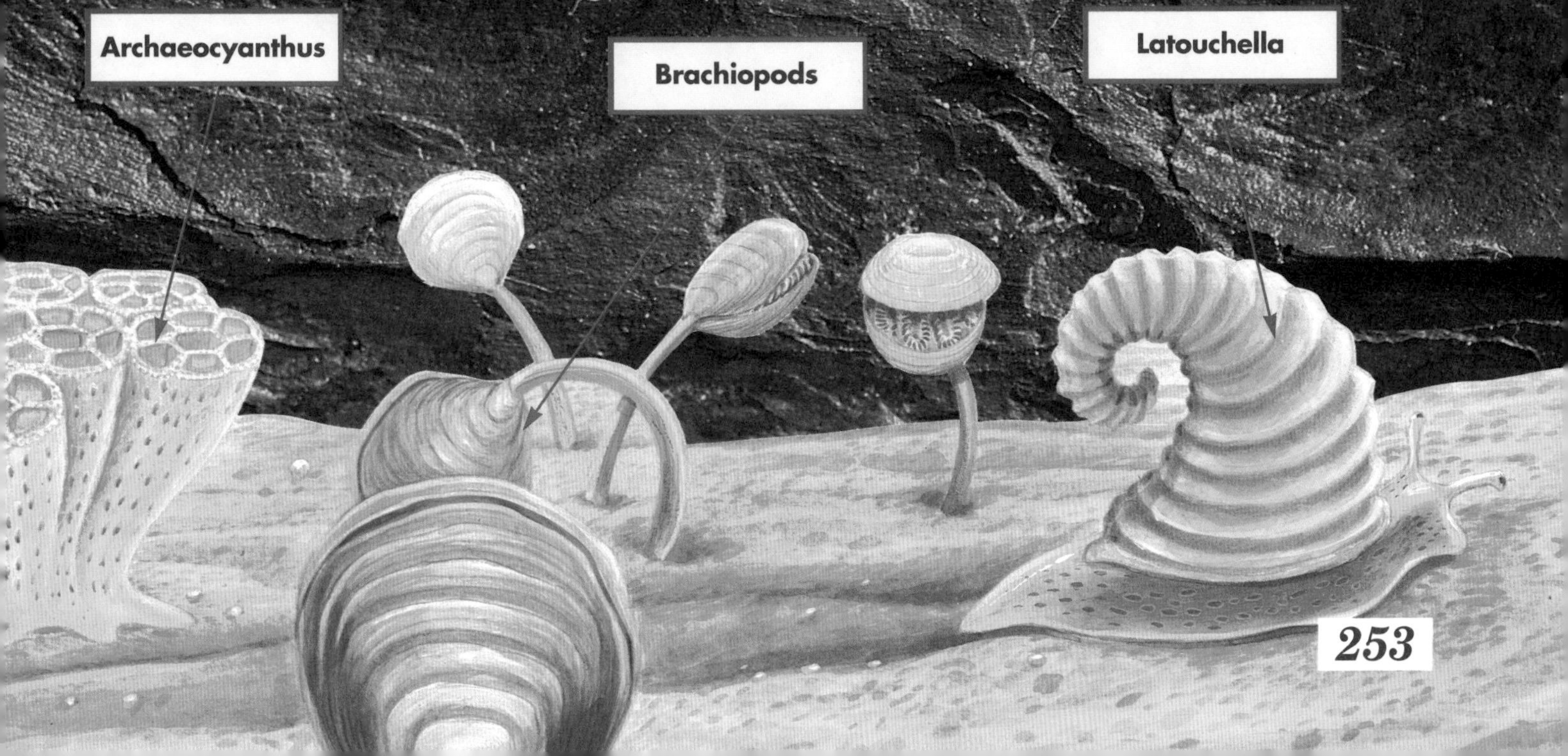

Archaeocyanthus

Brachiopods

Latouchella

GIANTS OF THE PAST

Albertosaurus on the attack! In the forests of Late Cretaceous North America, the huge meat-eater has spotted a young *Ankylosaurus* and is trying for a swift kill. Once the youngster is in reach of *Albertosaurus'* huge claws and knife-like teeth it will stand no chance. But the adult *Ankylosaurus* are putting up a strong fight, hitting the huge predator with their tail clubs.

255

3-D Gallery 72

PINACOSAURUS

On a dried-out lake bed in Late Cretaceous Mongolia, two *Pinacosaurus* are dying of thirst. They have come for water only to discover that the lake is dry. Weak, and lacking the strength to defend themselves, they will be easy prey for a hungry *Alectrosaurus*.

Prick up your ears

Prehistoric mammals could hear a wide range of sounds – from the shrillest squeak to the deepest rumble.

Unlike dinosaurs, prehistoric mammals had fleshy ears on the outside of their heads. Like mammals now, they could prick up their ears and even swivel them around to help them hear better.

Cranioceras could swivel its big ears to listen out for enemies.

SOUND TRAP

Human ears are small, flat and barely move at all. Big ears are much more effective, collecting a wider range of noises to funnel into the earholes. Animals with very large ears use them rather like satellite dishes to home in on their prey.

CAUGHT IN THE WAVES

Bats today have incredibly good hearing. Millions of years ago, the first bats were just as sharp-eared. *Icaronycteris* (<u>ih</u>-car-on-<u>ik</u>-ter-is) lived more than 65 million years ago. Like today's bats, it probably found its prey by a system called echolocation. As they fly, bats send out bursts of very high frequency sound. Anything in the path of the soundwaves sends back an echo to the bat's big ears. This helps the bat to locate the object and, if it is an insect, to swoop in and eat it.

Imagine being able to move your ears from side to side to pick up sounds more clearly, like this Dire wolf can.

RUMBLING ABOUT

Today's elephants and other large animals may be able to hear lower sounds than humans. One of the earliest elephants, *Deinotherium* (<u>dine</u>-oh-<u>thee</u>-ree-um), was gigantic. It lived 40 million years ago and was twice as tall as a man. Like today's elephants, it could probably hear very low sounds. And it could communicate with other *Deinotherium* in low sounds too. These sounds are pitched so low that human ears are unable to pick them up. But we can sometimes feel the sounds as a strange, rumbling sensation.

RECORD BREAKERS

● The jack rabbit has the longest ears of any rabbit. They are over 20cm long.

● An African elephant (left) has the largest ears in the world. Each one measures up to 1.8m wide.

● A long-eared bat has the largest ears compared to its body size. Its ears are around 4cm long and its body only 5cm long.

Bats hunt in the dark and live in dark places, such as caves. They catch their prey, and find their way around in the dark, by sending out powerful bursts of sound that are too high-pitched for the human ear to pick up. These soundwaves travel out from the bat's mouth, sending an echo back to its ears if they hit anything. That is how bats can fly in the dark without bumping into things, and how they catch insects they cannot see!

'Living fossils'

A small number of plants and animals have barely changed since prehistoric times – we call them 'living fossils'.

Animal and plant species usually survive for a time and then they die out. Normally a species exists for a few million years and then its place is taken by new, more successful types. But some species seem to change very little.

The coelacanth today (left) has changed little from its ancestor (below) which lived 400 million years ago.

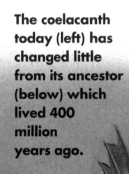

ALIVE TODAY
Some of these unusual 'living fossils' are described here. They range from strange fish that lurk deep down in the depths of the ocean, to familiar insects that scuttle around the garden.

IN THE SWIM
Turtles are surviving members of a very ancient group of reptiles. One of the largest prehistoric turtles was the giant *Archelon*, which lived 80 million years ago. It grew up to 3.7m long. Like the living leatherback turtle, it probably had a thick coat of rubbery skin which hung from its bony frame. *Archelon* had a sharp beak too, and probably fed on jellyfish – just as the leatherback does. Turtles have stayed the same for so long because they have no natural enemies.

Leatherback turtle

DEEP DOWN
A weird-looking fish was caught off the coast of South Africa over 50 years ago. Scientists were thrilled to discover it was a coelacanth. The first coelacanths lived 400 million years ago. They were related to the earliest fishes that walked on land. Coelacanths seem to have survived so well and changed so little because they live in the deep waters of the Indian Ocean, where they are almost alone and without competitors. They are an extremely rare type of fish even today.

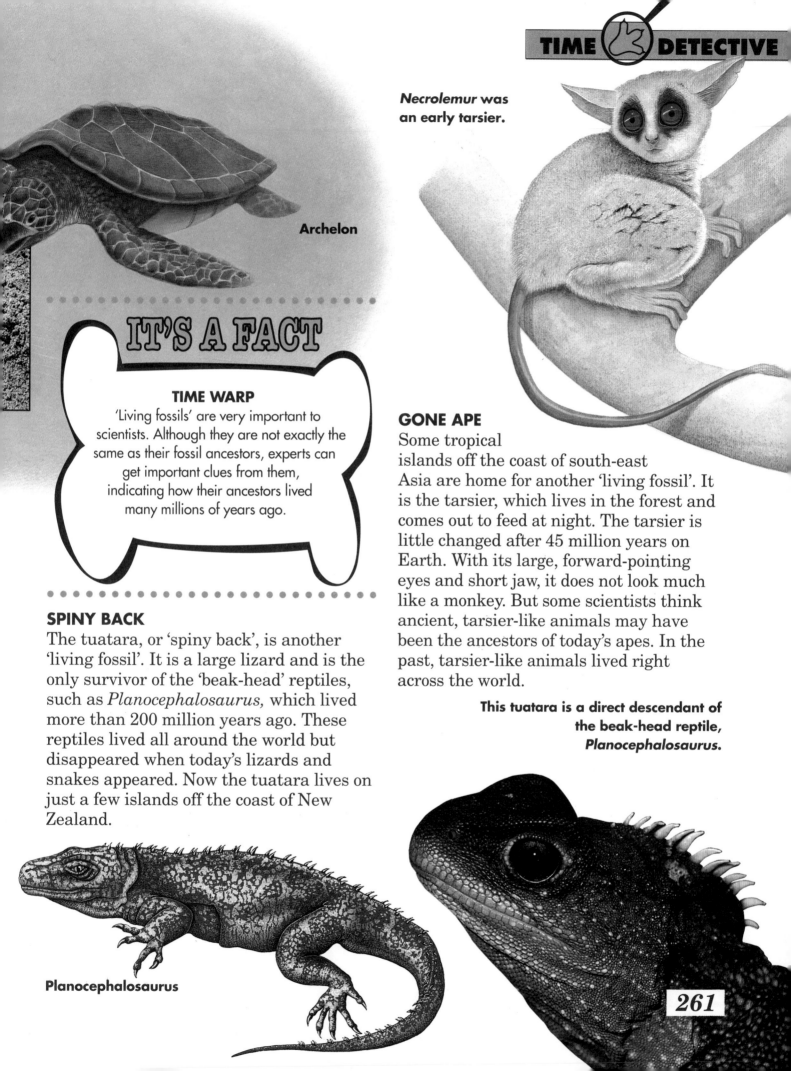

Necrolemur was an early tarsier.

Archelon

IT'S A FACT

TIME WARP
'Living fossils' are very important to scientists. Although they are not exactly the same as their fossil ancestors, experts can get important clues from them, indicating how their ancestors lived many millions of years ago.

GONE APE
Some tropical islands off the coast of south-east Asia are home for another 'living fossil'. It is the tarsier, which lives in the forest and comes out to feed at night. The tarsier is little changed after 45 million years on Earth. With its large, forward-pointing eyes and short jaw, it does not look much like a monkey. But some scientists think ancient, tarsier-like animals may have been the ancestors of today's apes. In the past, tarsier-like animals lived right across the world.

This tuatara is a direct descendant of the beak-head reptile, *Planocephalosaurus*.

SPINY BACK
The tuatara, or 'spiny back', is another 'living fossil'. It is a large lizard and is the only survivor of the 'beak-head' reptiles, such as *Planocephalosaurus,* which lived more than 200 million years ago. These reptiles lived all around the world but disappeared when today's lizards and snakes appeared. Now the tuatara lives on just a few islands off the coast of New Zealand.

Planocephalosaurus

261

SLOW SHUFFLE

Shuffling across the shallows of some North American and Indian seashores is another 'living fossil'. It is the horseshoe crab, which has hardly changed over 430 million years. Horseshoe crabs are not true crabs. They are related to spiders and scorpions. One of the main reasons why they have survived for so long is that they are protected by their hard shells. Many attackers simply may have felt they were not worth bothering about. Under the horseshoe crab's tough outer casing is only a very small body.

SCUTTLING AROUND

The familiar ground beetle that scuttles about the garden has looked the same for around 230 million years. *Protorabus* was the first-known ground beetle. Fossils 135 million years old have been found in central Asia. Prehistoric ground beetles must have fed on insects and grubs, just like today's ground beetles. They have survived well because they are successful hunters.

Horseshoe crab

IT'S A FACT

SHARKS THE SAME?

Today's sharks are 'living fossils' that have stayed more or less the same since prehistoric times. The teeth of today's Port Jackson shark are almost identical to fossilized shark teeth that are 150 million years old.

Ground beetle

The gingko tree is a 'living fossil' plant. It grows wild in one tiny area of China. But because gingko trees look so ornamental, they are planted in parks and gardens across the world. They are decorative, but the fruits, produced by the female trees, smell dreadful when they rot. Because of this, only male trees are generally grown.

Prolibytherium

PIGMY PREY

The last large animal to be discovered by scientists was found only about 100 years ago. It was the okapi, a primitive kind of giraffe, which has survived from prehistoric times. The earliest member of the okapi family was *Prolibytherium*, which lived 25 million years earlier. It had huge, leaf-shaped antlers. But apart from that it looked very like an okapi today. Okapis now live deep in the forests of Africa where few predators can find them.

Okapi

263

A DAY IN THE LIFE OF
ICHTHYOSAURUS

THE GREAT FEMALE ICHTHYOSAURUS GIVES BIRTH TO ONE CALF... AND A FEW MINUTES LATER, A SECOND ONE.

150 MILLION YEARS AGO, IN THE SEAS THAT COVERED WHAT IS NOW NORTHERN EUROPE, A POD OF ICHTHYOSAURUS IS FEEDING OFF A SHOAL OF SMALL FISH.

ALTHOUGH THE SURVIVING BABY ICHTHYOSAURUS IS ONLY A FEW HOURS OLD, IT KNOWS HOW TO CATCH THE FOOD IT NEEDS.

THE POD GORGES ITSELF ON THE PLENTIFUL SUPPLY OF SMALL FISH AND PLANTS, UNAWARE OF THE DANGER LURKING BELOW.

THE POD HAS BEEN SPOTTED BY A HUNGRY LIOPLEURODON, ONE OF THE MASTERS OF THE DEEP.

IT IS BIG ENOUGH TO ATTACK EVEN THE LARGEST ICHTHYOSAURUS.

THESE UNDERWATER CREATURES ARE NOT FISH. AS SOON AS THEY ARE BORN, INSTINCT MAKES THEM SWIM TO THE SURFACE TO FILL THEIR LUNGS WITH AIR.

A HUNGRY GEOSAURUS SPOTS THE LITTLE CREATURES AND ZOOMS IN FOR THE KILL. ONE ESCAPES BUT THE OTHER IS CAUGHT BY THE RAZOR-SHARP TEETH OF THE CROCODILIAN KILLER.

THE LIOPLEURODON IGNORES THE BABY ICHTHYOSAURUS AND GOES STRAIGHT FOR ITS MOTHER.

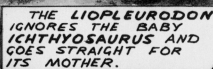

EVEN AS THE MOTHER ICHTHYOSAURUS DIES, THE REST OF THE POD SWIMS QUICKLY AWAY.

HAVING EATEN THEIR FILL, THEY SWIM UP TO THE SURFACE TO TAKE IN AIR.

WILL THE RECENTLY BORN ICHTHYOSAURUS LIVE TO GAIN MATURITY? PERHAPS. BUT IT'S QUITE LIKELY THAT IT WILL MEET THE SAME FATE AS ITS BROTHER IN THE CUT-THROAT WORLD OF THE JURASSIC SEAS.

Improve and test your knowledge with...
FACT FILE

Dimetrodon holds all the answers.
See how you score in the quiz.

5 A *Prolibytherium* had:
a) a long, thin nose
b) leaf-shaped antlers
c) big ears

4 What was the first-known ground beetle called?
a) coelacanth
b) tarsier
c) *Protorabus*

It's magic!

In 1922 Sir Arthur Conan Doyle, creator of Sherlock Holmes and author of The Lost World, astounded a meeting of the Society of American Magicians in New York by showing them a film of living dinosaurs. This actually turned out to be the special effects scenes from the film of The Lost World that was currently being made. The film was finally released in 1924.

3 *Pteranodon* was as heavy as:
a) a small child
b) a calf
c) an elephant

Minicroc

Alligatorellus was a tiny crocodile, only 30 cm long, from the Late Jurassic Period in Europe. Not very fierce, it only ate insects.

2 What is a tuatara?
a) a large lizard
b) a big turtle
c) a flat fish

1 *Archelon* grew up to:
a) 8.3m long
b) 1.5m long
c) 3.7m long

Thunderbones

When native Americans first found the bones of the giant brontotheres, they thought they were from the great birds of their myths that brought thunder.

6 **Diplocaulus** had a head like:
a) a rugby ball
b) a football
c) a boomerang

7 **Ankylosaurus'** most important weapon was:
a) its sharp teeth
b) its tail club
c) its horn

8 **Icaronycteris** found its prey by:
a) noselocation
b) earlocation
c) echolocation

9 An African elephant's ears are:
a) 90cm wide
b) 1.8m wide
c) 2.5m wide

10 Where did life first start?
a) in the water
b) on Mars
c) in volcanoes

Food for Triassic plant-eaters?

The first flowers appeared during the Cretaceous Period – or that's what experts believed... But the latest research indicates that there may have been flowers, such as this ancient water-lily, 100 million years earlier! Triassic dinosaurs may have enjoyed a more varied and colourful diet than we thought!

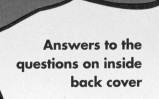

Answers to the questions on inside back cover

ASK THE EXPERT

Dr David Norman of Cambridge University answers your dinosaur questions

Did swimming reptiles suffer from the bends?

Any swimming creature that breathes air and dives to a great depth risks getting the 'bends'. This painful, sometimes fatal, condition is caused by bubbles in the blood. Oxygen dissolves in the blood at high pressure and the deeper the water, the greater the pressure. If an animal comes up too quickly from the ocean depths, the oxygen dissolved in the blood can form bubbles. Whales, which dive to great depths, breathe out before they dive so that less air is in their lungs.

Would dinosaurs have eaten mushrooms?

I see no reason why some dinosaurs could not have eaten mushrooms. They are very nutritious, and certainly existed in the Age of the Dinosaurs.

In most books the horned dinosaurs are called ceratopsians. But in DINOSAURS! they are called ceratopians Why?

The reason for calling horned dinosaurs ceratopians is that this is the correct spelling! This comes from knowing the meaning of the word. Ceratopsian is often used in dinosaur books, even though technically it is incorrect. I like to use the correct name.

Were there any prehistoric electric fish, like electric eels and electric rays?

Rays did exist in the Mesozoic seas, so maybe electric rays did too. We haven't found fossils of prehistoric electric eels however, so perhaps only cartilaginous fishes had electric relatives.

EUPARKERIA

Euparkeria was probably the first animal to run on two legs.

The small, agile flesh-eater, *Euparkeria,* usually walked on all four legs. But when it spotted a likely looking meal, in the shape of a tiny mammal-like reptile, it probably reared up on its hind legs and sprinted after its prey.

RULING REPTILES

Euparkeria was an important animal because it had features which were shared by both crocodiles and dinosaurs. It was an early member of a large group called the archosaurs (<u>ark-o-saws</u>) which ruled the Earth for millions of years. These animals were widespread during the Triassic Period.

TOOTHY REPTILES

Euparkeria belonged to the thecodont archosaurs, a group of reptiles that had their teeth anchored in sockets.

TAKEN BY SURPRISE

Euparkeria was about the size of a red fox. It skulked among the undergrowth in the warm, moist climate of Triassic South Africa. Hidden from view, it waited for the welcome rustle of small feet. As *Euparkeria* reared up for a better look, the startled victim took flight and the hunter leapt into action. *Euparkeria* could sprint off on its powerful legs to capture its prey.

TWO LEGS BEST

Its ability to run on two legs gave *Euparkeria* a big advantage over reptiles with all four feet firmly on the ground. It could move more quickly and so catch more food.

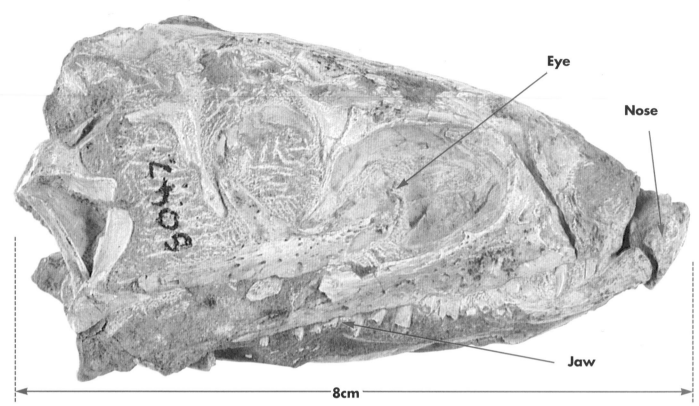

Eye

Nose

Jaw

8cm

TAIL LIFT

Its strong hind limbs were curved and powerful for quick acceleration. As it ran, *Euparkeria* lifted its tail for better balance.

TEETH AND SKULL

Euparkeria had the teeth of a hunting animal. Set deeply into its jaw, they could stand up to the struggles of its victims. And they were sharp and jagged, ideal for tearing through flesh. *Euparkeria* had two openings in its skull, one in front of its eyes and another in its jaw, which made its skull light and strong.

EARLY ARMOUR

Like the crocodiles and some of the dinosaurs which lived later, *Euparkeria* had bony plates all along its back. This simple armour was arranged in double rows along its backbone to give *Euparkeria* some protection against attacks from larger predators.

Is it true that archosaurs are still alive today?

The first archosaurs appeared in the Late Permian Period, over 250 million years ago. During the Late Triassic Period, two important lines evolved, the crocodylotarsi and ornithosuchia. These were the ancestors of the crocodiles and birds that survive today.

STRAIGHT UP

Before Early Triassic times, most reptiles moved with their elbows and knees sprawled outwards. As they walked along their bodies were close to the ground. *Euparkeria*'s legs were tucked partly beneath its body and were more efficient.

LEG ADVANTAGE

The dinosaurs, birds and mammals that lived after *Euparkeria* were even better able to support their body weight because their legs were positioned in a more upright position under their bodies.

MONSTER FACTS

- **NAME:** *Euparkeria* (yoo-par-kee-ree-a) means 'true Parker's'
- **GROUP:** reptile
- **SIZE:** up to 1m long
- **FOOD:** meat
- **LIVED:** about 240 million years ago in the Early Triassic Period in South Africa

Euparkeria **was a keen hunter and often caught smaller prey such as these** *Ericiolacerta.*

SIZE WISE

←1m→

271

AMMOSAURUS

Ammosaurus was as long as a small car and knee-high to an adult human.

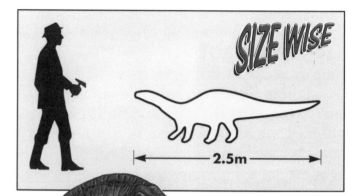

SIZE WISE

2.5m

Near the end of the last century, bridge builders in Connecticut, USA, came across the fossilized bones of a dinosaur in a quarry. The dinosaur was named *Ammosaurus*. Some time later, when the bridge was knocked down, even more fossils were uncovered.

LONG-BODIED

Like its relative *Anchisaurus*, *Ammosaurus* was a plant-eating prosauropod. It probably walked on four legs most of the time because its long neck and body made it difficult to balance on two legs. Whether it walked on two or four legs, *Ammosaurus* always kept its tail held off the ground.

HIGH AND LOW

Ammosaurus was able to reach low-growing plants and could also stretch up high to reach succulent shoots and leaves.

QUICK RETREAT

Ammosaurus looked for food on the muddy shores of the lakes in the Connecticut Valley. If attacked by a predator, it probably struck out fiercely with its five-fingered hands, tipped with sharp claws. Sometimes, of course, *Ammosaurus* decided to run away rather than fight!

MONSTER FACTS

- **NAME:** *Ammosaurus* (am-oh-saw-rus) means 'sand reptile'
- **GROUP:** dinosaur
- **SIZE:** 2.5m long
- **FOOD:** plants
- **LIVED:** about 205 million years ago in the Early Jurassic Period in Arizona and Connecticut, USA

CLADOSELACHE

Cladoselache was an early shark, shaped like a torpedo.

Big-eyed *Cladoselache* swam in the open seas of the Devonian Period alongside other fierce predators such as the monstrous *Dunkleosteus*. It moved its streamlined body swiftly through the water as it pursued its prey.

SNUB-NOSED AND SPINY

Unlike the shark of today, *Cladoselache* had a rounded snout and its jaws were at the front rather than underneath. But as with today's sharks, when old teeth dropped out, new ones moved up to replace them. *Cladoselache*'s fins spread out from a broad base and tiny horizontal fins near its tail acted like rudders for steering. Some specimens show that this shark also had spines at the front edges of its fins to help it cut through the water.

CANNIBAL INSTINCTS

Fossils of *Cladoselache* suggest that it was not very choosy about its victims. Remains of a variety of fish, including some of its own kind, have been found in its gut.

MONSTER FACTS

- **NAME:** *Cladoselache* (<u>klad</u>-oh-sel-<u>la</u>-<u>kee</u>) means 'stem shark'
- **GROUP:** fish
- **SIZE:** 50cm-1.2m long
- **FOOD:** other fish
- **LIVED:** about 370 million years ago in the Late Devonian Period in Europe and North America

SIZE WISE

50cm-1.2m

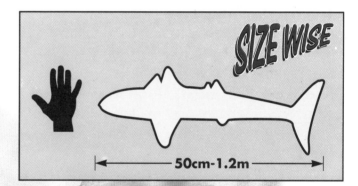

Changes in the sea

The Ordovician Period lasted from 505 to 438 million years ago. During this time there was no life on land. But in the seas, all sorts of exciting life was developing.

The animals that were important in the Cambrian Period continued to develop in the Ordovician. The trilobites and the shellfishes were especially successful.

SUCCESSFUL SHELLFISH

Nautiloids appeared in the Ordovician Period. They looked like squids wrapped in horn-shaped or coiled shells. Nautiloids were successful and still exist today. A modern relative is the *Nautilus*.

LIKE STARFISHES AND SEA LILIES

Calcichordate (<u>kal</u>-see-<u>kor</u>-date) is another fascinating fossil. It was related to the starfishes and sea lilies. In fact it looked like a sea lily that had fallen over.

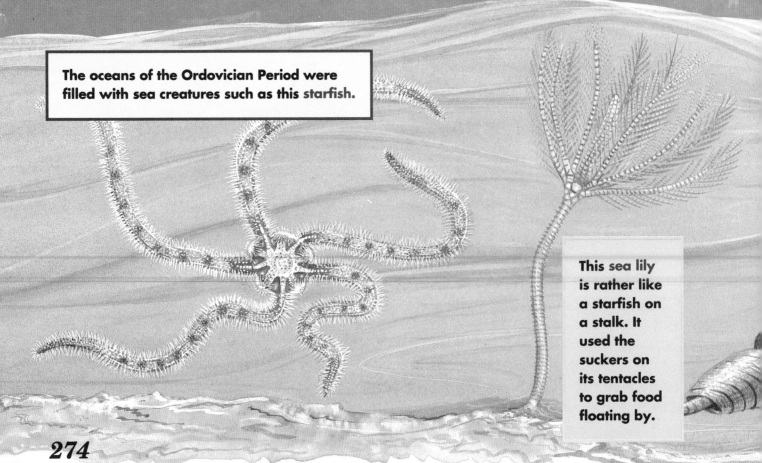

The oceans of the Ordovician Period were filled with sea creatures such as this **starfish**.

This **sea lily** is rather like a starfish on a stalk. It used the suckers on its tentacles to grab food floating by.

These fossils of 'tuning fork' graptolites help scientists to date rocks accurately.

OLD ROCKS OF WALES

The most famous Ordovician rocks are found in Wales. These rocks are shales and volcanic lavas. In Ordovician times, the continent of North America was moving towards northern Europe, pushing up the mud from the ocean floor to form black shale rocks above the water. The volcanic rocks were also created by the movements of the continents. The black shale contains fossils called graptolites. These graptolites were formed when tiny sea creatures died and sank to the ocean floor. Graptolites are used to date Ordovician rocks.

OUR ANCESTORS?

Some scientists think that calcichordates developed into the first animals with backbones. (We are animals with backbones.) Calcichordates had a body with a small mouth and tentacles at one end, and a tail at the other. If we think of the tail as a backbone, these little creatures were very like primitive fishes.

The background picture shows how the shoreline would have looked in Ordovician times.

Is it true that the Ordovician and Silurian Periods are named after tribes?

Yes. They are named after tribes that once lived in Wales – the Ordovices and the Silures. The rocks that tell the story of these periods were first found and studied in Wales. Of course, the tribes lived millions of years after the Ordovician and Silurian Periods named in their honour.

A calcichordate's mouth and tentacles faced forward and it could use its stalk-like tail to push itself along the seabed.

Arandapsis, an early jawless fish, swam in the waters of the Silurian seas. The Silurian was the period following the Ordovician.

First life on land

In Silurian times the world was covered by seas, mud flows, reefs and volcanoes.

The Ordovician Period ended in a mass extinction, and the Silurian Period, which lasted from 438 to 408 million years ago, began.

SILURIAN CLUES

Once again, the rocks in Wales were studied and these gave scientists clues to what happened during the Silurian Period. We know that at this time the continents of North America and Europe moved closer towards one another. The ocean bed continued to buckle and fold.

CHANGING SEAS

Large areas of shallow seas formed. At the beginning of the Period the sea level rose. This flooded the lands near the coast and made shallow seas over them. Scientists think an Ice Age occurred about half way through the Silurian Period.

IT'S A FACT

GREAT LAKES REEF

In the Silurian Period, a huge circular reef existed in the northern USA. You can still see the circular rock structure it formed in the curving shorelines of the five Great Lakes.

MASS DEATH . . .

At the end of the Ordovician Period there was a mass extinction. It was a big one, and killed off about half of all animal species. It is this period of extinction that palaeontologists use to mark the end of the Ordovician and the beginning of the Silurian Period.

. . . AND NEW LIFE

All sorts of animals were wiped out during this time. Ordovician trilobites died off, but new Silurian trilobites quickly evolved. New graptolites and new brachiopods evolved too.

SPONGE REEFS

As the shallow Silurian seas became warmer, vast areas of reef developed. These reefs were not made of coral, like the reefs you can see today, but were made of sponges called stromatoporoids (strow-mat-o-pore-oydz) that built themselves up in layers.

SIMPLE FISHES

Very simple fishes without jaws became quite widespread in the Silurian seas. But it was not until the Devonian Period that the true Age of the Fishes began.

NEW LANDS TO CONQUER

So now we've had a glimpse of life in the Silurian seas, let's see what's happening on land. Here a greenish tinge seems to be collecting at the shoreline and moving up towards the barren lands.

THE FIRST PLANTS

Plants were the first living things on land, and *Cooksonia* was probably the first land plant. *Cooksonia* had a network of tubes which carried water around it. This meant it could live away from the water's edge.

Pterygotus

Pharyngolepis

Dartmuthia

Creatures, such as the giant sea scorpion, *Pterygotus*, and the jawless fishes, *Pharyngolepis* and *Dartmuthia*, lived in the Silurian seas.

277

GIANTS OF THE PAST

EUPARKERIA

Lying in wait among the ferns on a warm day in Early Triassic South Africa, two *Euparkeria* hear a rustling noise nearby. Turning swiftly, one spots a fleeing *Ericiolacerta*. The little reptile stands no chance as *Euparkeria* gathers speed, sprinting along on its powerful hind legs.

EUSTREPTOSPONDYLUS

In the warm climate of the Jurassic, a mother and baby *Lexovisaurus* are peacefully eating the lush vegetation. Suddenly, the peace is disturbed by three *Eustreptospondylus*. They pounce on the young *Lexovisaurus* and start tearing it apart. The poor mother can do nothing to save the baby.

Fabulous fur

Australian fur seal

Thick or thin, soft or whiskery, body hair makes mammals different from other creatures.

All mammals have hair of some kind, even whales. The amount varies from a bear's thick fur coat to the fine hairs on a human's arm. Fur is not just for show. Since prehistoric times mammals have relied on fur and hair to protect them from heat and cold. In icy weather or baking sun, air trapped between the hairs of an animal's coat keeps its body temperature even.

The ancient beaver, *Palaeocastor*, probably had two fur coats to keep it warm and dry.

TWO TYPES OF FUR
Many mammals have two coats of fur. The undercoat is usually short and dense and keeps the animal warm. The longer 'guard coat' adds waterproofing.

Woolly mammoth

WATERPROOF FUR
To keep it warm and waterproof, today's fur seal has a coat which consists of a thick underfur and coarse outer hairs. Seals in prehistoric times, such as *Acrophoca*, must have needed to keep warm too. Living seals have sleek coats of fur which are kept oily by grease glands under their skin. The oil prevents the fur from getting waterlogged.

282

Morganucodon

Fur has to be kept clean to do a good job of keeping animals warm.

THE BIG FREEZE

Because hair does not usually fossilize we are not sure exactly what prehistoric animals' fur looked like. However, some hair has been found with the bones of mammoths. It is thick and shaggy, with long hairs known as 'guard hairs'.

CHANGING COLOUR

New research shows that the woolly mammoth's fur has gone red over millions of years. It was probably dark brown when the mammoth was actually wearing it!

HAIRY HORN

The horn of the woolly rhinoceros was not really a horn at all. It was made of tough hair matted together into a horn-shaped mass.

THE CAT'S WHISKERS

Many mammals today have whiskers to help them feel objects or sense movements. Ancient mammals, such as *Morganucodon*, also had whiskers, as holes in their nose bones show.

283

Trapped in tar!

The tar pits of Rancho La Brea in Southern California held an incredible secret for many thousands of years.

Around Los Angeles in Southern California, between the Pacific Ocean and the mountains behind the coast, is a narrow strip of land where oil is trapped in the rocks. The oil has been there for many thousands of years and is still there today.

STICKY PUDDLES

In some places the oil is not trapped below the ground very securely. It seeps up to the surface through cracks and along faults in the rocks. When this happens, the oil spreads out on the ground as a long, black puddle. Under the warm Californian sun some of the oil evaporates away to leave behind a sticky pond of thick tar.

IT'S A FACT

HORSING AROUND

The remains of horses have been found at Rancho La Brea. Horses first evolved in North America, but became extinct there over 15,000 years ago, so for thousands of years there were no horses in North America. Then, in the sixteenth century, they were brought back by European settlers to where they'd first evolved.

TRAPPED!

These sticky puddles occurred in the past, too, when prehistoric beasts roamed freely across what is now the city and suburbs of Los Angeles. Rain showers left puddles of water on top of the tar layers. Animals, looking for a drink, wandered into the shallow water and their feet sank into the tar. Bellowing in anger, they discovered they couldn't move.

BITER BIT!

The noise attracted the meat-eating beasts, always on the look-out for animals in distress. The meat-eaters then became stuck as well. Scavenging birds flew in for a feast, but were unable to lift off because their feathers were clogged with tar.

WHAT IS IN THE PIT?

How do we know this happened? Because at Rancho La Brea near Los Angeles a tar pit full of prehistoric beasts has been discovered. Found in the tar were the bones of many animals known to live in North America around 35,000 years ago, plus the remains of animals from South America that had migrated northwards.

Thirsty plant-eaters wandered into the shallow tar pits for water and became stuck. Their cries were heard by meat-eaters which came to hunt them and also became trapped.

BIG ICE-AGE BEASTS

The big animals that became trapped included the giant sloth *Glossotherium*, the American mastodon, the imperial mammoth and other, now extinct, types of camel, bison and horse.

GREEDY MEAT-EATERS

The meat-eaters that were attracted by the squirming victims included the great sabre-toothed cat, *Smilodon,* and the extinct dire wolf, *Aenocyon.*
There were also meat-eaters we know today, such as coyotes and lynx, and a type of lion, but these skeletons are less common. Perhaps these more intelligent hunters were careful and avoided becoming stuck. The scavenging birds included a vulture, *Teratornis,* as well as hawks and eagles.

STICKY BONES

Tar helps to preserve things very well. So the bones of these unfortunate animals have survived tens of thousands of years and have not decayed away. Many of these bones lie there to this day, waiting for the palaeontologists to excavate them.

285

CITY SITE

Now, let us jump forward 35,000 years to the present day. The oil is still rising up through the ground and the tar pits are still there, although they are not as active as they once were. The landscape of yellow grasses with pine and cypress trees, backed by the purple haze of the distant hills, has changed, however. Now the pits lie in the centre of Los Angeles.

ANCIENT AND MODERN

Wilshire Boulevard hums and bustles close by, tower blocks cast their shadows across the tar and the Hollywood sign looks down from the hills. The only mammoths and ground sloths that exist at Rancho La Brea now are skeletons and life-sized sculptures.

RANCHO LA BREA

Rancho La Brea (*brea* is Spanish for tar) was discovered by the Spanish explorer Gaspar de Portolá in 1769. The first European settlers in California used to take tar from the pits to seal the roofs of their houses and make them waterproof.

ANIMAL SITE

Towards the end of the last century the Hancock family, on whose estate the tar pits lie, recognised that the bones in the tar were those of extinct animals. The site was given to Los Angeles county in 1913 and excavations have continued there ever since.

These sculptures of ground sloths are based on skeletons found in the tar pits.

286

Perhaps excavations in the tar pits, like the one shown left, will find still more creatures.

The skeleton of a baby mastodon (right) from Rancho La Brea.

The sabre-toothed cat, *Smilodon*, shown below, has become the state fossil of California.

Tar pits still exist today right in the middle of the large, bustling city of Los Angeles in Southern California, USA.

A PALAEONTOLOGIST'S DREAM

One block of tar, about the size of a small truck, had 50 dire wolf skulls and 30 sabre-toothed cat skulls in it. There have been over 200 prehistoric animals and plants identified at the site so far.

COME AND SEE

In 1977 George C. Page donated money to build a museum on the site so that the area could be properly excavated. The George C. Page Museum of La Brea Discoveries contains skeletons of all the types of animal found there.

IT'S A FACT

STATE FOSSIL

The great sabre-toothed cat *Smilodon californicus* was found in the Rancho La Brea tar pits. It was so spectacular and became such a popular attraction that it has been adopted as the state fossil of California.

287

"DARWIN PUBLISHED HIS BOOK "ORIGIN OF SPECIES" IN 1859. IT CAUSED QUITE A STIR!

SAYS BIRDS ARE DESCENDED FROM REPTILES!

THE MAN'S **MAD!**

NATURAL SELECTION— RUBBISH!

TOO MANY MISSING LINKS FOR THIS TO HOLD WATER!

BUT PROOF THAT THERE **WERE** MISSING LINKS CAME VERY SOON! IN 1860, A GERMAN SCIENTIST NAMED HERMAN VON MEYER EXAMINED A FOSSILIZED FEATHER....

SENSATIONAL! THIS MUST BE FROM THE VERY FIRST BIRD! I SHALL CALL IT ARCHAEOPTERYX.

EVENTUALLY, PROFESSOR RICHARD OWEN BOUGHT IT FOR THE BRITISH MUSEUM....

THIS FOSSIL IS A **VITAL** NEW DISCOVERY— WE MUST HAVE IT FOR OUR COLLECTION!

THE DISCOVERY OF ARCHAEOPTERYX, SO SOON AFTER DARWIN'S BOOK WAS PUBLISHED, WAS NOT SEEN AS SO IMPORTANT THEN AS IT IS NOW. TODAY PEOPLE REALISE THAT DINOSAURS ARE NOT JUST EXTINCT CURIOSITIES....

...THEY WERE ALL LINKS IN THE CHAIN OF ANIMAL LIFE ON EARTH. ONCE AGAIN, DARWIN THE PIONEER WAS PROVED RIGHT!

Improve and test your knowledge with...

FACT FILE

Follow the footprints on the mammoth's back and answer the questions posed

Fossil count

At the last check, there were about 2,100 different dinosaur specimens stored in various museums throughout the world.

Rice and bones for lunch?

On early dinosaur hunting expeditions in North America, the staple food was rice. Edward Drinker Cope and Charles Sternberg, two great dinosaur hunters of the time, hated the stuff. However, they found that they could make a thick paste from it that protected fossil bones on their journey home!

1 Who is the museum in Rancho la Brea named after?
a) George C. Page
b) Bill Clinton
c) Abraham Lincoln

2 Stromatoporoids were:
a) corals
b) small fishes
c) sponges

3 The fossilized bones of *Ammosaurus* were found in:
a) a car park
b) a firing range
c) a quarry

4 What did *Palaeocastor* have to keep it warm?
a) a hot water bottle
b) two fur coats
c) a big jumper

5 *Euparkeria* was about the size of a:
a) brown cow
b) red fox
c) black dog

6 *Cladoselache* was shaped like:
a) a box
b) a boat
c) a torpedo

7 The tar pits were caused by:
a) oil from under ground
b) careless drivers
c) leaking pipes

8 The Silurian Period was named after:
a) a Welsh tribe
b) a sea lily
c) an ancient rock

9 How many different animals and plants have been found at La Brea so far?
a) under 100
b) around 3,000
c) over 200

10 The state fossil of California is:
a) *Smilodon Californicus*
b) Smiley Bear
c) Californian seal

Jurassosaurus nedegoapeferkimorum

This dinosaur has a very long name because it has been named after the leading actors in the film 'Jurassic Park'. It is the world's oldest armoured dinosaur and was found in China.

Thick ribs

We can often tell if an animal was a water dweller because of its thick ribs. Thick ribs help to adjust the buoyancy of an animal while it swims.

Five-toed footprints

The first ever five-toed dinosaur footprints to be found in Britain were discovered in late Jurassic rocks in Dorset in 1988. They were probably made by a sauropod.

Answers to the questions on inside back cover

ASK THE EXPERT

Dr David Norman of Cambridge University answers your dinosaur questions

How old is the oldest monotreme fossil?

The oldest known monotreme (egg-laying mammal) was recognised from teeth and a partial skull which was similar to that of a platypus. These early fossil remains date from the Oligocene of Australia. Before that time, there was no fossil evidence of monotremes, though their history should be traceable back to Jurassic times.

Are there fossil tadpoles?

Yes, there are fossils of immature amphibians. Most, which date back to the Carboniferous Period, are not strictly tadpoles, but are more accurately described as 'larvae'. The name tadpole is used rather exclusively for the young larvae of frogs and toads. However, newts and salamanders produce young that are known as larvae. These have frilly external gills. Some small fossils obtained from shallow ponds and lakes include creatures which have carbonised remains of external gills – these are almost certainly amphibian larvae.

Cretaceous Iguanodon fossils were found in a coal mine dating from the Carboniferous. Why?

The remains of Iguanodons were found in a seam of clay which was from Cretaceous times. The reason they were found in a mine which contained coal, dating from much earlier times, is rather complicated. It seems that the coal formed in layers within limestone rocks. Millions of years later the limestone began to dissolve, creating caverns in the limestone. Millions of years after the dinosaurs had been buried in Cretaceous times, the caverns collapsed and the dinosaurs slipped into these caverns, to be discovered in recent times by coal miners.

Basilosaurus was a whale. So why does its name sound like that of a dinosaur?

Perhaps the first discoverers thought *Basilosaurus* was a giant lizard. It looked very like the huge mosasaurs that were seen at the end of the Cretaceous Period.

INDOSUCHUS

Indosuchus was a huge, fierce meat-eating dinosaur built very much like the great _Tyrannosaurus rex_.

Experts were excited when dinosaur fossils were discovered in India. _Dravidosaurus_, one of the last stegosaurs, and the sauropod, _Barapasaurus_, were among early finds in the last century.

FLESH-EATER

Indosuchus was named in 1933. Only a fragment of its skull and some teeth were found. However, these were enough to show palaeontologists that _Indosuchus_ was a flesh-eater.

ANCHORS AND MEAT HOOKS

As long as today's elephant, _Indosuchus_ walked on two powerful legs. Like _Tyrannosaurus rex_, its arms were tiny compared with the rest of its body. As it thundered along, _Indosuchus_ held its arms and hands close against its body. Experts think that the hands were used to grip the ground when the tyrannosaurid heaved itself up from a resting position or as meat hooks to hold down prey.

WALKING TALL

Indosuchus walked upright with its back level and its body balanced by a tail held stiffly behind. It had a large head, but 'windows' or openings in the skull made the head light enough to be moved from side to side as _Indosuchus_ scanned the landscape for its next meal.

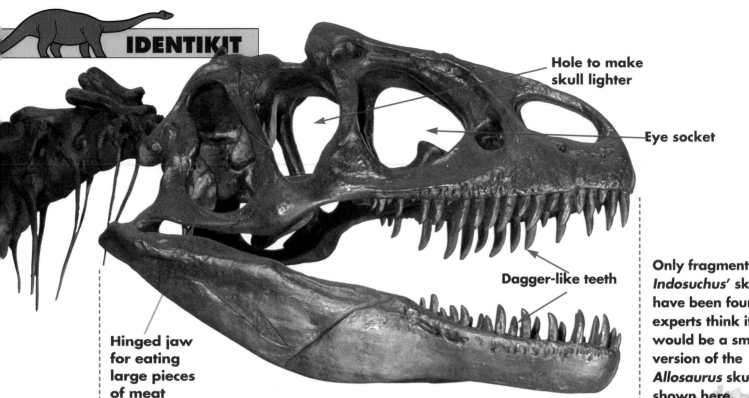

Hole to make
skull lighter

Eye socket

Dagger-like teeth

Only fragments of
Indosuchus' skull
have been found bu
experts think it
would be a smaller
version of the
Allosaurus skull
shown here.

Hinged jaw
for eating
large pieces
of meat

90cm

SHOCK ABSORBER

When *Indosuchus* attacked its prey, its
skull and neck were flexible enough to
bear the brunt of the collision. But the
shock of the impact and the struggles of
the victim meant that *Indosuchus* lost a
few teeth in every battle. A flesh-eater
without teeth would be a sorry sight and
Indosuchus had a special way of dealing
with the problem.

Is it true

**that India was once
joined to Africa?**
Yes. India was once part of the
'supercontinent' of Gondwana. About
145 million years ago, northern and southern
continents began to divide and India drifted away
from Antarctica and Africa. The large island which
was to become India moved northwards and
eventually joined with Asia. But it kept on moving
northwards, crushing the land up into great folds,
which became the Himalaya Mountains.

NEW TEETH FOR OLD

We have to look after our teeth. If our second, or permanent, teeth are damaged, they have to be repaired or replaced with false teeth. *Indosuchus* had no such problem. When scientists took an X-ray of the dinosaur's skull fragments, they saw that small teeth were tucked out of sight, deep in the jaw. When a tooth fell out, a new tooth came to the surface to replace it.

BITING FIT

Some of *Indosuchus*' teeth were as long as the middle finger of a human hand. Sharp and pointed, each tooth had a jagged edge to cut through the skin of its victim. After receiving several savage bites, the prey of *Indosuchus* was probably too weak to move and lay completely helpless.

MONSTER FACTS

- **NAME:** *Indosuchus* (<u>in</u>-doh-<u>soo</u>-kus) means 'Indian crocodile'
  GROUP: dinosaur
- **SIZE:** up to 6m long
- **FOOD:** meat
- **LIVED:** about 75 million years ago in the Late Cretaceous Period in central India

THAT SMELLS GOOD!

Sometimes it was not necessary for *Indosuchus* to go out looking for food. Dinosaur flesh gave off a very powerful smell and when a dinosaur died, by accident or naturally, the rotting carcass would attract many hungry creatures. Large meat-eaters, such as *Indosuchus* and *Tyrannosaurus rex,* were not too proud to scavenge a tasty, dead dinner.

SIZE WISE

6m

295

DEINOGALERIX

***Deinogalerix* was a hairy, hunting hedgehog.**

This extraordinary meat-eating mammal lived during the Miocene Epoch about 10 million years ago. It lived on an island which is now joined to the land mass we call Italy.

AMBITIOUS HUNTER

On its island home, *Deinogalerix* did not have to compete for food with many other hunters. It was able to hunt bigger prey than today's hedgehogs, catching small lizards and mammals rather than insects and worms.

NOSE TWITCHER

When out searching for prey, *Deinogalerix* scuttled along in the undergrowth on four short legs with its whiskery nose twitching. Its jaw was filled with sharp teeth and it used its pointed front teeth to bite its victims, spearing an arm or leg and leaving them helpless.

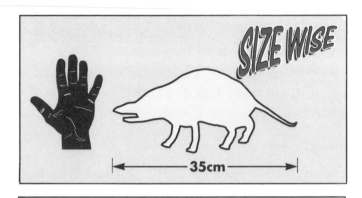

SIZE WISE

35cm

MONSTER FACTS

- **NAME:** *Deinogalerix* (dine-oh-gal-er-ix) means 'terrible hedgehog'
- **GROUP:** mammal
- **SIZE:** about 35cm long
- **FOOD:** small lizards and mammals
- **LIVED:** about 10 million years ago in the Miocene Epoch in southern Italy

HAIRY HEDGEHOG

Unlike today's hedgehog, *Deinogalerix* had a coat of long rough hair rather than spikes. But the prospect of such a hairy mouthful did put off predators and gave it some protection.

296

ANTARCTOSAURUS

Antarctosaurus was as long as two buses parked end to end.

his huge sauropod is known from only a few fossils, but experts think that it was probably related to *Diplodocus*. Ten times heavier than a modern elephant, *Antarctosaurus* was about three times taller than a man. In comparison with the rest of its body, this gigantic plant-eater had a tiny head.

ARMOURED BACK

Several fragments of *Antarctosaurus'* skeleton have been found in different parts of South America. Some experts think that *Antarctosaurus* may have had armour plating like the Argentinian sauropod *Saltasaurus*. This would certainly have put off any carnivore that was not deterred by its enormous size and tried to leap on to its back. And so *Antarctosaurus* was probably left alone to browse among the treetops in peace.

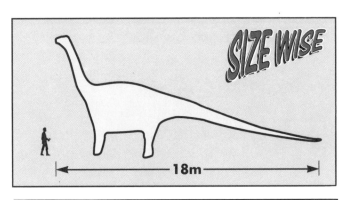

SIZE WISE

18m

MONSTER FACTS

- **NAME:** *Antarctosaurus* (ant-<u>ark</u>-toe-saw-rus) means 'southern reptile'
- **GROUP:** dinosaur
- **SIZE:** up to 18m long
- **FOOD:** plants
- **LIVED:** about 80 million years ago in the Late Cretaceous Period in South America and possibly Asia

TOOTHY PEGS

When it came to eating, *Antarctosaurus* was a nibbler rather than a muncher. With its few peg-like teeth, it nipped off juicy leaves and swallowed them whole. Its small skull and long neck enabled *Antarctosaurus* to reach the top branches other dinosaurs could not reach.

Devonian world

Fishes ruled the seas during the Devonian Period, but insects were the miniature monsters that ruled the dry parts of the world.

 he Devonian World lasted from 408 to 362 million years ago. The oceans were ruled by huge predatory fish. Animals and plants began to flourish on dry land.

THE CHANGING WORLD

If you could travel back in time to Devonian Earth, you would find a very different world to ours. There were only two main land masses. One was Laurasia, which was made up of North America, Europe and most of Asia. The other land mass was Gondwana, which was made up of South America, Africa, Australia, India and Antarctica.

SUPERCONTINENT

Much of Laurasia and some of Gondwana was covered by shallow seas. During this Period the two great land masses moved together to form one supercontinent called Pangaea.

THE AGE OF FISHES

Fossils show that Devonian waters swarmed with life. There were seaweeds and coral reefs. Worms and trilobites burrowed in the mud at the bottom of the lakes and oceans. Above them swam the shellfishes. The early jawless fishes were joined by fishes with spines, with bony plates of armour, or with fleshy-based fins which they used to haul themselves out of the water.

FIRST LAND ANIMALS

During the Devonian Period, plants evolved into bigger, more varied types such as clubmosses, horsetails and ferns. They spread away from swamps and lake shores to form the first dry-land forests. This 'green carpet' began to be inhabited by the early cousins of millipedes, centipedes, insects, mites and spiders.

FOOD FOR FISHES

There were many strange and exciting fishes living in the Devonian. There were also water plants and smaller animals that were food for the fishes. Seaweeds, such as *Fucus* (brown wrack), *Ulva* (green sea-lettuce) and *Ceramium* (red hair-weed), thrived. You can still see similar seaweeds today.

Dunkleosteus

Pteraspis

Ulva

Ceramium

Fucus

298

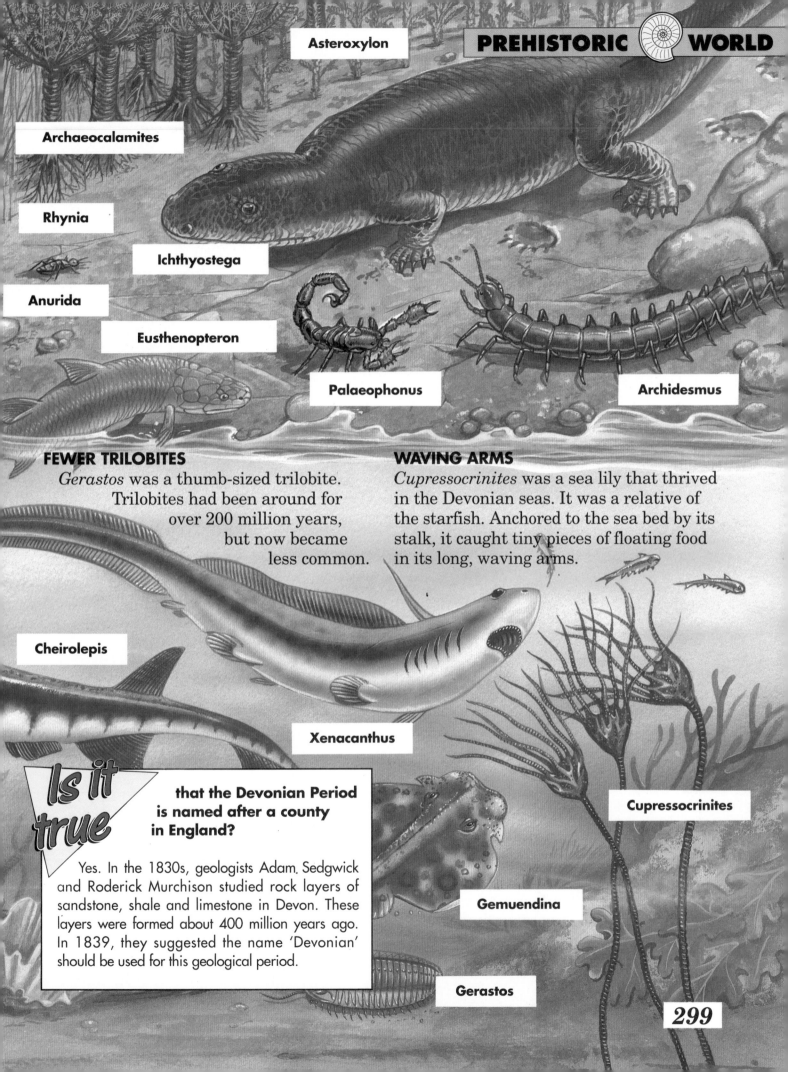

Asteroxylon

Archaeocalamites

Rhynia

Ichthyostega

Anurida

Eusthenopteron

Palaeophonus

Archidesmus

FEWER TRILOBITES

Gerastos was a thumb-sized trilobite. Trilobites had been around for over 200 million years, but now became less common.

WAVING ARMS

Cupressocrinites was a sea lily that thrived in the Devonian seas. It was a relative of the starfish. Anchored to the sea bed by its stalk, it caught tiny pieces of floating food in its long, waving arms.

Cheirolepis

Xenacanthus

Cupressocrinites

Is it true

that the Devonian Period is named after a county in England?

Yes. In the 1830s, geologists Adam Sedgwick and Roderick Murchison studied rock layers of sandstone, shale and limestone in Devon. These layers were formed about 400 million years ago. In 1839, they suggested the name 'Devonian' should be used for this geological period.

Gemuendina

Gerastos

NO JAWS

Jawless fishes, such as *Pteraspis*, were still around in the Devonian Period. *Pteraspis* was an amazing-looking fish, with a head shield and spines on its back. Its mouth was underneath a long snout. Experts think it was a powerful swimmer.

GREAT JAWS

The terror of Devonian seas was the giant *Dunkleosteus*. It had massive jaws and at 9m long was bigger than today's Great White Shark. It was a placoderm, meaning 'plated skin', and had bony plates of armour on its head and on the front of its body. Another placoderm was *Gemuendina*, which had a flattened body like that of a ray. *Gemuendina* was as long as a human foot. The Devonian Period also saw the appearance of sharks, such as *Cladoselache* and *Xenacanthus*. The sharks have hardly changed since then.

Terrifying *Dunkleosteus* was an enormous armoured fish.

STEPS ON TO LAND

Ray-fins, common fishes today, first appeared in Devonian times. There was the wide-mouthed, sharp-toothed, 50cm-long hunter *Cheirolepis* and the fish-finger-sized *Moythomasia*. There were also lobe-fins such as *Eusthenopteron*. These had lungs for breathing air and could probably drag themselves on to the land using their fins.

FOUR LEGS FOR WALKING

It was only a short step from lobe-finned fishes to four-legged land animals. The lobe-fins evolved legs and feet, and *Ichthyostega* walked from the water as the first amphibian.

IT'S A FACT

THAT THERE WAS A DEVONIAN SWORDFISH

The swordfish design, of a long, flat snout with spikes along either side, appears many times during the evolution of the fishes. Even the jawless fishes of Devonian times had their 'swordfish'. It was called *Doryaspis* and was as big as a human hand. Strangely, its mouth was above its sword-snout, and it had saw-teeth on its bony 'side-wings' too!

Cheirolepis

SPREADING ACROSS THE LAND

Ichthyostega did not walk on to an empty landscape. New kinds of land plants were evolving. These were 'vascular' plants, which means they had a system for circulating liquids through their stems, just as blood is transported around the human body.

EARLY PLANTS

Rhynia was about 50cm tall. It had a central stem with small, twig-like side parts. The early land plants also included the clubmosses, such as *Asteroxylon,* which was about 1m tall and looked like a leaf-covered cactus. It had a thick stem and small side arms.

Gemuendina

Xenacanthus

BIGGER AND BETTER

During the Devonian Period, plants grew even taller. There were 10m-high horsetails, such as *Archaeocalamites*, with its umbrella-like leaves. Another plant group, the ferns, made their first appearance. By the end of the Devonian Period, giant ferns, such as *Archaeopteris*, towered 20m above the land.

MINIBEASTS ON LAND

Ichthyostega was not the only animal on land. Down among the miniature jungle of the clubmosses, a collection of minibeasts was on the prowl.

THE VERY FIRST INSECTS

Crawling among the fronds were centipedes and millipedes, like *Archidesmus*, mites and the very first insects. *Rhyniella*, like many early insects, had no wings. *Anurida* was a Devonian springtail. Scorpions, like *Palaeophonus*, could sting their prey and rip it apart with their claws. By the end of the Devonian, there was truly life on land.

301

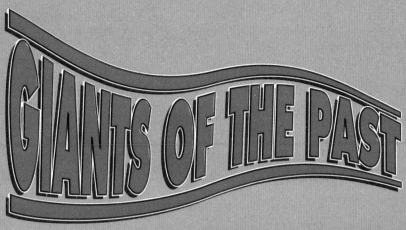

GIANTS OF THE PAST

A small pack of meat-eating *Jubbulpuria* excitedly gathers round a dinosaur's corpse. But there will be no free meal for them today - they have been spotted by gigantic *Indosuchus* and with a few quick strides of its powerful hind legs it is upon them. The terrified little dinosaurs scatter, but it is too late for one, as *Indosuchus* sinks its long, jagged teeth into its flesh.

LUFENGOSAURUS

200 million years ago in southern China, a group of ravenous *Lufengosaurus* gathers beside a river. These giant reptiles use their rough-edged teeth to strip leaves off branches and they have spotted a huge clump of leafy trees on the other side of the bank. But how can they reach them? Throwing caution to the wind, they plunge into the river and strike out for the other side as their hunger gets the better of them.

Dinosaur artist

Discover how a professional illustrator brings dinosaurs to life.

 inosaur artists have to turn fossil skeletons into living creatures. We asked Mike Dorey to talk about his job.

'A Day in the Life of Brachiosaurus' being created by dinosaur artist Mike Dorey.

HOW DID YOU BECOME AN ILLUSTRATOR?

"I always liked drawing – I used to do strip cartoons when I was 4! I studied at art college. Then I went to London to get a job as an illustrator. I drew strip cartoons for comics and did drawings for books, television and even pop videos."

WHY DID YOU START DRAWING DINOSAURS?

"I used to do strip cartoons for a famous comic called *Eagle*. One story was called 'The Land of the Dinosaurs'. I did lots of dramatic drawings of *Tyrannosaurus rex* and wanted to do more dinosaur illustrations."

HOW DO YOU DRAW A DINOSAUR?

"Before I start, I look at as many different drawings by other artists as I can. I also look very carefully at models and skeletons of dinosaurs."

HOW DO YOU BRING A DINOSAUR BACK TO LIFE?

"To make a dinosaur drawing really alive, I have to understand how the dinosaur might have moved. When I've worked that out, I can draw it in action."

WHAT'S YOUR FAVOURITE DINOSAUR?

"I like *Styracosaurus* best. It looks so dramatic with all those horns!"

HOW DO YOU DO 'HISTORY IN PICTURES?'

"An author writes the words and I plan the pictures to go with them. Then I draw it all out in pencil. At that stage we show the rough artwork to our dinosaur expert David Norman to check. Then I go over it in black ink. I use blue or black for the shadows and shading and then paint in the colour and write the words in black."

WHAT ARE THE HARDEST BITS?

"The trickiest bit is to decide what colours the dinosaurs should be. No one really knows. Another difficult thing is to show how big they were, so I try and put a tree in for scale. Or I paint them as if I am looking up at them."

A chilling death?

Why the dinosaurs became extinct is one of the great unsolved mysteries of science. Was it because the weather got too cold for them?

DETECTIVE WORK

Theories are fine but they must be backed up with evidence. Time detectives look at rocks and fossils for clues.

During the Age of the Dinosaurs different species of dinosaurs lived alongside each other.

Why aren't there any dinosaurs today? Dinosaurs lived successfully for around 170 million years. Then, 66 million years ago, they all vanished.

FAST OR SLOW?

There are plenty of theories about why dinosaurs died out. Some of them are silly. Others are more sensible. There are two major 'sensible' theories. One is that the dinosaurs were killed off suddenly by a world disaster, such as a meteorite hitting the Earth or violent volcanic eruptions. The other theory is that they died out slowly over a period of time because the climate changed.

FOSSIL RECORD

So let's see what evidence there is for dinosaurs dying out because the climate changed. The fossil record shows that different species of dinosaur from the same family lived alongside each other.

 **What is ? A FOSSIL RECORD**

When someone writes down what happens it is called a record. A diary is a kind of record. Fossils in the rocks are the record of what happened to plants and animals millions of years ago. That's why palaeontologists call it the fossil record, or F.R. for short.

THE BEGINNING OF THE END?

In North America, for example, towards the end of the Cretaceous Period, several different kinds of duckbilled dinosaurs, such as *Prosaurolophus*, *Corythosaurus* and *Saurolophus*, lived side by side. But at the very end of the Cretaceous only *Saurolophus* was left. The same was true of the ceratopians.

PLENTY TO EAT

The kinds of plants in the Jurassic and Early Cretaceous fossil record show that the climate was warm with plenty of rain. These were ideal conditions for lush, green tropical forests to flourish. So dinosaurs who ate the plants did well. And dinosaurs who ate the dinosaurs who ate the plants did well too!

By the end of the Cretaceous, species had died out and were not replaced.

Rainforest (above) and woodland.

SLOW EXTINCTION

Triceratops, *Chasmosaurus* and *Styracosaurus* lived at the same time, but by the end of the Cretaceous only *Triceratops* was left. For scientists who support the slow extinction theory, the fossil record from North America is evidence that the dinosaurs died out gradually, species by species. But what was the cause?

PLANT CLUES

Dinosaur bones are not the only fossils found. Plants leave fossils too. Plants can tell us a lot about the Earth millions of years ago and about changes that may have caused the death of the dinosaurs.

COOLING DOWN

In the middle of the Cretaceous Period, the plants began to change. They became more like the woodlands of today's cooler climates. Scientists now believe that the Earth's climate changed and cooled drastically during the Late Cretaceous Period.

TIME DETECTIVE

THE CHANGING SEASONS

Not only did the climate cool, it changed from cold to warm at different times of the year. The changing seasons had arrived. So why was there such a great change in the weather at that time? Some scientists think it was because the continents were on the move again.

THE DIVIDING LAND

Australia was being pushed away from Antarctica. A great surge of cold water pushed up towards the equator, cooling the land. At the same time, the broad, shallow seas around the continents drained away exposing more land. The climate became drier and gradually much cooler.

that dinosaurs were not the only animals to become extinct in the Late Cretaceous?

Yes. There was a mass extinction in the Late Cretaceous. Among the animals that died out were the curly-shelled ammonites, the large marine reptiles such as mosasaurs and ichthyosaurs, and the flying reptiles such as the pterosaurs.

145 MYA

Late Jurassic. The land masses were drifting further apart.

66 MYA

Late Cretaceous. The oceans filled gaps between the continents.

Twentieth century

Today, there are great stretches of ocean.

LOSING HEAT

Experts think that the dinosaurs could not adapt to the new conditions on Earth for several reasons. Large dinosaurs were probably endothermic or 'cold-blooded'. They could not create heat from food as mammals can. Once a large cold-blooded dinosaur lost heat from its body during cold weather, it was probably almost impossible for it to get warm again. Dinosaurs did not have feathers or fur to keep them warm when it got cold. Once they lost heat they did not have enough energy to look for food and they may simply have starved to death.

TOO COLD FOR DINOSAURS

Many other animals managed to survive the great cooling of the Earth. Some of them, such as mammals and birds, had fur or feathers to keep them warm. Others probably slept through the coldest times of the year. They dug burrows, or crawled into crevices and hibernated, just as today's dormouse does. But most dinosaurs were too big to dig burrows or crawl into holes. Dinosaurs had dominated the Earth for millions of years but they faced the colder weather with very little to protect them.

310

THE RIGHT THEORY?

The long, slow cooling may have been too much for the dinosaurs to bear. They were used to warm weather, with no sudden changes of temperature. It had been like that for millions of years. The dinosaurs had to cope with many changes: different plants to eat, cooler weather and extremes of warm and cold weather. Many scientists think that the dinosaurs simply could not adapt to the new conditions, and so they gradually died out, species by species. But is that the right theory? In the next issue, you can see the evidence for the theory that the dinosaurs were killed off suddenly, in one great disaster.

A dormouse can protect itself from the cold weather by hibernating in its nest.

Unlike other animals, the dinosaurs could not cope with the changing climate and they began to disappear.

311

Improve and test your knowledge with...

FACT FILE

Fascinating facts
to read and
10 fun questions
to answer!

Lowland beasts
Nearly all the dinosaur skeletons that have been found are of animals that lived in lowlands, by rivers or near the sea. Dinosaurs that lived in mountain areas would not have stood much chance of becoming fossilized in hard, rocky ground.

1 What was the most distinctive feature of *Stegoceras*?
a) its sharp claws
b) its flattened skull
c) its enormous horns

2 *Antarctosaurus* ate:
a) succulent dinosaur meat
b) crisp insects and centipedes
c) juicy plants and leaves

3 *Icaronycteris* is the oldest known:
a) bat
b) bird
c) dinosaur

4 Dinosaurs may have died out because:
a) the weather got too cold
b) people hunted them
c) they couldn't swim

5 In the Devonian seas *Ulva* was:
a) a red sea-cabbage
b) a yellow sea-cauliflower
c) a green sea-lettuce

6 The hedgehog *Deinogalerix* ate:
a) small lizards and mammals
b) fishes and seashells
c) leaves and bark

7 *Hypohippus* was:
a) a small hippopotamus
b) an early horse
c) a giant lizard

8 *Indosuchus* means:
a) Indian dinosaur
b) Indian teeth
c) Indian crocodile

9 *Dunkleosteus* was as big as:
a) today's Great White Shark
b) a double-decker bus
c) a green sea-lettuce

314

Serves them right!

In 1877 two railwaymen sent the famous dinosaur expert, Othniel Charles Marsh, some bones that they had found in Colorado, USA. This was the beginning of the great American dinosaur discoveries. Marsh sent a large sum of money in return, but the two men could not cash the cheque. They had used false names because they had found the bones while working in the railway's time!

Roman Dino

A dinosaur leg bone was studied in 1677 by the Reverend Robert Plot of Oxford, who deduced that it was the bone of an elephant brought to Britain by the Romans.

The whale that walked

Palaeontologists believe they have finally discovered the missing link between whales and land-dwelling mammals. They have found the 50-million-year-old fossil of a mammal that could both walk and swim. Ambulocetus, as they have called it, had short thick legs and large webbed feet for swimming. When the whales took to the sea full time, the front legs evolved into paddles and the back legs disappeared altogether.

Dino route

The longest dinosaur trackway ever discovered lies outside Lisbon in Portugal. It is 120m long and is made up of Cretaceous iguanodont footprints. A new road has had to be rerouted to avoid them.

10

Lufengosaurus lived in:
a) Orlando
b) southern China
c) northern India

If a big dinosaur fell into a river, would it float or sink?

Big dinosaurs were surprisingly light. They may even have had air-filled pockets along their backbones to reduce their weight. If this was the case, then huge dinosaurs would have floated incredibly well if they fell into water.

If dinosaurs were covered with feathers, why haven't we found fossils of the feathers?

Some scientists think dinosaurs may have been covered with feathers but it is very rare to find fossils of soft tissue, such as feathers. Feathers are made of keratin, which rots away quickly after death. Most dinosaurs died on land and were then washed into rivers and lakes. This meant that feathers rotted away before they could be preserved. However, *Archaeopteryx* feathers have been preserved in fine, sticky mud. As you can see, it is very difficult to find evidence for or against the feather theory, but I still do not believe that dinosaurs had feathers!

Would adult dinosaurs have recognised their own babies?

It is likely that the dinosaurs, such as hadrosaurs, which built nests and fed their babies, did recognise their young. However, it is just as likely that many dinosaurs laid their eggs and left, paying their young no more attention. They never recognised them. Perhaps that is why some dinosaurs were cannibals, eating their own kind.

Were any dinosaurs poisonous, like snakes are?

Nobody knows whether dinosaurs had snake-like venom. There is no evidence, and my guess is that dinosaurs were not venomous. But dinosaur spit may have been dangerous. Like that of animals today, it probably contained unpleasant chemicals.

MICROCERATOPS

Tiny *Microceratops* lived among terrifying predators such as *Tarbosaurus* and *Velociraptor*.

he bare, arid earth of modern Mongolia is a treasure trove for fossil hunters. In prehistoric times Mongolia must have teemed with animal life.

NIPPING AROUND

Fossils discovered in Mongolia show that a great variety of dinosaurs lived there over 70 million years ago. Huge carnivores and egg-eaters lived alongside gentle plant-eaters and herds of bonehead dinosaurs. Nipping around the feet of its large neighbours was little *Microceratops*.

FAMILY MATTERS

Imagine a piglet that walks on two legs, has a beak-nose and a delicate neck-frill and you will have some idea of what *Microceratops* looked like. It belonged to the family of protoceratopians, which included *Protoceratops* and *Leptoceratops*. *Microceratops* was lively and active and experts think it was a lot like the primitive ceratopian *Psittacosaurus,* which was about 2m long and also lived in Mongolia. Like *Microceratops, Psittacosaurus* had a parrot beak and could walk on two legs.

SMALL AND SWIFT

Microceratops was one of the smallest dinosaurs. It measured about 80cm. Its back legs were quite slender and its feet were long and narrow. This suggests *Microceratops* was a fast runner.

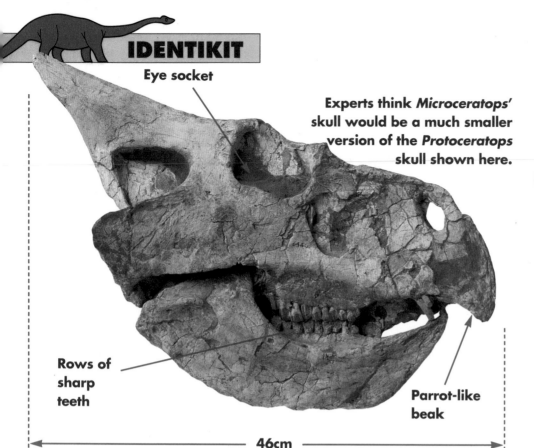

Eye socket

Experts think *Microceratops'* skull would be a much smaller version of the *Protoceratops* skull shown here.

Rows of sharp teeth

Parrot-like beak

← 46cm →

BEAKS AND TEETH

Like its relatives, *Microceratops* probably nipped off shoots with the hard edge of its horny beak. With the teeth in its cheeks, it sliced up food with a scissor-like action. When *Microceratops* balanced on its back legs, its forearms could grasp stems above its head and pull them down to its mouth.

HAPPY TO SHARE

It did not need the same quantities of food as big plant-eaters and was probably happy to share its juicy supper with larger plant-eaters such as *Homalocephale*.

FRILLED TO SEE YOU

Microceratops has a short, solid frill at the back of its skull. Muscles attached to the frill probably helped move the powerful jaws. A frill also helped a dinosaur to recognise members of its herd.

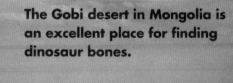

The Gobi desert in Mongolia is an excellent place for finding dinosaur bones.

IT'S A FACT

AMERICAN DISCOVERY

It was an American team of scientists that first discovered the rich fossil resources of Mongolia. A team led by Roy Chapman Andrews and Walter Granger made the first expedition in 1922.

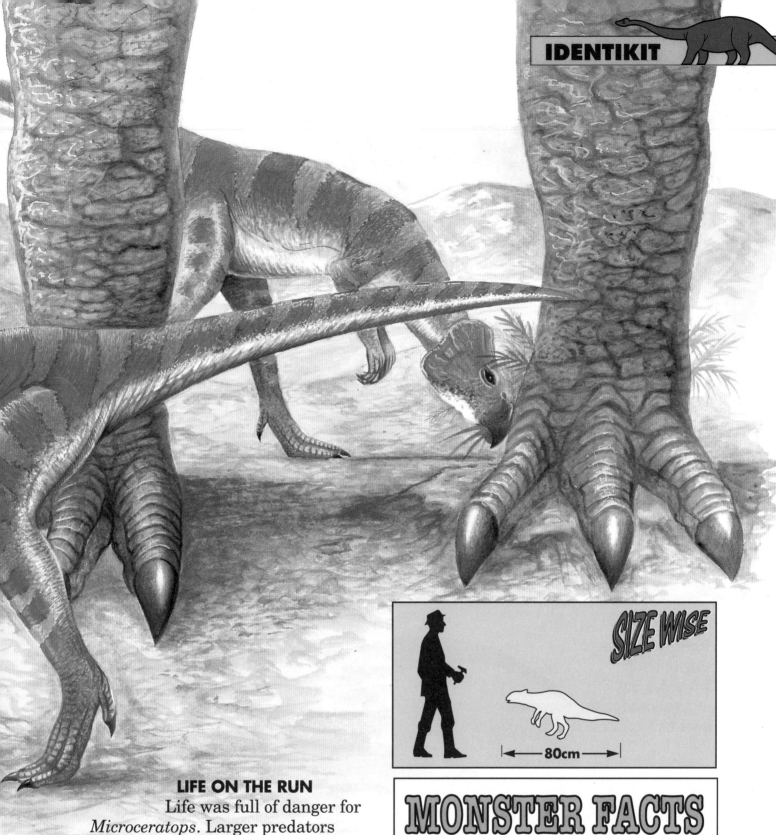

SIZE WISE

←——— 80cm ———→

LIFE ON THE RUN

Life was full of danger for *Microceratops*. Larger predators such as *Velociraptor* were always ready to pounce, and egg-stealing *Oviraptor* hovered hopefully around its nests. Living in a herd gave *Microceratops* some protection. Alerted to a sound, the group could run through the undergrowth to safety. The youngest or the slowest dinosaurs were most likely to be caught.

MONSTER FACTS

- **NAME:** *Microceratops* (my-crow-<u>serra</u>-tops) means 'tiny horned face'
- **GROUP:** dinosaur
- **SIZE:** 80cm long
- **FOOD:** plants
- **LIVED:** about 75 million years ago in the Late Cretaceous Period in Mongolia and China

319

DEINOCHEIRUS

Two gigantic arms are the only fossils of *Deinocheirus* found so far.

n a wet day in southern Mongolia, Polish scientists were amazed to find some huge bones sticking out from the top of a small hill. They were part of the shoulder, arms and claws of a mysterious dinosaur.

THE LONG ARM
This extraordinary find puzzled all the experts. Long, slender limbs and three-fingered hands were a feature of the ostrich dinosaurs, the ornithomimosaurs. But, at 2.4m long, this arm was bigger than any ornithomimosaur arm palaeontologists had ever found.

FINGERS AND THUMBS
The experts found that none of the *Deinocheirus'* fingers could fold inwards to grasp objects.

SIZE WISE

UNKNOWN

GIANT CLAWS
Deinocheirus could not grip tightly, but it could do immense damage with its enormous claws. Each claw was as long as a human head and was curved and pointed like a huge hook. Even so, scientists are not sure whether or not *Deinocheirus* was a meat-eater.

UNSOLVED MYSTERY
Deinocheirus' appearance remains a mystery. Its arms are so unusual that scientists have found it hard to imagine what the rest of its body looked like. It may have been as tall as a giraffe!

MONSTER FACTS
- **NAME:** *Deinocheirus* (dye-no-kye-rus) means 'terrible hand'
- **GROUP:** dinosaur
- **SIZE:** unknown
- **FOOD:** probably meat
- **LIVED:** about 75 million years ago in the Late Cretaceous Period in southern Mongolia

BOROGOVIA

Borogovia was a nimble hunter of small mammals.

Borogovia was a two-legged predator about 2m long. It moved stealthily through the forest. If a small creature scurried through the undergrowth, *Borogovia* was alerted instantly. It had forward-facing eyes to help it see tiny shapes, even when the light was fading.

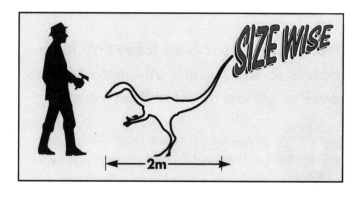

SIZE WISE

2m

SPEEDY SPRINTER

Lizards, snakes and small mammals can move quickly, but this did not always keep them safe from *Borogovia*. It could sprint forward to catch its prey, taking massive strides with its long, slim legs.

HANDS AND FEET

Borogovia carried extra hunting equipment on its hands and feet – sharp claws. It grasped hold of its prey with hook-shaped claws while its jagged teeth did their deadly work. As *Borogovia* ran, its weight was supported by three toes. Like *Troodon*, it probably had a large, swivelling claw on its second toe.

MONSTER FACTS

- **NAME:** *Borogovia* (<u>bore</u>-oh-<u>go</u>-vee-a) is named after the 'borogove' in Lewis Carroll's poem 'Jabberwocky'
- **GROUP:** dinosaur
- **SIZE:** up to 2m long
- **FOOD:** meat
- **LIVED:** about 80 million years ago in the Late Cretaceous Period in Mongolia

321

Galloping wonders

Horses have evolved from tiny leaf-eaters to the superb athletes of today over a period of 50 million years.

Horses are marvellous. They can be trained to obey commands, can run like the wind, carry riders, leap over fences, prance elegantly to music, and pull a carriage or a cart.

THE HORSE FAMILY

All horses today, from tiny Shetland ponies to huge carthorses, belong to a single species, *Equus caballus*. There are six other horse-type animals, also named Equus, which make up the living members of the horse family, the equids (e-kwids).

A LONG HISTORY

Horses were probably first tamed and used by people over 6,000 years ago in Asia. But the story of the horse family begins over 50 million years ago, during the Early Eocene Epoch, when equids first appeared. At this time, horses were dog-sized, forest-dwelling, leaf-eaters. When grasses appeared and spread across the lands, horses evolved to take advantage of this new food source. There were many equid species in prehistoric times, especially in North America.

Is it true

that the zebra is a striped horse?

Yes. Or, more accurately, it's a striped equid. Zebras are extremely similar to horses, apart from the colour and pattern of their coat. In fact, the seven living members of the horse family are very close relatives and are all called Equus:

- Horse: *Equus caballus*.
- Wild Mongolian or Przewalski's horse: *Equus przewalski*.
- Plains zebra: *Equus burchelli*.
- Mountain zebra: *Equus zebra*.
- Grevy's zebra: *Equus grevyi*.
- Asian ass: *Equus hemionus*.
- African ass: *Equus africanus*.

FOUR KEY CHANGES

Horses have evolved in four main ways. All the factors have contributed to make today's horses very fast.

Bigger: horses got bigger, and so stronger and better able to defend themselves.

Longer: horses' legs got longer, so they could move further, faster.

Slimmer: legs became slimmer, too, which saved weight and helped agility.

Fewer: the toes were reduced to one.

FIT FOR THE JOB

Their necks became long and well muscled to cope with grazing on the open grasslands. Their jawbones became long and deep to carry large, hard-wearing teeth, excellent for chewing tough grass.

SUPER SENSES

Horses evolved into alert animals with sharp eyesight, keen hearing, a good sense of smell and a fairly large brain.

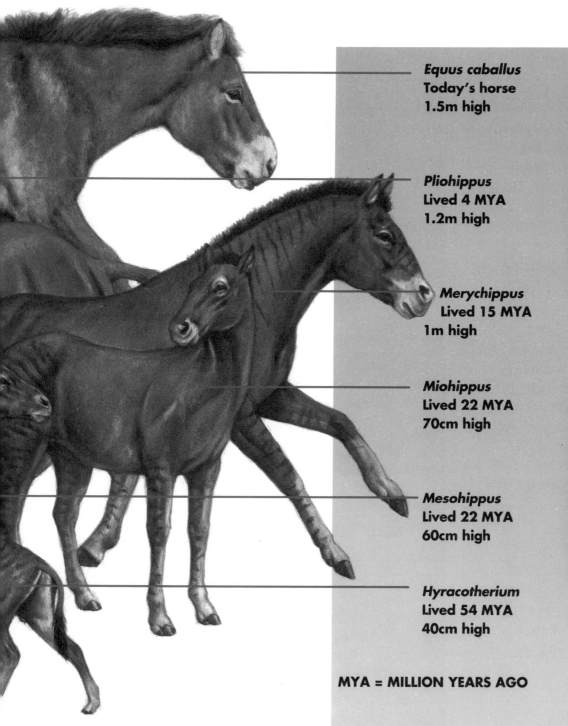

Equus caballus
Today's horse
1.5m high

Pliohippus
Lived 4 MYA
1.2m high

Merychippus
Lived 15 MYA
1m high

Miohippus
Lived 22 MYA
70cm high

Mesohippus
Lived 22 MYA
60cm high

Hyracotherium
Lived 54 MYA
40cm high

MYA = MILLION YEARS AGO

Today's horse can gallop at up to 60kph.

For 6,000 years, man has used horse power.

Is it true

that the horse stands on its toenails?

Yes. The hoof of a horse is equivalent to a cat's claws or your fingernails. All three are made of the same stuff, keratin, which is hard and tough, yet light. The hoof is like a wrap-around toenail. The modern horse has only the third toe on each foot, so you could say that it stands on four third toenails.

FIRST HORSE

Hyracotherium, the first horse, was only 40cm high. It lived in North America and Europe 54 million years ago and had a short neck, curved back, short, slim legs and a long tail.

FOURTEEN TOES IN TOTAL

Hyracotherium had four toes on its front feet and three on its back feet, each tipped by tiny hooves.

LIVING IN FORESTS

Hyracotherium lived in forests in the low undergrowth. It probably ate soft leaves, using its small, low-crowned teeth set in its short jaws. *Orohippus* was a tiny descendant of *Hyracotherium* that lived in the Eocene Epoch. It had bigger teeth and could cope with chewing tougher leaves in drier woodland.

TALLER AND STRAIGHTER

Mesohippus, which means 'middle horse', was larger than *Hyracotherium*, at 60cm high. It also had a longer neck, straighter back and larger teeth. It lived in North America about 38 million years ago. It had three hoof-tipped toes on each long leg.

TOWARDS THE SINGLE TOE

Living about 22 million years ago, *Miohippus* was bigger still. Its feet were beginning to take on the appearance of today's horse's hoof. On each foot there were three toes, but the middle one was larger and longer than those on either side. *Miohippus*' cheek teeth were large and ridged, which helped it chew the tough plants that grew in the dry climate.

GRASSLAND GRAZERS

Grasses first evolved during the Miocene Epoch, and spread across the landscape in the dry climate. *Merychippus*, from North America 15 million years ago, was one of the first grass-eating or grazing horses and had long, ridged cheek teeth that kept on growing as they wore down.

ALMOST THERE

Merychippus was 1m tall and had one main hoof on each foot. *Pliohippus* was 1.2m tall and looked like today's horse. It had lost its outer toes. It lived in the Pliocene Epoch about 4 million years ago.

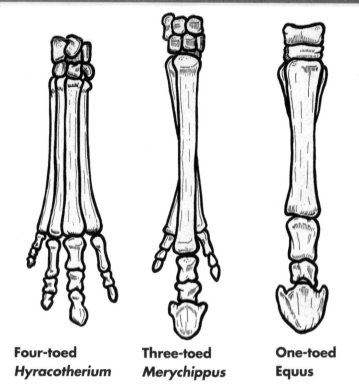

Four-toed
Hyracotherium

Three-toed
Merychippus

One-toed
Equus

A Suffolk Punch (right) is given some new shoes to give its hoofs a longer lease of life.

A herd of *Pliohippus* (left) gathers by the river to drink.

A herd of grazing *Mesohippus* (inset).

HORSES TODAY

The species of horse we know today first appeared around two million years ago. It spread worldwide, although horses died out in North America until Spanish invaders introduced some in the 16th century. By the end of the Pleistocene Ice Ages, there were only a few Equus species, in Asia and Africa. Later, humans tamed the horse and took it all over the world.

325

GIANTS OF THE PAST

A group of *Microceratops* is resting in the shade of some rocks when they are surprised by *Tarbosaurus*. The enormous predator, its mouth gaping wide, is hungry for fresh meat. The *Microceratops'* best chance of escape is to hide in cracks in the rocks where the huge *Tarbosaurus* cannot reach them. But, half-awake, some of the tiny creatures may not be quick enough to escape the long, curved teeth of this terrifying carnivore.

MICROCERATOPS

Dragons and griffins

Were dinosaurs the inspiration for mythical monsters and beasts?

ong before people knew anything about dinosaurs, they made up stories about amazing monsters.

FRIEND OR FOE?

Dragons are mythical animals. In the West they are terrifying creatures that breathe fire. In the East, the dragon brings good luck.

A MYSTERY EXPLAINED

Dragon stories may have been invented to explain the discovery of giant bones, which clearly belonged to something bigger than any living animal. We now know these huge bones belonged to dinosaurs.

BIRD FEET

When some strange footprints were found in America in the early 19th century, people thought that they belonged to a huge bird from Noah's Ark. The myth of the huge birds lasted for years until the fossilized footprints were proved to belong to a dinosaur.

A Chinese dragon. People used to think that dinosaur bones belonged to strange beasts such as dragons.

MISTAKEN IDENTITY

The gentle plant-eating dinosaur, *Protoceratops*, may have inspired another ancient legend. It is thought that fossils of this frilled ceratopian were found by the Ancient Greeks or Romans. The mythical beast, the griffin, was invented to explain them. This terrifying creature had wings, the head of an eagle and the body of a lion.

NO ROOM ON THE ARK

The disappearance of the dinosaurs 66 million years ago has given rise to all sorts of stories and myths. One of them is about Noah and his Ark. It is said that as all the animals went in two by two, the Ark became too full and the poor dinosaurs were left behind to be washed away by the flood!

TODAY'S DINO MYTHS

It is a myth that the flying reptiles, the pterosaurs, and the sea reptiles, the mososaurs, are dinosaurs. But many people go on calling them dinosaurs when they are not.

A mythical griffin

Protoceratops

MYTHICAL NAMES

Some dinosaurs have been named after beasts and people in myths. These include: *Titanosaurus* – after the giant Titans in Greek myths; *Garudimimus* – after Garuda, a mythical Asian bird (right); *Harpymimus* – after the Harpy, a winged monster from Greek myth; *Camelotia* – after King Arthur's court at Camelot; *Gryposaurus* – which means 'griffin reptile'; *Rhoetosaurus* – after Rhoetos, a giant from Greek myth.

Death from the skies

A BLOCK OF ROCK

A giant meteorite is a block of rock about 10km in diameter. There are many rocks of different sizes flying around the Solar System. If one of these rocks comes near the Earth, gravity will pull it in. It then tears through the Earth's atmosphere burning white hot and crashes down on to the Earth. The bigger the meteorite, the bigger the crash. A giant meteorite could penetrate deep into the Earth causing great destruction.

WORLD-WIDE DESTRUCTION

The impact would be so great that the hot rocks deep in the Earth's crust would be exposed. Seawater would quickly rush in to fill the hole and would turn to steam in the heat. Gigantic sea waves 1km high would spread outwards from the point of impact, flooding the nearby continents. A mixture of powdered rocks and water vapour would turn the whole sky black.

A brilliant white streak streams across the sky. An intense flash of light silhouettes the trees, hills and mountains. Violent vibrations shake the ground. A blast of air tears up everything in its path. Is this nuclear war? No. This is what scientists believe would happen if a giant meteorite crashed into the Earth.

DARKNESS OVER EARTH

Once the winds, earthquakes and giant waves had died down, the Earth would be quiet, cold and dark. The darkness could last for months or even years.

If a giant meteorite hit the Earth it would be devastating.

TWILIGHT OF THE DINOSAURS

What would have happened to the dinosaurs if a meteorite had crashed into the Earth? The first impact would have killed large numbers of animals. But most would have survived and continued with their day-to-day lives. confused by the cold and dark.

GOOD FOR MEAT-EATERS

The plant life would begin to die out in the dark and cold conditions. Eventually there would be nothing for the big plant-eating dinosaurs to eat and they would starve to death. The meat-eaters that survived the meteorite crash would have had lots of food at first. There would be the dinosaur corpses from the crash and the weak, starving plant-eaters would have been easy targets. But in time the food would have run out for the meat-eaters as well.

SUNLIGHT RETURNS

Eventually, after months or even years of darkness, the skies would begin to clear. A watery sun would shine down on the devastated landscape and life would slowly begin to return to the Earth. But by this time, the dinosaurs would have all died out.

Scientists investigate a meteorite crater in the 1920s.

What is? A METEORITE

A meteorite is a chunk of rock that falls to Earth from space. It begins life as a meteoroid. Most come from the band of asteroids around the Sun. Thousands of meteoroids enter the Earth's atmosphere every day, but most burn up before they crash into our planet. Meteorites are the ones that do not burn up and so reach the Earth.

Were these dinosaurs killed by a giant rock from outer space?

A TELL-TALE LAYER

Are we sure that all this actually happened? Not really, but there is plenty of evidence to suggest that it did. In the 1970s scientists found that the top layer of rock of the Cretaceous Period was rich in an element called iridium. Iridium is rare at the Earth's surface but quite common in meteorites. If a meteorite had struck the Earth at that time, it would have left a lot of iridium in the rocks.

These Cretaceous rocks contain a lot of an element called Iridium. Iridium is found in meteorites.

LOST ITS MARBLES

In these Cretaceous rocks, scientists have found a great many tektites. Tektites are tiny balls of glass, which are formed when splashes of molten rock cool down and become solid. Scientists believe they could have been produced when a meteorite blasted through the Earth's crust and reached the molten rock below.

CRACKED CRYSTALS

Crystals of the mineral called quartz are hard and tough. But the pieces of quartz found in the iridium-rich layer of rock are cracked and twisted. They have been subjected to a tremendous force — something like a vast explosion.

BUT WHERE IS THE HOLE?

If a massive meteorite struck the Earth, then it must have left some sort of a scar. Scientists have found a crater that is big enough and of the right age on the coast of the Yucatan Peninsula in Mexico. It is tens of kilometres in diameter. It is now buried, but scientists know it is there because their instruments can detect it deep in the Earth's crust. The thickest beds of tektites are found in this area.

The Yucatan Peninsula in Mexico, where scientists have found a massive meteorite.

GIGANTIC WAVES

In northern Mexico and in Texas, USA, scientists have found some strange rocks. They are made up of things usually found in the sea and some fossilized wood, all mixed up, swirled around and spread out as sediment. Some experts say that all this was left behind by the gigantic waves that swept across the land when a meteorite hit the Earth.

FOREST FIRES

In other parts of the world, including Denmark and New Zealand, the fossil wood in the top layer of Cretaceous rocks looks as if it has been burned. This may be because the intense heat of a meteorite's explosion caused massive forest fires.

DOES THAT PROVE IT?

The meteorite theory has convinced many scientists. But there are other theories. Some experts believe that all this evidence could also be explained by massive volcanic activity caused by the moving continents.

A *Tyrannosaurus rex* has died of starvation. It makes a tasty meal for some prehistoric rats.

INDIAN LAVA

Most of India is made up of lava produced by volcanoes during the Cretaceous Period. Massive volcanic explosions could have blocked out the sun with a layer of dust. The resulting cold and dark conditions could have killed off the dinosaurs.

THE FINAL STRAW

Some scientists believe that the dinosaurs died out slowly as the Earth's climate changed to become much colder. An event such as a gigantic meteorite crashing into the Earth, or massive volcanic eruptions, may have been the disaster that finally pushed the weakened dinosaurs over the edge and into extinction. So perhaps both theories are right!

Is it true

that volcanoes are made when the Earth moves?

Yes. There are massive slabs of rock, known as 'plates', in the Earth's surface. When these slide around, hot, molten rock (magma) from deep underground is forced up to the surface. It spews out at the point where the plates meet and forms a volcano. When magma reaches the surface, it is called lava. When volcanoes erupt, lava can flow out and destroy whole towns.

A YEAR IN THE LIFE OF
MEGALOCEROS

TWELVE THOUSAND YEARS AGO, IN THE COUNTRY WE NOW CALL IRELAND, A GROUP OF MEGALOCEROS IS GRAZING PEACEFULLY.

THE SCENT IS ALSO PRODUCED BY A GLAND IN THE MALE'S FEET. HE SCRAPES THE GROUND TO SPREAD THE SMELL...

...WHICH IS RECOGNIZED BY FEMALES AND OTHER MALES.

THE YOUNGER MALE IS LOOKING FOR LAND TO MARK AS HIS TERRITORY. HE FACES THE OLDER ONE...

...BUT ONE LOOK AT THOSE MAGNIFICENT ANTLERS TELLS HIM HE WOULD BE FOOLISH TO CHALLENGE THIS MALE FOR HIS TERRITORY, ESPECIALLY NOW, DURING THE MATING SEASON.

WITH NO FEMALE NOW WILLING TO MATE WITH HIM, AND UNABLE TO DEFEND TERRITORY AGAINST MALES WITH ANTLERS, THE OLD STAG HAS TO LEAVE THE HERD.

IF HE IS LUCKY HE WILL DIE NATURALLY. BUT IT'S MORE LIKELY HE WILL BECOME FOOD FOR CARNIVORES.

THE MALE MEGALOCEROS HAS MAGNIFICENT ANTLERS.

THE FEMALES NEVER GROW ANTLERS.

THE FEMALE MEGALOCEROS LIKES THE LARGE MALE AND, LATER, WILL ALLOW HIM TO MATE WITH HER.

AN ADULT MALE HAS HIS OWN TERRITORY.

HE MARKS IT BY RUBBING THE SPECIAL SCENT GLAND ON THE SIDE OF HIS HEAD AGAINST PLANTS AND TREES.

A YEAR LATER, MONTHS AFTER THE FEMALE HAS GIVEN BIRTH, THE BREEDING SEASON COMES ROUND AGAIN.

HER OLD MATE HAS SHED HIS ANTLERS, BUT NO NEW ONES HAVE GROWN IN THEIR PLACE. NOW HE IS POWERLESS TO STOP ANOTHER MALE FROM MARKING THE TERRITORY AS HIS OWN.

THE REMAINS OF MEGALOCEROS WERE FIRST FOUND IN IRELAND SEVERAL CENTURIES AGO. THAT'S WHY IT IS SOMETIMES CALLED THE IRISH ELK.

THE ANTLERS WERE USED AS GATEPOSTS, AND EVEN AS A TEMPORARY BRIDGE TO SPAN A STREAM!

FACT FILE

Ichthyosaurus holds all the answers. See how you score in the quiz.

Don't make it look real!
Jim Danforth, the sculptor and animator, made some very accurate dinosaur models for the film 'When Dinosaurs Ruled the Earth'. However, the producer did not find them frightening enough, and sent him away to create something dragon-like and, of course, totally fictitious.

1 *Edmontosaurus* lived as far north as:
a) The Arctic Circle
b) The Antarctic
c) The North Pole

2 *Indricotherium* was bigger than:
a) eleven elephants
b) four elephants
c) one elephant

3 In which direction did *Borogovia*'s eyes face?
a) forwards
b) backwards
c) sideways

4 What is a tektite?
a) a kind of bicycle
b) a ball of natural glass
c) a volcanic eruption

5 *Garudimimus* was named after:
a) a mythical bird
b) an aeroplane
c) a dragon

6 Tiny *Microceratops* ate:
a) ants and termites
b) microwave meals
c) plants

7 When did the dinosaurs become extinct?
a) in the Cretaceous Period
b) in the Devonian Period
c) in the Dark Ages

8 *Megaloceros*' antlers have been used as:
a) surfboards
b) gateposts and bridges
c) signposts

Pearly pinks
Shrews have pink teeth. The pink colorations can still be seen in fossil shrew teeth from the Oligocene.

Meet Thomashuxleya

Sometimes fossil animals are named after famous people. The Argentinian palaeontologist Florentino Ameghino took this to extremes, giving his finds names like Thomashuxleya, after the great Victorian naturalist Thomas Huxley, and Josepholeidya after Joseph Leidy, the American dinosaur expert.

Dino dreams

Edward Drinker Cope, the famous 19th-century American dinosaur hunter, was so badly affected by the bad food and water on field trips that his sleep was broken by nightmares about being savaged by the very dinosaurs that his expedition was seeking.

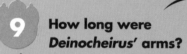

9 How long were *Deinocheirus'* arms?
a) 24cm
b) 24km
c) 2.4m

10 Horses were first tamed over:
a) 6,000 years ago
b) 6 million years ago
c) 600 years ago

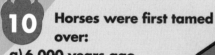

Longest tusk
The largest mammoth tusk so far found is in the Franzens Museum in Brno, Slovakia. It is 5.02 m long.

Answers to the questions on inside back cover

ASK THE EXPERT

Dr David Norman of Cambridge University answers your dinosaur questions

Could dinosaurs eat tree bark, like today's deer?

Of course, it is possible that some of the plant-eaters ate, or scraped, tree bark. Ornithischians had sharp beaks which would probably have been capable of scraping bark. Naturally, if they did this it would have killed the tree. Unfortunately, we do not have fossil evidence to support this idea.

Land animals evolved from sea animals, so why did some, such as plesiosaurs, go back to the sea?

Land animals developed a number of features that are also useful for life in the sea. They developed tough, waterproof skin, strong legs and air-breathing lungs. Waterproof skin insulates an animal's body against the effects of water which can be troublesome to animals with leaky skins. Legs are useful as strong paddles for swimming. Lungs enable the animal to breathe air, removing the need for leaky gills. Lungs also provide an inbuilt buoyancy tank which helps the animal to float. Many land animals, such as penguins, whales and seals, as well as the marine reptiles, have used these features to re-invade the water.

How high did pterosaurs fly?

Probably like birds today, pterosaurs flew as high as they could. They would mainly have been limited by the availability of oxygen. Above about 4,500m the air is rather thin because it contains less oxygen, so this may well have been the upper limit for most pterosaurs.

Do you know what dinosaur meat would have tasted like?

Frankly, I have no idea. But crocodile meat tastes rather like chicken, and since crocodiles and birds are the nearest relatives of dinosaurs, perhaps dinosaur meat was a bit like chicken.

DINOSAURS!
DISCOVER THE GIANTS OF THE PREHISTORIC WORLD

BRACHYCERATOPS

**No trace of a fully grown
Brachyceratops has yet been found.**

Five or six skeletons of this horned plant-eater have been found in Alberta, Canada and Montana, USA. But these all belong to young dinosaurs. Adults probably grew to be about 4m long – about the size of today's rhino.

HUNGRY HERD

Near the end of the Age of the Dinosaurs, Alberta swarmed with a huge variety of animal life. Boneheaded and duckbilled plant-eaters browsed along rivers banks and in the lush, swampy forests. Large herds of horned dinosaurs tramped through the vegetation and covered great distances in their search for food. For protection they probably lived in huge packs. Predators were always waiting to attack.

SENDING SIGNALS

Brachyceratops had a short face with a horn which curved upwards from its nose. The sharp point of the horn could inflict a fatal wound if it pierced the body of another dinosaur. Within a herd, the nose horn was probably also a sort of 'flag' that helped animals to recognise each other. *Brachyceratops* may have tossed its head and waved its horn at a rival to try and frighten it away.

341

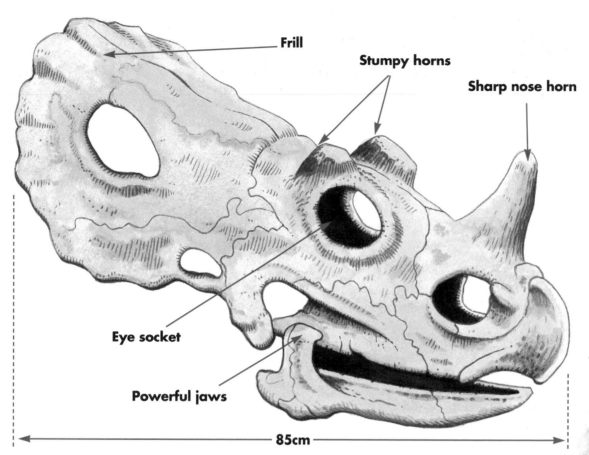

Frill

Stumpy horns

Sharp nose horn

Eye socket

Powerful jaws

←——— 85cm ———→

Brachyceratops had a sharp horn on its nose and two small stumpy horns above its eyes. It had a very impressive frill around its neck, and strong jaws for munching up tough plants.

SHOWING OFF

Like other ceratopians, *Brachyceratops* had a distinctive neck frill. When it dropped its head forward the frill stood up and could be seen more clearly. By nodding its head up and down and swinging it from side to side, *Brachyceratops* used its frill to warn off rivals and predators, and probably to attract females.

BROW HORNS

Several *Brachyceratops* skulls have been found. One skull was badly shattered and had to be carefully restored, like fragments of a precious vase. The skulls show *Brachyceratops* had a tiny stumpy horn above each eye.

BIG BUT NIMBLE

Brachyceratops walked on broad feet, which helped to support its weight when it wandered through muddy swamps. In spite of its size, *Brachyceratops* moved quite nimbly, especially when it was being chased by a predator.

Is it true **that ceratopians were once mistaken for buffaloes?**

Yes. When Othniel Charles Marsh was shown the remains of some large, bony horns discovered in Colorado, USA, at the end of the last century, he thought they belonged to an extinct buffalo. He even named them *Bison alticornis* which means 'high-horned buffalo'. These were, in fact, the remains of the well-known horned dinosaur *Triceratops*.

WHEN THE CHEWING GETS TOUGH...

Brachyceratops found tough plants as tempting as lush shoots. It was able to nip off stems with its narrow beak and let its powerful jaws munch them to a digestible pulp. Deep in its cheeks, rows of slicing teeth worked like a pair of scissors to shred up the food.

SIZE WISE

4m

Brachyceratops shows off its impressive neck frill.

MONSTER FACTS

- **NAME:** *Brachyceratops* (brak-ee-serra-tops) means 'short horned face'
- **GROUP:** dinosaur
- **SIZE:** up to 4m long
- **FOOD:** plants
- **LIVED:** about 80 million years ago in the Late Cretaceous Period in the USA, Canada and India

The tale of the

The great whales, sea-cows and seals are mammals that have lived in the sea for millions of years.

The first four-limbed animals on land were the amphibians, which evolved from fishes. Over millions of years amphibians evolved into reptiles and reptiles evolved into mammals. After the death of the dinosaurs, mammals took over the land. Then, about 50 million years ago, a strange thing happened. Some mammals returned to the water.

MAMMALS IN THE SEA

Like mammals on land, marine (sea) mammals are warm-blooded, breathe air and feed their babies on milk. But they are completely at home in the sea. There are three groups of marine mammals: the cetaceans, including whales and dolphins; the sirenians, including manatees, which are also called sea-cows; and the pinnipeds, including seals and sea-lions.

WEBBED-FEET WHALE

Whales were the first mammals to return to the sea, over 50 million years ago. The earliest, *Pakicetus*, probably looked like a large otter – 2m long with webbed feet on its four limbs. Next came *Protocetus*, which had huge, fearsome teeth and very small back legs. Then, about 40 million years ago, *Basilosaurus* terrorised the seas. It was fully fitted for watery life.

BACK LEGS GONE

Basilosaurus had the stream-lined shape of a whale. It was over 20m long with an eel-like body. Its front legs had evolved into proper whale flippers. At its rear end there were probably flukes – the 'tail' of a whale. The flukes were not the whale's legs.

Cetotherium

Prosqualodon

Eurhinodelphis

Kentriodon

Pakicetus

whale

LONG GONE
The rear limb bones of *Basilosaurus* had almost disappeared. They were tiny and hidden inside its body. These whales belonged to a group which has died out.

TEETH AND WHALEBONE
Today there are toothed whales, including killer whales and dolphins, and baleen whales, such as humpback whales and blue whales. The baleen whales have large, brush-like fringes of baleen (whalebone) in their mouths. These act like a sieve for filtering small food, such as krill, from the sea.

SAWS AND SWORDS
One of the first toothed whales was *Prosqualodon*. It lived about 35 million years ago, was about 2.4m long and looked like a dolphin with a saw on its nose! *Eurhinodelphis* had a fierce-looking, sword-shaped mouth lined with sharp teeth. It was an early dolphin, 2m long, from 25 million years ago.

Is it true that whales breathe air?

Yes. The whale is a mammal, so it breathes air. It has a hole in the top of its head called a blowhole. It is a whale's nostril – the hole it breathes through. The whale can breathe air even when only a small part of its head is above the water. All whales today are designed like this. When a whale breathes out through its blowhole, the warm breath and water spray like a fountain into the ocean air. This is called the blow. Many years ago, sailors who spotted this fountain were known to cry: 'There she blows!'

MORE LIKE TODAY
By the Miocene Epoch, 15-10 million years ago, whales and dolphins looked very like they do today. *Cetotherium*, a baleen whale, was only 4m long but looked like today's Pacific grey whale. The grey whale is probably the most ancient design of whale still alive today.

By the Miocene Epoch dolphins, such as *Kentriodon*, looked much like dolphins do today.

Dolphin

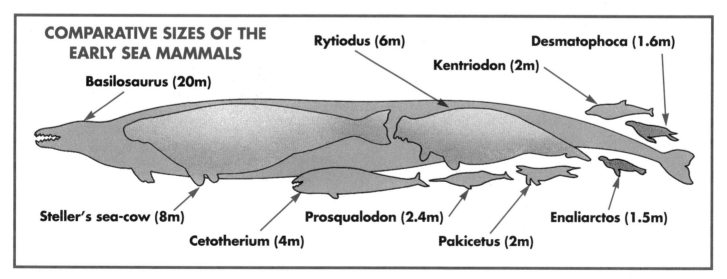

COMPARATIVE SIZES OF THE EARLY SEA MAMMALS

Basilosaurus (20m)
Rytiodus (6m)
Desmatophoca (1.6m)
Kentriodon (2m)
Steller's sea-cow (8m)
Cetotherium (4m)
Prosqualodon (2.4m)
Pakicetus (2m)
Enaliarctos (1.5m)

COWS OF THE SEA

There are only four species of sea-cows today. Three are manatees from Africa and the Americas and one is the dugong from South-East Asia and Australia. They are all plant-eaters and live in coastal waters, estuaries and rivers. Sea-cows look like tuskless walruses. They have tubby bodies, flipper-like arms, no legs and whale-type tail flukes. They are peaceful, slow-moving animals.

Steller's sea-cow

A NEW LOSS

Steller's sea-cow, was 8m long. This huge, slow creature lived in cold northern seas in the last few million years. It had no teeth and ate only seaweed. We know this because it was discovered alive in 1741. But only 30 years later it was extinct – hunted for its flesh and the fatty blubber that kept its body warm.

Rytiodus

Prorastomus

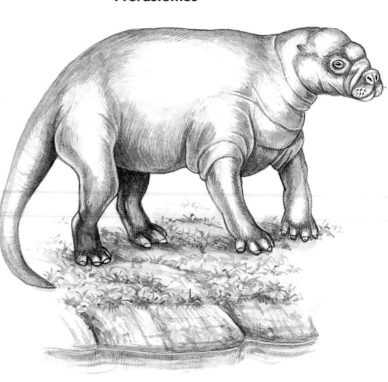

UNDERWATER ELEPHANTS

Sea-cows appeared in the early Eocene, just after the whales. Like cows on land, they grazed on plants. But their plants were the great underwater meadows of seagrasses that grew in the warm coastal waters. You might even call them sea-elephants since they may have evolved from the same ancestors as the elephants!

FEW REMAINS

One of the first sea-cows was *Prorastomus*. Its fossils date back to the middle of the Eocene Epoch and suggest *Prorastomus* still had four legs and a long tail. By the time of *Rytiodus*, 40 million years ago, sea-cows looked much as they do today. *Rytiodus* was 2m longer than today's sea-cow and had tusks to grub up seabed roots.

THE 'FLIPPER-FEET'

The third group of sea mammals is the pinnipeds, 'wing-footed' or 'flipper-feet'. They are fast, agile hunters with sharp, fish-gripping teeth and streamlined bodies. Their limbs have evolved into short, broad, webbed flippers. There are three main kinds today: the sea-lions and fur seals (eared seals), which swim with their front flippers; true seals (earless seals), which swim with their rear flippers; and the walrus, which swims with both sets of flippers and has long tusks.

Enaliarctus **lived 25 million years ago.**

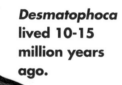

Desmatophoca **lived 10-15 million years ago.**

IT'S A FACT

THAT SEA-COWS MAY BE MERMAIDS

Sea-cows sometimes lie in the sea with just their heads sticking up. They also make eerie noises that sound like humming and wailing. Sailors, scanning the horizon, may have mistaken a sea-cow for a singing woman with a fish-like tail. This may have started the mermaid legend!

Elephant seal

Many millions of years ago, there were several species of elephant seal. Now there is only one.

PROPER SEA-LIONS

One of the first proper sea-lions was *Desmatophoca*. It was about 1.6m long and lived 10-15 million years ago around the coasts of Asia and North America. *Allodesmus,* which lived at about the same time, was 5m long. It probably looked like today's elephant seals.

STARTER SEALS

The sea-lion and seal group probably began as dog-like carnivores related to today's otters. Gradually, they took to life in the water, diving after fish along the coast. *Enaliarctos* was about 1.5m long and lived 25 million years ago. It was midway between an otter and a sea-lion – it had webbed feet and a tail.

ONE WALRUS LEFT

By the end of the Pliocene Epoch, 2 million years ago, there were several types of walrus. But only one survives today. The true seals are a success story in recent evolution. There are 19 species of seal today including the rarest, which is the Mediterranean monk seal.

349

GIANTS OF THE PAST

A herd of *Brachyceratops* peacefully grazes in the lush, swampy forests of North America. The herd tries to stay close together whenever possible to stop the weak and vulnerable members being picked off by predators. If a predator attacks, the adults will defend. They lower their heads to display their enormous neck frills and frighten the attackers away. If this fails, they can attack with their sharp horns.

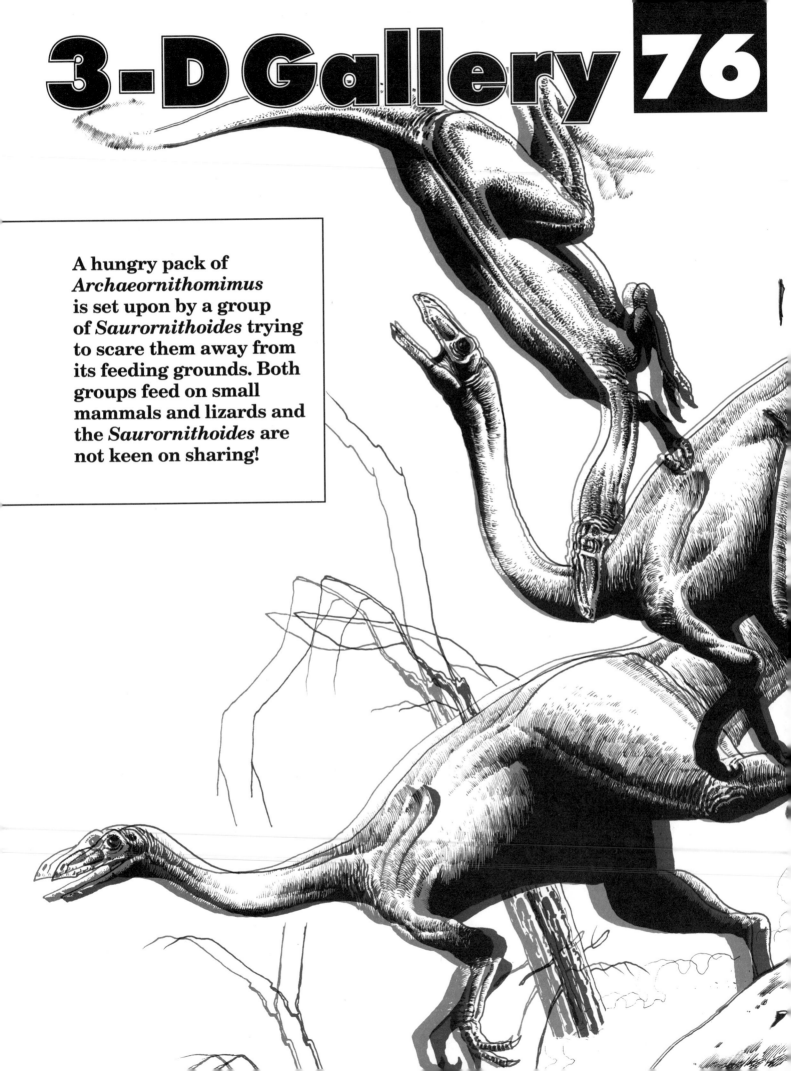

A hungry pack of
Archaeornithomimus
is set upon by a group
of *Saurornithoides* trying
to scare them away from
its feeding grounds. Both
groups feed on small
mammals and lizards and
the *Saurornithoides* are
not keen on sharing!

ARCHAEORNITHOMIMUS

Giants and Monsters

Amazing prehistoric animals inspired many myths and legends.

Spellbinding stories about mythical animals have thrilled people for centuries. The monsters and the stories told about them may not be real, but they can have a grain of truth in them. This is because they were often invented to explain evidence of strange creatures from prehistoric times.

One of the photographs claiming to prove that Nessie really exists.

A unicorn is like a horse but it has a long horn in the middle of its head.

LOCH NESS MONSTER

Tales of giant serpents and monsters lurking in oceans and lakes are found in many parts of the world. In Scotland a huge lake called Loch Ness is famous as the home of such a monster. Stories about the Loch Ness monster have been told for hundreds of years and many people claim to have seen 'Nessie'.

NESSIE THE PLESIOSAUR?

If Nessie exists, it may be a member of the plesiosaur family, such as the fish-eating reptile *Elasmosaurus* which lived over 70 million years ago and had a very long neck. Loch Ness has been searched by experts with scientific equipment but Nessie has not been found.

ONE EYE

There are lots of stories about one-eyed giants. One of the most famous is Cyclops – a giant shepherd who ate humans. People may have thought this fearsome monster existed when they found huge mammoth skulls. Mammoth skulls have a hole in the centre where the trunk joins the skull. It looks like a giant eye socket!

The Loch Ness monster might look like this _Elasmosaurus_.

ABOMINABLE SNOWMEN

Stories of man-like hairy creatures have been told for over 150 years. In Asia these hairy giants are called Yeti; in the USA they are known as Bigfoot; and in Canada as Sasquatch. Stories of these monsters could have been inspired by the bones of giant prehistoric apes.

UNICORN HORN

The unicorn is a mythical beast with the bite of a lion and the kick of a horse. It has one long, slender horn that grows in the centre of its forehead. It appears in lots of pictures and coats of arms from the Middle Ages. The story of the unicorn could have sprung from the prehistoric rhinoceros _Elasmotherium_, which had a horn as big as a man.

Are these the Devil's fingers or some fossils?

FEARSOME FINGERS

When strange, pencil-shaped fossils were found in Germany in the Middle Ages, people thought they were the Devil's fingers. In fact, they were fossilized belemnites – squid-like animals from the Jurassic Period.

Is this proof that Bigfoot exists?

MYTHICAL NAMES

Prehistoric animals are sometimes named after ancient myths and legends.

• _Icaronycteris_ – a bat that lived 50 million years ago, named after a boy in a Greek legend. Icarus made wings from feathers and wax. When he flew too near the sun, the wax melted and he fell to the ground.

• _Quetzalcoatlus_ – a huge pterosaur, which was named after the Aztec god of the air, Quetzalcoatl.

• _Ramapithecus_ – a monkey-sized tree-dweller. It was named after Rama, a hero from Indian mythology.

The dinosaurs today

If the dinosaurs had survived they would have continued to evolve. What would they be like today?

In the Triassic Period there were dinosaurs such as *Plateosaurus*, *Coelophysis* and *Melanorosaurus*. The world changed and in the Jurassic Period there were different dinosaurs such as *Apatosaurus*, *Stegosaurus* and *Allosaurus*. In the Cretaceous Period there were dinosaurs such as *Triceratops*, *Iguanodon* and *Tyrannosaurus*. But 66 million years ago, in the Cretaceous Period, the dinosaurs all died out.

AN IMAGINARY MODERN WORLD

But let's imagine that the dinosaurs did not die out 66 million years ago. What would they look like now? The changes that have taken place on the Earth during the past 66 million years mean that the dinosaurs of today would be very different from any that we know from the fossils. Let's try to imagine the way some of these dinosaurs would have evolved.

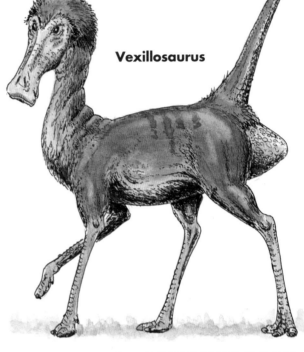

Vexillosaurus

Picusaurus

WHERE THE DINOSAURS ROAM

Look at the sprintosaur, *Vexillosaurus*. This evolved from the duckbilled dinosaurs that lived at the end of the Cretaceous Period. It looks a bit like a modern antelope. It needs strong teeth to chew grass and long legs for running away from its enemies. There were no dinosaurs like this in the Triassic, Jurassic or Cretaceous Periods because there were no grasslands then.

IN THE TREES

Here is a nauger called *Picusaurus*. It is a very small dinosaur that lives in trees. It looks like a woodpecker, with strong toes for clinging to the wood and front teeth that form a sharp point for pecking into tree trunks. Its ancestors were small, two-footed, meat-eating dinosaurs.

DINOSAUR MOUTHFUL

The wasp-eater, *Vespaphaga*, lives in trees and raids the nests of wasps. It is covered with thick scales to protect it from the wasp stings and its mouth is a long tube that can reach into the wasps' nest and feed on the grubs. There were no wasp-eating dinosaurs in the Age of the Dinosaurs because the wasps did not evolve until the end of the Cretaceous Period.

Vespaphaga

PANDASAUR

How about mountain-living dinosaurs? Up in the Himalayas there is a dinosaur called a *Multipollex*, which is a type of taddey. You would almost think that it was some kind of giant panda. Like the panda, it eats bamboo. It evolved from the hypsilophodonts – the swift, two-footed, plant-eating dinosaurs of the Cretaceous Period. There were no taddeys during the Age of the Dinosaurs because there was no bamboo at that time and, besides, the Himalayas did not form properly until 50 million years ago!

Multipollex

ONE-LEGGED SHRIMP-EATER

The *Cribrusaurus* feeds on tiny shrimps and shellfish that live in shallow ponds. Its teeth are very close together like the teeth of a comb. It uses them like a sieve to catch its food. It takes a mouthful of water and after the water flows out between the teeth the tiny animals are left behind. This cribrum has a lot in common with today's flamingo.

Cribrusaurus

Is it true

that birds are really surviving dinosaurs?

Birds are extremely closely related to dinosaurs. Some scientists think they are so similar that we should regard birds as dinosaurs that have survived until today.

357

THE BIGGEST MEAT-EATER

Remember how the meat-eaters evolved in Cretaceous times? They became bigger and bigger and their forelimbs became smaller and smaller. Just take a look at *Tyrannosaurus rex*. If these meat-eaters had survived after the Cretaceous Period, we might have ended up with something like the gourmand. *Ganeosaurus*, a type of gourmand, is an enormous meat-eater which is 17m long and weighs 15 tonnes. Its forelimbs have vanished.

CUNNING HUNTER

When you look at a dinosaur fossil, you will notice that the back is usually curved, with the head and tail pulled towards each other. This is what happens when a dinosaur's body dries out in the sun before it is buried. *Necrosimulacrum*, a type of springe, relies on this for hunting. It lies on a mudbank pretending to be dead, with its head and tail pulled back. When scavenging birds or pterosaurs come to eat it, it lashes out with its long killing claw. Springes such as *Necrosimulacrum* evolved from the vicious-clawed troodonts.

SWEET TOOTH

Nectar, the sugary substance produced in flowers, is a food that does not need much digesting. Any animal that eats nectar does not need a very big gut, or a very big body in fact. The gimps – an example is the *Melexsorbius* shown here – are the smallest dinosaurs ever. They are only 20cm long. They clamber about in trees and feed only on nectar, which explains their small size.

Necrosimulacrum

Ganeosaurus

DUMB DINOS
None of these imaginary dinosaurs is very clever. Springes are cunning hunters, but are not really intelligent. It could be that there would be intelligent dinosaurs by now if the dinosaurs had not died out.

THINKING TROODONTS
Back in the Cretaceous Period the troodonts were quite cunning hunters. They had big brains, for dinosaurs, and had hands that could grip things. It could be that now, 66 million years later, they would have evolved into intelligent beings. If they had, they would look rather like humans, standing on two legs and with a big round head to house the brain.

ALL IN THE MIND
All these creatures are, of course, imaginary. There are no dinosaurs today, but it is fun to think about what they would look like if there were. Think about it yourself, and see what kind of imaginary modern dinosaur you can dream up.

Melexsorbius

IT'S A FACT

THAT WE WOULD NOT BE HERE IF THE DINOSAURS HAD NOT DIED OUT

If the dinosaurs had not died out at the end of the Cretaceous Period, the world would be a very different place today. Mammals, including ourselves, were able to evolve as they did precisely because the dinosaurs became extinct.

359

Improve and test your knowledge with...
FACT FILE

Dimetrodon holds all the answers.
See how you score in the quiz.

Far-flung animals

The first vertebrate fossil to be found in Antarctica was the skull of Lystrosaurus from the Triassic Period. It was found in 1969. Other Lystrosaurus fossils were found in South Africa and India, proving that in Triassic times all these continents were joined together.

Big print

The only known footprint of Tyrannosaurus rex was found in New Mexico about 10 years ago, but it lay unidentified in a fossil collection until 1993. It is about 90cm long and shows three broad toes and a little toe that touches the ground at the back.

5 Was *Kronosaurus*:
a) as small as a mouse
b) the size of a pig
c) as big as two elephants

4 *Brachyceratops'* name means:
a) 'plant-eater'
b) 'short horned face'
c) 'broken horn'

3 *Quetzalcoatlus* is named after:
a) an Aztec god
b) a Greek god
c) a piece of clothing

2 How did *Conchoraptor* eat the eggs it stole?
a) lightly boiled
b) by cracking them in its beak
c) by dropping them

1 What did *Eryops* eat?
a) fish and chips
b) fish and whales
c) fish and baby amphibians

362

Rich reptile

A fossil plesiosaur found in Australia was mineralised with the semi-precious stone, opal.

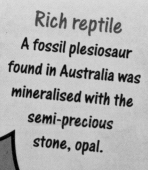

A big beast

In 1989 two Indian palaeontologists found the leg bones of a gigantic meat-eating dinosaur. They called it Bruhathkayosaurus. From these leg bones, they estimate that the animal was probably 20m long and weighed twice as much as T rex.

6 Was *Cribrum*:
a) an imaginary dinosaur
b) a type of seaweed
c) a meat-eating bird

7 *Pakicetus* was:
a) a swimming dinosaur
b) a pterosaur
c) an early whale

8 *Basilosaurus'* front legs evolved into:
a) flippers
b) flappers
c) floppers

9 Steller's sea-cow ate:
a) whales
b) seaweed
c) ammonites

10 A whale breathes through:
a) its skin
b) its blowhole
c) its tail

Too many skeletons

In 1993 an expedition in Wyoming ran into trouble. There were so many dinosaur skeletons that the team had to leave most of them in the ground!

Answers to the questions on inside back cover

363

Dr David Norman of Cambridge University answers your dinosaur questions

ASK THE EXPERT

Did pterosaurs nest in trees?

It is not known if pterosaurs ever nested in trees. Pictures usually show them nesting on the ground. It seems likely that the very large pterosaurs would have made nests on the ground; nevertheless it is possible that some of the small ones, such as *Pterodactylus,* could have nested in trees. There is no evidence for nest-building in trees from the Jurassic or the Cretaceous Periods.

Vultures can use rocks to break bones. Could dinosaurs do this?

There is no evidence that dinosaurs used rocks to break up the bones of animals they had killed. Crocodiles can swallow bones with very little difficulty. They then soften them in their stomachs, before crushing them with powerful contractions of their gut muscles. Maybe this is what dinosaurs did.

Why are children better at pronouncing dinosaur names than grown-ups?

Children are good at pronouncing dinosaur names because they find them interesting and pay a lot of attention to them. Adults usually don't bother to find out how to pronounce the names correctly.

Did dinosaurs have any parasites?

At the time of the dinosaurs there would definitely have been parasites – animals that live on other animals. Parasites would have lived on the inside of dinosaurs (in the guts or other organs) or on the outside (burrowing under the skin, between the toes or under the claws). Healthy dinosaurs, like our pets today, would not have noticed this normal 'parasite load'.

DINOSAURS!
DISCOVER THE GIANTS OF THE PREHISTORIC WORLD

NOASAURUS

When *Noasaurus* hunted in packs, these little dinosaurs were able to attack half-grown sauropods.

Noasaurus was a small, active theropod that was a successful hunter. Large plant-eaters such as *Saltasaurus,* which lived in South America at the same time as *Noasaurus*, needed to keep a protective eye on young or sickly members of their families to protect them from these predators.

SURPRISE ATTACK

A pack of meat-eaters such as *Noasaurus* would spring a sudden attack on their unwary victims, completely overpowering them within a matter of minutes.

UNIQUE FEATURE

Among the scattered fossils of *Noasaurus* was part of a skull, pieces of backbone and two foot bones. But the most exciting find was a large claw, about as long as your thumb. When experts examined this closely, they found that it was unique.

CLEVER CLAWS

At the back of the claw there was a groove or pit where a powerful muscle was attached. This meant that the claw could be pulled back when *Noasaurus* was running and brought forward when it wanted to attack.

ATTACK AND DEFENCE

With its light frame, *Noasaurus* was probably able to leap into the air as it attacked. Several might leap on to the back of a plant-eater or attack its soft underside. The claws ripped the victim's flesh until it was too weak to fight. *Noasaurus* also used its claw as protection against larger, fiercer carnivores.

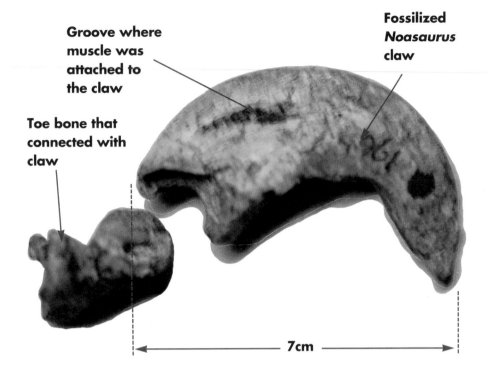

Groove where muscle was attached to the claw

Toe bone that connected with claw

Fossilized *Noasaurus* claw

No other dinosaur had a claw like this. *Noasaurus* could pull these large claws back when it ran, but it could stick them out when it attacked.

7cm

ARMS FOLDED

As it ran after its prey, with its body straining forward, *Noasaurus* was just shorter than the height of an adult human. Its arm bones have not yet been found, but *Noasaurus* probably kept its arms folded high up against its chest.

STRONG NECK

Noasaurus' neck was powerfully built and topped by a large, deep head. Its long, slender jaws were light, so this predator was able to move its head with ease.

TYPICAL TEETH

Lining the jaw were small, pointed teeth with the typical, jagged edge of a flesh-eater. Even the tough, armoured skin of *Saltasaurus* could be pierced by them.

IT'S A FACT

SOUTH AMERICAN DINOSAURS ARE HARD TO FIND

South America contains some of the most difficult country in the world. Dense vegetation and jungle make life hard for the fossil-hunter and most discoveries have been made in desert-like regions and grasslands. In spite of these difficulties, some exciting discoveries have been made in Argentina, Brazil and Uruguay.

NOASAURUS

When *Noasaurus* hunted in packs, these little dinosaurs were able to attack half-grown sauropods.

Noasaurus was a small, active theropod that was a successful hunter. Large plant-eaters such as *Saltasaurus,* which lived in South America at the same time as *Noasaurus*, needed to keep a protective eye on young or sickly members of their families to protect them from these predators.

SURPRISE ATTACK

A pack of meat-eaters such as *Noasaurus* would spring a sudden attack on their unwary victims, completely overpowering them within a matter of minutes.

UNIQUE FEATURE

Among the scattered fossils of *Noasaurus* was part of a skull, pieces of backbone and two foot bones. But the most exciting find was a large claw, about as long as your thumb. When experts examined this closely, they found that it was unique.

CLEVER CLAWS

At the back of the claw there was a groove or pit where a powerful muscle was attached. This meant that the claw could be pulled back when *Noasaurus* was running and brought forward when it wanted to attack.

ATTACK AND DEFENCE

With its light frame, *Noasaurus* was probably able to leap into the air as it attacked. Several might leap on to the back of a plant-eater or attack its soft underside. The claws ripped the victim's flesh until it was too weak to fight. *Noasaurus* also used its claw as protection against larger, fiercer carnivores.

Groove where
muscle was
attached to
the claw

Fossilized
Noasaurus
claw

No other dinosaur had a claw
like this. *Noasaurus* could pull
these large claws back when it
ran, but it could stick them out
when it attacked.

Toe bone that
connected with
claw

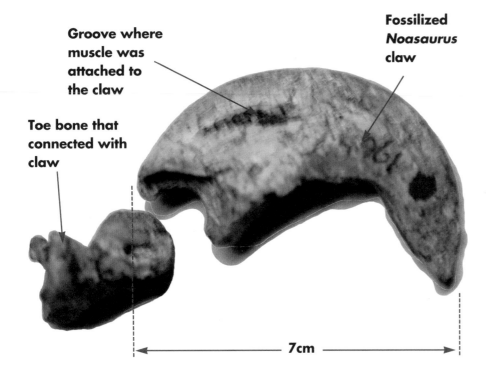

7cm

ARMS FOLDED

As it ran after its prey, with its body
straining forward, *Noasaurus* was just
shorter than the height of an adult
human. Its arm bones have not yet been
found, but *Noasaurus* probably kept its
arms folded high up against its chest.

STRONG NECK

Noasaurus' neck was
powerfully built and topped
by a large, deep head. Its
long, slender jaws were
light, so this predator was able
to move its head with ease.

TYPICAL TEETH

Lining the jaw were small,
pointed teeth with the
typical, jagged edge of
a flesh-eater. Even
the tough,
armoured skin
of *Saltasaurus*
could be pierced
by them.

IT'S A FACT

SOUTH AMERICAN DINOSAURS ARE HARD TO FIND

South America contains some of the most
difficult country in the world. Dense
vegetation and jungle make life hard for
the fossil-hunter and most discoveries
have been made in desert-like regions
and grasslands. In spite of these difficulties,
some exciting discoveries have been made
in Argentina, Brazil and Uruguay.

NEW FAMILY ...

Other dinosaurs have been discovered that have hooked claws very like those of *Noasaurus*. *Deinonychus* is just one example. But experts think that *Noasaurus* belonged to a different family group from all the others.

... NEW NAME

Noasaurus' head was different from that of other dinosaurs. This difference, together with the unique way in which its claw worked, led Argentinian scientists to suggest that this agile little dinosaur was the only known member of a new family, which they named the noasaurids.

SIZE WISE

2.4m

Noasaurus was agile and fast. It had sharp claws and jagged teeth for tearing up the flesh of its victims.

MONSTER FACTS

- **NAME:** *Noasaurus* (noh-ah-saw-rus) means 'reptile from Noa'
- **GROUP:** dinosaur
- **SIZE:** up to 2.4m long
- **FOOD:** meat
- **LIVED:** about 70 million years ago in the Late Cretaceous Period in Noa, Argentina

DATOUSAURUS

The early sauropod, *Datousaurus*, was a giant among the dinosaurs of Jurassic China.

Datousaurus was discovered by a Chinese expedition at the end of the 1970s. Its huge body was balanced at each end by a long neck and tail. As *Datousaurus* wandered through thick forests of pines and tree ferns, it would have stopped for the occasional snack and reached high into the branches for the juiciest shoots.

SIZE WISE

14m

MONSTER FACTS

- **NAME:** *Datousaurus* (<u>dat</u>-oo-<u>saw</u>-rus) means 'Datou reptile' after the place where it was discovered.
- **GROUP:** dinosaur
- **SIZE:** up to 14m long
- **FOOD:** plants
- **LIVED:** about 160 million years ago in the Mid-Jurassic Period in Sichuan Province, China

WELL DESIGNED

Datousaurus' skull was strong and its jaws were lined with curved, spoon-shaped teeth. Like sheep and horses today, its teeth were designed for the plants it ate.

IN HERDS

Datousaurus was unlikely to be disturbed as it fed. Its size was probably enough to deter most predators. Experts also think that sauropods such as *Datousaurus* moved in herds which would also help to protect them.

LOOK AFTER BABY

A young *Datousaurus* travelling in the centre of this moving army was kept safe from predators by the massive, fully grown adults that kept guard around it.

368

SEYMOURIA

Seymouria was one of the first amphibians able to live almost entirely out of water.

*S*eymouria evolved when creatures were beginning to crawl from steamy swamps to hunt for food on dry land. It was an amphibian and well able to cope with life on land. To live on land, animals needed new features that would help them to survive. Their bodies had to be more waterproof and their limbs strong enough to bear their weight.

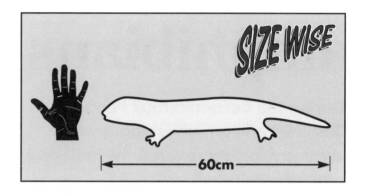

SIZE WISE

60cm

MONSTER FACTS

- **NAME:** *Seymouria* (see-<u>more</u>-ree-a) was named after Seymour in Texas, where it was found.
- **GROUP:** amphibian
- **SIZE:** up to 60cm long
- **FOOD:** fish, small mammals
- **LIVED:** about 270 million years ago in the Early Permian Period in Texas, USA

SPRAWLING GAIT
Beautifully preserved fossils show that badger-sized *Seymouria* had five-toed feet which helped it to keep its grip on the muddy ground. Its legs were almost at right angles to its body and it walked with a sprawling gait.

LONGER AND STRONGER
Its limbs were both longer and stronger than the first amphibians and it was probably able to move quickly.

LOOK AND LISTEN
Hunting small land creatures and insects, *Seymouria* needed well-developed senses and there is evidence that it could hear quite well.

Seymouria's strong limbs helped it to move quickly.

Swamps, coal and amphibians

During the Carboniferous Period, 362-290 million years ago, steamy, swampy forests covered the land and amphibians ruled.

Imagine standing up to your knees in murky water with your feet deep in mud. Every time you try to lift your foot out of the cold slime, there is a burst of bubbles and the stench of rotting vegetation. Around you is a dense bed of what look like yellow-green Christmas trees.

SILENT GREENERY

The really strange thing is the silence. Some distance away you can hear the slight movement of some water. The tops of the strange plants are swishing quietly in the wind. But that is all. There is no roar of an animal or hint of birdsong.

DUCK!

Suddenly, the shadow of some flying thing appears. You can also hear a loud 'frrrrm' – the rapid flapping of long, sparkling wings. A dragonfly swoops down and disappears between the stems of the plants. It is *Meganeura* – a dragonfly as big as a parrot!

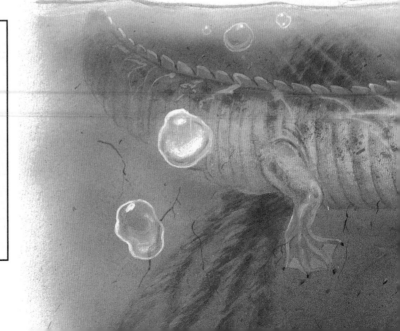

What is A DELTA?

A delta is a fan-shaped piece of land that sticks out into the sea. It is formed from very fine earth or silt washed down to the sea by rivers. When the river waters meet the sea they slow down and the silt they are carrying builds up at the mouth of the river. Some deltas are vast. One of the most famous is the Nile Delta in Egypt. The soil is good for farming, but deltas are often flooded.

Fossils of lizards (below) and horsetails (above) from Carboniferous times.

1 Horsetails, as tall as today's trees, grew out of the swampy Carboniferous waters.

2 Dragonflies, such as parrot-sized *Meganeura*, flitted among the tall plants.

3 Plants and trees died and fell into the swampy waters, eventually to form peat.

4 Beneath the waters swam *Eogyrinus*, an early amphibian.

DELTAS AND SWAMPS

Deltas were created in Carboniferous times, especially across northern Europe and North America. Huge mountain ranges, which had formed during the Devonian Period, began to be worn down by wind and rain. The rocks were ground down to a fine sand, called silt, which formed into areas of land when it hit the sea. This damp, swampy land was covered by dense forests filled with strange ferns, reeds and trees.

WHERE ARE YOU?

You are standing in the muddy waters of a Carboniferous delta. Dinosaurs, mammals and birds do not yet exist. The plants that surround you are giant horsetails. They are ancient relatives of the little, wispy plants you come across in ditches today.

THE AGE OF AMPHIBIANS

The Carboniferous Period is also called the Age of Amphibians. Conditions were just right for them. There was plenty of water where they could lay their eggs. Their tadpoles could hatch, develop in the water and then crawl on to land where there was plenty of food for them.

MONSTERS OF THE MURKY WATERS

Eogyrinus (ee-oh-gee-rine-us) was one of the many amphibians that thrived in Carboniferous times. It had a long, eel-like body and tail, and a head like a crocodile. It lived entirely in the water and probably swam through the horsetails by making 's' shapes with its body.

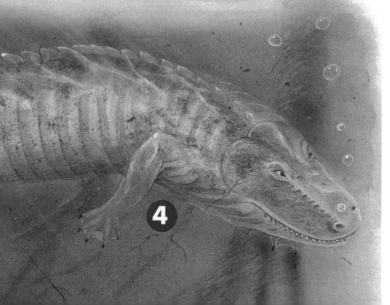

371

GREEN GLOOM

The trees in the Carboniferous forests were not like trees you can see today. They were actually giant versions of some of today's plants called horsetails and clubmosses. The branches and leaves of trees such as *Lepidodendron* (lep-i-doh-<u>den</u>-dron) and *Sigillaria* (sig-ill-<u>air</u>-ee-ah) formed a ceiling above the forest, plunging the forest floor into darkness.

FUTURE FUEL

Near the ground was a dense tangle of ferns growing in the damp soil. When plants and trees died, they became absorbed into the swamp and gradually turned into peat. Peat is made from squashed layers of rotting vegetation. When the peat itself becomes squashed by layers of mud and sand, it turns into coal.

CHANGING LANDSCAPE

The beds of giant horsetails would have covered the shallow Carboniferous waters. The higher ground would have been covered in different plants. These were a very primitive type of conifer, related to today's fir trees.

Westlothiana was one of the first reptiles on Earth.

Carboniferous forests were damp and swampy. When trees and plants died, they fell into the swamp, slowly turned into peat and then into coal.

Arthropleura was a gigantic millipede. It lived in the Carboniferous forest.

GIANT MILLIPEDE

Arthropleura, (<u>ah</u>-throw-<u>pler</u>-ah) was a millipede as long as you are. Some millipedes grew to be 2m long! They lived in the damp, swampy Carboniferous undergrowth.

A HINT OF THE FUTURE

Other, smaller animals lived on the forest floor too. Little lizard-like animals scampered around, using their tongues to 'taste' their surroundings. These were the early reptiles. One of these was *Westlothiana* (west-low-thee-<u>ah</u>-na). The Carboniferous Period saw the evolution of the first reptiles. They were the ancestors of both the dinosaurs and the mammals.

Is it true

that coal is made from trees and shrubs?

Yes. The coal that is burned today began life as plants about 300 million years ago in the Carboniferous Period. When dying trees and other plants fell into the Carboniferous swamps they were covered in mud. Eventually the plant remains dried out and formed something called peat. Deep in the ground, buried under layers of soil and rock, the peat was pressed down and heated until it eventually became coal. That is why coal often has to be dug out thousands of metres below ground. It is also the reason why miners sometimes find the fossils of tree trunks and plants in coal mines.

Coal miners

NOASAURUS

A mother *Saltasaurus* watches helplessly as a pack of *Noasaurus* attacks her baby. The young *Saltasaurus* is over 5m long but is no match for these little predators. With their vicious claws and jagged teeth the *Noasaurus* will make short work of the terrified youngster. Plodding plant-eaters must frequently have fallen victim to agile *Noasaurus* herds in South America 70 million years ago.

3-D Gallery 77

EUOPLOCEPHALUS

On a hot day in Late Cretaceous North America, a herd of *Euoplocephalus* takes a cooling dip in a peaceful lake. These heavily armoured dinosaurs usually swing their mighty tail-clubs to kill predators or fend off enemies. But the clubs are also useful for swishing water over their over-heated bodies.

Prehistoric dogs

Cynodesmus

The dogs we keep as pets are descended from the first dogs that lived about 40 million years ago.

Dogs are a great success story. They can live in many different environments and eat all sorts of food. Dogs belong to a family that includes foxes, wolves and coyotes. Most early dogs evolved in North America from Late Eocene times onwards.

OTHER RELATIVES
Dogs belong to a group called canids. Canids belong to a large group of carnivores that includes otters, weasels, cats, mongooses, seals and walruses.

SUPERB HUNTERS
Some dogs are superb hunters with sharp senses and great stamina. Running on the tips of their four-toed feet, they are able to chase prey over long distances.

IT'S A FACT

DOGS AREN'T FUSSY EATERS!
Dogs are usually omnivorous – they eat a wide range of meat, bones, fruit and insects. They rip flesh apart with long pointed teeth and crunch up tough food with powerful molars. So wherever they live, dogs are unlikely to go hungry.

DOGS IN DISGUISE
Hesperocyon (<u>hes</u>-per-oh-<u>sigh</u>-on) lived 35 million years ago and looked more like a mongoose than a dog. *Phlaocyon* (flay-oh-<u>sigh</u>-<u>on</u>) was a racoon-like dog that lived in North America in Miocene times. It ate seeds and birds' eggs, as well as small mammals and insects.

Osteoborus

Hesperocyon

A family of wolves today.

DOGS AND FOXES

Cynodesmus (<u>sigh</u>-no-<u>dez</u>-mus) was the first dog to look like the dogs we know. It was the shape of an American coyote and lived in the Late Oligocene. *Cerdocyon* (<u>ser</u>-doh-<u>sigh</u>-on) was an early fox that lived in Argentina, South America. Like its descendant, the crab-eating fox, it lived by eating almost anything it found.

SCAVENGING DOGS

Osteoborus (<u>oss</u>-tee-oh-<u>bore</u>-uss) was a bear-like scavenger. It lived in North America about 8 million years ago. After it became extinct, its scavenging lifestyle was continued by the prehistoric dire wolf. The dire wolf was larger than the members of the dog family shown here. It was 2m long and the others were about 80cm long.

Cerdocyon

Dogs, like this sheepdog, are intelligent and easy to train.

379

Mammoth deep freeze

Whole mammoths, deep-frozen for thousands of years, have been dug out of the ground in Siberia.

It is very rare to find more than the bones of an animal that died a long time ago. Normally, when a creature dies, all the soft flesh, hair and scales on its body rot away to leave just the bones. But, in special circumstances, this does not happen. Scientists were thrilled to discover whole mammoths frozen into the icy ground of Siberia in the far north of Russia. Their bodies had been preserved for thousands of years by the cold, just as food is preserved in your freezer.

This mammoth lived in Siberia 45,000 years ago. When it died, it was buried in the ice and became deep-frozen.

IN THE KNOW

Experts know a great deal more about the mammoth because of these amazing discoveries. They know not only almost exactly how it looked, but they have also been able to work out how it moved by studying the muscles. Scientists even know what mammoths ate from examining the food in the frozen stomachs.

WOOLLY MAMMOTH

About 25 deep-frozen bodies have been discovered. They all belong to *Mammuthus primigenius*, the woolly mammoth. Woolly mammoths were smaller than today's elephants. They were well adapted to coping with freezing temperatures. They had a long, warm coat and their ears were small to stop them from getting frost-bitten. They also had a fatty hump behind their heads. Like a camel's hump, this acted as an extra store of nourishment when food and water were scarce or buried under snow.

IT'S A FACT

PREHISTORIC PERFUME

Deep-frozen mammoths have been used in very strange ways. In 1809, a Russian government worker decided to make perfume from the soft marrow inside mammoth bones. He gathered together sackfuls of frozen bones. But they thawed too quickly and the marrow disappeared before he could collect it.

MELT DOWN

The first complete, deep-frozen mammoth to be studied was found in 1901. It was sticking out of a melting glacier on the banks of the River Berezovka in Siberia. The huge creature was perfectly preserved and scientists could see how it must have looked thousands of years ago.

MAMMOTH INVESTIGATIONS

Scientists were able to cut open and study the smallest parts of the mammoth's body. By examining its blood, scientists learned that it was closely related to the Asian elephant. By studying its stomach contents, they found that it mainly ate grass. Seeds in its food showed that this mammoth probably died in the autumn.

HOW IT HAPPENED

Like detectives, scientists have been able to piece together the last few hours of the Berezovka mammoth's life. The creature was grazing when it stepped on to a crevasse (a very deep crack) covered by a thin layer of soil. It plunged down into the gap and broke several bones. The mammoth made a desperate attempt to climb out by hooking its front feet into the earth in front of it. But the animal was too badly injured to heave its huge body out of the pit.

Woolly mammoths had hairy coats to keep them warm in the ice and snow.

This baby mammoth was discovered in 1977. The scientists called him 'Dima'.

BURIED BABY

In 1977, a baby mammoth was found in Siberia. He was nicknamed 'Dima'. Dima was buried under frozen earth and snow for 40,000 years and the weight flattened his body. One scientist wanted to see if a modern baby mammoth could be produced using some of Dima's body cells. They were planted inside a female Asian elephant but the experiment didn't work.

MAMMOTH FINDS

Hundreds of mammoth skeletons have been collected around the world. Scientists have already gathered a great deal of information about mammoths. But every time they examine a skeleton or body they make new discoveries.

THE BIG FREEZE

Experts used to think that mammoths died out at the end of the last Ice Age, about 10,000 years ago. But scientists working in the Arctic Circle discovered mammoth skeletons only 3,700 years old. They collected bones from Wrangel Island, off the north coast of Siberia, which proved that mammoths were living there when the pharoahs ruled Egypt.

MINI MAMMOTHS

When the last Ice Age ended, the world's climate got warmer. Mammoths preferred the cold so they moved further north to places such as Wrangel Island. They managed to live on for another 6,000 years. But, in order to survive, they had to change. Scientists discovered from teeth samples that the island mammoths evolved to become smaller.

A Stone Age painting of a mammoth. This was found on the walls of a cave in France.

ROCK ART

We also know what mammoths looked like because our Stone Age ancestors painted them on the walls of caves in France and Spain. People believed that if they drew a picture of the animal they wanted to kill, they could catch it more easily.

BONE HUTS

In 1965, a Russian farmer discovered a huge beehive-shaped hut that was completely built from mammoth bones. The hut was probably made 20,000 years ago. Experts think people used bones to build shelters because wood was scarce.

TRAMPLED ON

Experts thought cuts in the mammoth bones were made by hunters' spears. But similar marks have been found on elephant bones, which were made by other elephants trampling on the bodies. This might also explain the mammoth marks.

Is it true **that mammoths were seen in the 16th century?**

A strange animal was sighted in the 16th century, but no one knows if it really was a mammoth. In 1850, however, an expedition across Serbia reported seeing a 'large hairy elephant'. The local people told the expedition that they had seen many such animals. The Serbians called them 'mountains of meat'.

This hut belonged to a mammoth hunter. It is made entirely from mammoth bones.

A DAY IN THE LIFE OF STYRACOSAURUS

72 MILLION YEARS AGO DURING THE CRETACEOUS PERIOD, IN WHAT IS NOW NORTH AMERICA. A MALE AND FEMALE STYRACOSAURUS ARE INTENT ON EATING.

SUDDENLY, A THIRD BEAST APPEARS AND APPROACHES THE TWO STYRACOSAURUS. THE MALE OF THE PAIR KNOWS THAT THE INTRUDER IS ALSO A MALE.

AS HE MAKES HIS WAY ACROSS THE ARID GROUND, THE DEFEATED MALE SPOTS A GROUP OF STYRACOSAURUS AND HEADS TOWARDS THEM, HOPING TO FIND A FEMALE.

BUT SOMETHING TELLS THE STYRACOSAURUS THAT HE IS IN DANGER. JUST IN TIME HE SPINS ROUND ON HIS BACK LEGS WITH SURPRISING SPEED TO FACE THE KILLER.

DASPLETOSAURUS MISTIMES ITS ATTACK — AND PAYS THE PENALTY.

THE MALES USE THEIR SWEEPING FRILLS TO ATTRACT FEMALES AND TO THREATEN RIVALS. THE ONE WITH THE MOST IMPRESSIVE FRILL WILL SEE OFF THE OTHER, AND WIN THE RIGHT TO MATE WITH THE FEMALE.

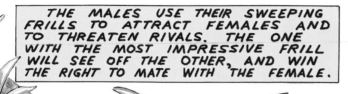

THE INTRUDER MAKES A BETTER DISPLAY THAN HIS RIVAL AND AMBLES ACROSS TO THE FEMALE...

... LEAVING THE LOSER TO SKULK AWAY.

THE STYRACOSAURUS PLODS ON UNAWARE THAT HE IS BEING TRAILED BY A RUTHLESS, SKILLED PREDATOR.

BUT AN EAGLE-EYED DASPLETOSAURUS, ONE OF THE MOST AWESOME KILLERS OF THE CRETACEOUS, SEES HIM.

WHEN DASPLETOSAURUS KNOWS FROM EXPERIENCE THAT THE TIME IS RIGHT, HE ATTACKS...

AS THE STYRACOSAURUS JERKS HIS HEAD UPWARDS, THE POINTED HORN ON HIS NOSE PIERCES THE SOFT FLESH OF DASPLETOSAURUS' UNDERBELLY.

AS THE DASPLETOSAURUS BLEEDS TO DEATH, THE STYRACOSAURUS FACES ANOTHER CHALLENGE...

... BUT THIS TIME, ONE OF HIS OWN MAKING.

THE SIGHT OF HIS MIGHTY FRILL AND BLOOD-STAINED HORN MAKES THE YOUNGER BEAST BACK OFF.

THE WINNER NOW HAS A MATE AND FORGETS HIS FIGHT WITH ONE OF THE DEADLIEST KILLERS OF PREHISTORIC TIMES.

Improve and test your knowledge with...

FACT FILE

Follow the footprints on the mammoth's back and answer the questions posed.

Is it a plane?

Scientists used to think that Pteranodon, with its 9m wingspan, was the biggest thing that could possibly fly. Then they discovered Quetzalcoatlus with its wing span of 11m.

Elephantine elephant

The biggest mammoth ever found consisted of a partial skeleton discovered at Mosbach in Germany. This enormous animal would have had a shoulder height of 4.5m, taller than a double-decker bus!

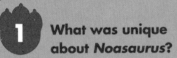

4 What did mammoths eat most of the time?
a) meat
b) frozen dinners
c) grass

7 What does the name *Megatherium* mean?
a) big bear
b) big beast
c) clever beast

1 What was unique about *Noasaurus*?
a) its claws
b) its nose
c) its tail

5 What is peat made from?
a) rotting vegetation
b) rotting flesh
c) pieces of coal

8 *Euoplocephalus* could splash itself with water using:
a) its trunk
b) its paws
c) its tail-club

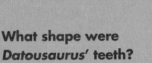

2 What shape were *Datousaurus'* teeth?
a) dagger-shaped
b) fork-shaped
c) spoon-shaped

6 What is a *Cerdocyon*?
a) a seal
b) a fox
c) a wolf

9 The dragonfly *Meganeura* was as big as:
a) a parrot
b) a fly
c) an ostrich

3 When did *Seymouria* live?
a) in the Cretaceous Period
b) in the Permian Period
c) in the Jurassic Period

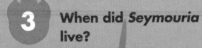

10 Early reptiles were ancestors of:
a) dinosaurs
b) horsetails
c) sharks

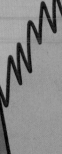

THE MALES USE THEIR SWEEPING FRILLS TO ATTRACT FEMALES AND TO THREATEN RIVALS. THE ONE WITH THE MOST IMPRESSIVE FRILL WILL SEE OFF THE OTHER, AND WIN THE RIGHT TO MATE WITH THE FEMALE.

THE INTRUDER MAKES A BETTER DISPLAY THAN HIS RIVAL AND AMBLES ACROSS TO THE FEMALE...

...LEAVING THE LOSER TO SKULK AWAY.

THE STYRACOSAURUS PLODS ON UNAWARE THAT HE IS BEING TRAILED BY A RUTHLESS, SKILLED PREDATOR.

BUT AN EAGLE-EYED DASPLETOSAURUS, ONE OF THE MOST AWESOME KILLERS OF THE CRETACEOUS, SEES HIM.

WHEN DASPLETOSAURUS KNOWS FROM EXPERIENCE THAT THE TIME IS RIGHT, HE ATTACKS...

AS THE STYRACOSAURUS JERKS HIS HEAD UPWARDS, THE POINTED HORN ON HIS NOSE PIERCES THE SOFT FLESH OF DASPLETOSAURUS' UNDERBELLY.

AS THE DASPLETOSAURUS BLEEDS TO DEATH, THE STYRACOSAURUS FACES ANOTHER CHALLENGE...

...BUT THIS TIME, ONE OF HIS OWN MAKING.

THE SIGHT OF HIS MIGHTY FRILL AND BLOOD-STAINED HORN MAKES THE YOUNGER BEAST BACK OFF.

THE WINNER NOW HAS A MATE AND FORGETS HIS FIGHT WITH ONE OF THE DEADLIEST KILLERS OF PREHISTORIC TIMES.

Improve and test your knowledge with...

FACT FILE

Follow the footprints on the mammoth's back and answer the questions posed.

Is it a plane?
Scientists used to think that Pteranodon, with its 9m wingspan, was the biggest thing that could possibly fly. Then they discovered Quetzalcoatlus with its wing span of 11m.

Elephantine elephant
The biggest mammoth ever found consisted of a partial skeleton discovered at Mosbach in Germany. This enormous animal would have had a shoulder height of 4.5m, taller than a double-decker bus!

1 **What was unique about *Noasaurus*?**
a) its claws
b) its nose
c) its tail

2 **What shape were *Datousaurus'* teeth?**
a) dagger-shaped
b) fork-shaped
c) spoon-shaped

3 **When did *Seymouria* live?**
a) in the Cretaceous Period
b) in the Permian Period
c) in the Jurassic Period

4 **What did mammoths eat most of the time?**
a) meat
b) frozen dinners
c) grass

5 **What is peat made from?**
a) rotting vegetation
b) rotting flesh
c) pieces of coal

6 **What is a *Cerdocyon*?**
a) a seal
b) a fox
c) a wolf

7 **What does the name *Megatherium* mean?**
a) big bear
b) big beast
c) clever beast

8 ***Euoplocephalus* could splash itself with water using:**
a) its trunk
b) its paws
c) its tail-club

9 **The dragonfly *Meganeura* was as big as:**
a) a parrot
b) a fly
c) an ostrich

10 **Early reptiles were ancestors of:**
a) dinosaurs
b) horsetails
c) sharks

386

Look at my crest

Crests seem to be quite common in meat-eating dinosaurs. A new dinosaur, found in Kunming in China, was similar to Dilophosaurus, except this one had one crest instead of two.

Dinosaurs on top

The film 'Jurassic Park' won a host of awards and is one of the most successful films ever made – so perhaps dinosaurs still rule the world after all!

Expecting a lot

An exhibition called 'Dinosaurs Live' was recently held in Memphis Zoo, USA. It featured a number of mechanical, model dinosaurs. Some people asked for their money back when they found that the dinosaurs were not alive.

Answers to the questions on inside back cover

ASK THE EXPERT

Dr David Norman of Cambridge University answers your dinosaur questions

Did dinosaurs hunt by smell?

It is very unlikely that dinosaurs hunted by smell. It is really only mammals that have a well-developed sense of smell. Snakes and some lizards can pick up chemical smells on their forked tongues. But there is no evidence dinosaurs had forked tongues. Meat-eating dinosaurs used their eyesight and strong legs to hunt successfully.

Some pictures show Stegosaurus with four spines on its tail, others show it with eight. Which is true?

Some stegosaurs had four spines (*Stegosaurus stenops*) on the tail, while others had eight (*Stegosaurus ungulatus*). It is one of the differences that has been used to tell stegosaur species apart.

How would Deinonychus manage with a broken claw?

If a deinonychosaur broke a claw, it would probably try attacking with its good claw until the other one had healed. If it was unable to attack and kill its prey, then it would have starved to death, unless it could keep up with the pack and scavenge from the remains of the pack's kills. This is very unlikely.

What's the difference between a mammal and a mammal-like reptile?

Mammals have two sets of teeth: one set of milk teeth, showing that the animal was breast-fed when young; and one permanent set. The earliest mammals, show this distinctive feature and this is the reason why they are identified as mammals. Reptiles, even mammal-like reptiles, replace their teeth more or less continuously.

SECERNOSAURUS

This duckbilled hadrosaur lived in South America, a long way from most of its North American relatives.

ecernosaurus was the first hadrosaur to be found in South America, although fossils of *Kritosaurus* have since been found in a region called Patagonia. Most other hadrosaurs have been found far away to the north. This is why *Secernosaurus* was named 'separate reptile'. Although the fossils of this dinosaur were discovered in 1923, it lay unnoticed in a museum for 56 years. Eventually it was studied, described and given its name by the American palaeontologist Mike Brett Surman.

SMALLER THAN AVERAGE

It was *Secernosaurus'* hip bones that gave experts a vital clue to its size. As the bones were not much more than 80cm wide, scientists could tell that the dinosaur was quite small, probably about the same length as today's rhinoceros. Hadrosaurs *Kritosaurus* and *Edmontosaurus* were three to four times that size.

BIG SPLASH

The deep tails and paddle-like hands of hadrosaurs suggest that they could swim. Without armour or sharp claws for protection, *Secernosaurus* had to run away when a predator appeared. By plunging into deep water it was safe from attack. Some experts believe that *Secernosaurus* migrated to South America from North America. *Secernosaurus* would have been able to swim across any areas of water it met during this long journey.

ROUGH AND READY

Secernosaurus had broad rows of self-sharpening cheek teeth to crush and slice up mouthfuls of rough and chewy vegetation. Large herds of hadrosaurs probably travelled together and filled their wide beaks with mouthfuls of food as they moved along.

IDENTIKIT

Grinding teeth

Eye socket

Toothless beak

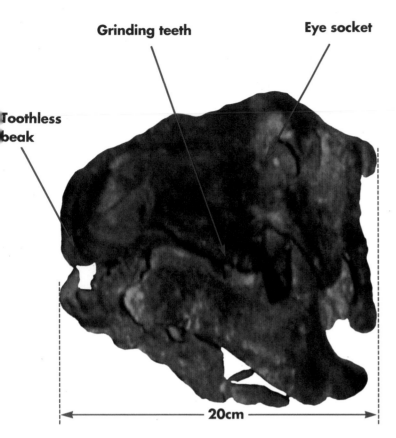

◄——— 20cm ———►

No one has yet discovered a complete *Secernosaurus* skull. This is the skull of a *Probactrosaurus*, which experts think was similar to that of *Secernosaurus*.

FLAT HEAD
Although only the back part of *Secernosaurus'* skull was found in Argentina in 1923, it was enough to show scientists that, unlike other hadrosaurs such as *Lambeosaurus* and *Bactrosaurus*, it did not have a head crest.

BLOW YOUR OWN TRUMPET
Secernosaurus may have had a nose sac like *Edmontosaurus*. Animals often make sounds to communicate with each other. When *Edmontosaurus* called and bellowed, it inflated its nose sac. This made the sound much louder, as it echoed around the sac. Imagine a whole herd of dinosaurs calling to each other at sunrise – like a deafening dawn chorus!

AMONG THE FLOWERS
Today, the lush, steamy rainforests of South America contain a vast range of exotic and colourful plants. During the Late Cretaceous Period in Argentina, when *Secernosaurus* was alive, the first flowers ever seen on Earth began to bloom.

LOTS TO EAT
Secernosaurus was fortunate to have a very wide choice of food. It ambled along among the coniferous trees and the ferns using its sharp back teeth to munch up pine needles, twigs and seeds, as well as the new flowering plants.

390

ELAPHROSAURUS

Elaphrosaurus may have been an ancestor of ostrich dinosaurs like Struthiomimus.

Found in rich fossil beds in Tendaguru, Tanzania, the remains of *Elaphrosaurus* did not include a head. Even without this vital clue, experts were able to see many similarities between this theropod and the ornithomimosaurs that lived about 70 million years later. *Elaphrosaurus* shared its home in eastern Africa with huge plant-eaters like *Barosaurus* and *Brachiosaurus*.

NOT SO FAST

Elaphrosaurus stood on two legs with its tail held out stiffly behind its body. Its bones were hollow and this lightweight frame enabled *Elaphrosaurus* to move nimbly. However, experts think that in a race against *Dromiceiomimus*, one of the later, speedy ostrich dinosaurs, it would certainly have come second!

MYSTERIOUS TEETH

It is hard to tell if *Elaphrosaurus* had a horny beak or teeth. Many small theropod teeth were found in the same area as this dinosaur. *Elaphrosaurus* may have fed on small, fast-moving animals, such as lizards, which it would have gripped tightly in its jaw.

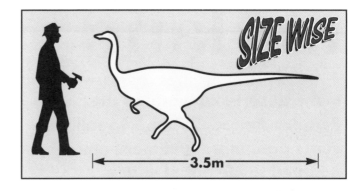

SIZE WISE

3.5m

MONSTER FACTS

- **NAME:** *Elaphrosaurus* (ee-<u>laf</u>-roe-<u>saw</u>-rus) means 'lightweight reptile'
- **GROUP:** dinosaur
- **SIZE:** up to 3.5m long
- **FOOD:** small mammals, insects
- **LIVED:** about 150 million years ago in the Late Jurassic Period in Tanzania, Africa

Elaphrosaurus had hollow bones and was probably a fast runner.

At home on land

In the desert-like world of the Permian Period, 290 to 245 million years ago, more and more animals adapted to life out of water.

uring the drier Permian Period seas drew back and left more land exposed. Great deserts appeared. The soft, lush vegetation that grew in the swamplands during the Carboniferous was replaced by stringier plants that were harder to digest. Vast forests of firs and tall pine trees grew.

RED BEDS
Perm is a place in Russia where many fossils have been found. The Permian Period takes its name from Perm but many discoveries from that time have been made in other parts of the world. Some of the most exciting finds come from South Africa and the 'red beds' of Texas, USA.

ON TO LAND
Land masses began to drift towards the north, and icy glaciers shifted southwards. In this changing world, shallow ponds and lakes disappeared and some animals moved on to land and made their homes there.

NEW FREEDOM
Like reptiles of today, they laid their eggs on land and had waterproof skins. As they no longer needed to lay eggs in water, these animals could leave the swamps and enjoy the freedom of living on dry land. Among the most successful of these new groups were the mammal-like reptiles.

DIFFERENT DINNERS
One special group of early mammal-like reptiles were the pelycosaurs, including some amazing sail-back reptiles. There was *Edaphrosaurus*, a herbivore with blunt, peg-like teeth and a skin-covered sail on its back. *Dimetrodon* also had a tall sail but it was a flesh-eater, with sharp teeth set in a curved jaw.

These two mammal-like reptiles were very different. *Titanosuchus* was a predator with sharp teeth and strong jaws while *Moschops* was a large, slow plant-eater.

Titanosuchus

Shansisuchus was a fearsome meat-eater.

Plants in the Triassic landscape included horsetails, gingkos, ferns and conifers.

GONE FISHING

Triassic seas were very busy. Swimming, fish-eating reptiles, such as *Nothosaurus*, paddled along with their arms and legs and pierced their prey with sharp teeth. Dolphin-like ichthyosaurs, such as *Mixosaurus* and *Ophthalmosaurus*, swam in shallow waters all over the Triassic world.

ROOTING ABOUT

Rhynchosaurs, such as *Scaphonyx*, thrived from the Mid to Late Triassic Period. *Scaphonyx* was able to scratch up tough roots with its hind feet and little tusks.

SOCKET-TOOTHED REPTILES

The most important reptiles in the Triassic were the flesh-eating thecodonts – 'socket-toothed reptiles'. This group gave rise to the crocodilians, dinosaurs and pterosaurs. *Shansisuchus* was an early thecodont. It was the biggest animal alive at the time, and a fearsome meat-eater. *Euparkeria* was a smaller thecodont, which sprinted after prey on its hind legs.

THE DINOSAURS ARRIVE

One of the first dinosaur groups to appear were the saurischians. This group included the large prosauropods, such as *Plateosaurus*, and flesh-eaters such as *Coelophysis*. Early ornithischians also appeared. These were small, nimble, plant-eating dinosaurs such as *Lesothosaurus*. One of the earliest dinosaurs found so far is *Eoraptor*. Many mammal-like reptiles and thecodonts, and all the rhynchosaurs, became extinct. Now dinosaurs began their 160-million-year rule.

GIANTS OF THE PAST

A herd of duckbilled *Secernosaurus* is peacefully grazing in the South American jungle. Suddenly, one hears a noise and alerts the others to possible danger. They scatter – some decide to swim to safety and leap into the water, others take their chances on dry land.

SECERNOSAURUS

3-D Gallery 78

ALAMOSAURUS

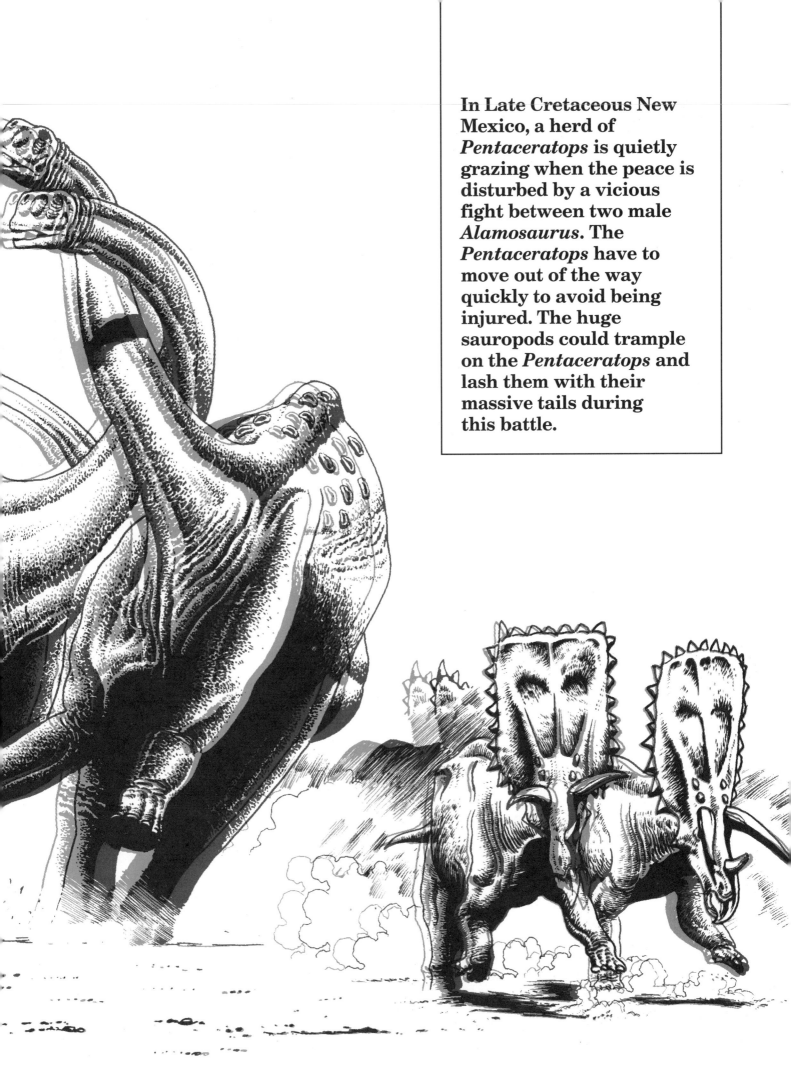

In Late Cretaceous New Mexico, a herd of *Pentaceratops* is quietly grazing when the peace is disturbed by a vicious fight between two male *Alamosaurus*. The *Pentaceratops* have to move out of the way quickly to avoid being injured. The huge sauropods could trample on the *Pentaceratops* and lash them with their massive tails during this battle.

Watch it!

Seeing is so important that many different kinds of eyes evolved millions of years ago.

nimals need good eyesight to help them survive. They have to watch out for danger and to search for food. Creatures need different kinds of eyes, depending on how and where they live. Today there is an incredible variety of eyes throughout the animal world, just as there was many millions of years ago.

MULTI-VISION

The eye of an insect is quite different from ours. It is made up of hundreds of tiny, simple eyes that all work together. This kind of eye is very good at detecting movement. A dragonfly has an amazing 30,000 tiny eyes within each eye. Over 360 million years ago giant dragonflies the size of seagulls darted about. They used their keen sight to track prey and avoid predators. In the seas, trilobites watched the underwater world with similar eyes.

UP AND ABOUT

Some creatures have eyes on stalks to help them see better. Land snails have existed since the Age of the Dinosaurs. Their eyes are on the tips of their 'horns'. Swimming scallops have survived for millions of years, too. Each scallop has many tiny eyes that are dotted around the edges of its shell.

SEEING IS BELIEVING

Some of the strangest eyes belong to creatures that lurk in the depths of the sea. The nautilus has hardly changed for 400 million years. It has a single eye, without a lens, which operates a bit like a very simple camera. Light enters the eye and allows the nautilus to detect movement but it cannot focus to see things distinctly. When it is too bright, the nautilus closes the opening so it is almost shut.

The primitive snail *Pleurotomaria* lived in the Age of the Dinosaurs. It had a spiral, pointed shell and eyes on the end of its horns. It was about 5cm high.

EAGLE-EYED

An eagle has incredibly sharp sight. Its eyes can pick out tiny details far smaller than we can see. It can do this because its eyes are able to magnify what it sees. They can zoom in on something, a bit like a telephoto camera lens. Today's eagle relies on good eyesight to spot movement at a great distance. If it sights a likely meal, it can then swoop in and pounce on its prey at high speed. Prehistoric birds of prey must have had extra-sharp eyes, too.

IT'S A FACT

OUT OF SIGHT

Certain creatures can see things which are invisible to us. Piranha fish have developed special sight to track prey in murky water. They can see the invisible infra-red remote-control beams that make televisions and videos work, too. Similar hunting fish existed in prehistoric times. They probably had infra-red sight as well.

SEEING IN THE DARK

Night hunters have to be able to see in the dark. Some have large eyes to help them. The tarsier monkey has survived unchanged since prehistoric times. Its eyes are so big, they fill most of its head.

This scallop has tiny blue eyes around the edge of its shell. It can tell light from dark and detect movement.

Trilobites had eyes made up of lots of little eyes, much like today's insects. They were the first creatures on Earth to develop efficient eyes like this.

403

Blue Babe

The amazing story of how an Ice-Age bison was found in a gold mine.

When Walter Roman began his day's work in his gold mine near Fairbanks, Alaska, USA, in 1979, he hoped he might find some gold. In fact, he found a very different sort of treasure.

BURIED TREASURE

As he hosed away the frozen mud and silt to get at the gold-bearing gravel beneath, he noticed legs and hoofs sticking out of the wall of frozen mud in front of him. Not bare bones, but the actual legs of an animal, with flesh and skin on them.

CALL IN THE EXPERTS

Walter Roman called in the palaeontologist Dale Guthrie from Fairbanks University. Guthrie began to excavate the animal from the slowly thawing ground. It was very muddy work, but eventually he uncovered an amazing mummified Ice-Age bison. It had been perfectly preserved in the frozen mud.

MUD, GLORIOUS MUD

Buried in the surrounding mud were all sorts of clues about the bison and when and how it had lived. Dale Guthrie studied the layers of mud around the mummified bison and worked out that it had lived about 36,000 years ago.

BLUE SKIN

As the bison was dug out, tiny blue spots appeared all over it. Minerals on the skin turned blue as they came into contact with air. So Guthrie named it Blue Babe.

A COLD DEATH?

At first, Guthrie thought that Blue Babe might have died of cold and starvation. But when he began to study the mummy he found clues to a different story.

Cave paintings made by prehistoric hunters illustrate a bison, which they hoped to kill.

CLUE 1 Examining the mummy in his laboratory, Dale Guthrie found the marks of long, deep scratches. They were along the skin on Blue Babe's rump and they looked as if they had been made by very sharp claws. Perhaps Blue Babe had been killed by a predator. But what sort of animal could attack and kill a large bison? Wolves hunting in a pack might have been able to surround a bison weakened by cold and hunger. But wolves do not use their claws to cut and rip their prey.

What is? A MUMMY

A mummy is a dead animal or human whose flesh and skin have been preserved. This sometimes happens naturally when a carcass is frozen in the ground or dries out very quickly in desert conditions. Sometimes bodies are mummified on purpose. The ancient Egyptians mummified human and animal bodies with special chemicals to preserve them. Frozen mummies are rare. Blue Babe was the first North American mummy to be studied in detail.

water flowing downhill

Blue Babe

Dale Guthrie has worked out how the body of Blue Babe must have been buried in order that, 36,000 years later, it could be dug out of the mud as a perfectly preserved mummy. He thinks the bison died on a slope and that the carcass was covered by cold water flowing down the incline in the spring. The cold water was full of particles of silt and earth, which gradually built up around the bison. The cold, wet silt on top of Blue Babe and the icy ground below kept the body frozen and prevented it decomposing or being attacked by scavengers.

CLUE 2 Guthrie also discovered that some tooth marks had punctured Blue Babe's hide, especially round the nose. What creature had managed to bring this huge animal down using teeth and claws? Dale Guthrie began to think about what large predators lived in Alaska 36,000 years ago.

GOT IT!

Suddenly, Dale Guthrie realised that the tooth and claw marks were those of lions. When Blue Babe was alive, lions lived in Alaska. Ice-Age Alaskan lions must have killed Blue Babe!

TOOTH DETECTIVE

The puncture marks made by teeth were exactly the same distance apart as the canine teeth of an Ice-Age lion's skull in the university museum. The teeth marks were around the nose because lions kill large prey by biting it around the nose in an air-tight grip in order to suffocate it.

PIECE OF EVIDENCE

Then a piece of a lion's tooth was found embedded in Blue Babe's thick hide. It was more proof of Guthrie's theory. It seems that one of the lions must have broken a tooth when it bit the bison.

JIGSAW COMPLETED

Gradually, Dale Guthrie completed his time-detective work using his knowledge of biology and palaeontology. He managed to fit all the jigsaw pieces of the 36,000-year-old puzzle together. This is what he worked out probably happened to Blue Babe.

THE WHOLE STORY

Long, long before the Egyptians built the pyramids or there were any people in North America, a male bison grazed. It was the beginning of an Alaskan winter. From time to time it raised its head and, with the wariness of a grass-eater, looked around.

Alaska is icy today, but was warm grassland 36,000 years ago.

Although Blue Babe was much bigger than the lions, it stood no chance against their hunting skills.

THE ENORMOUS BULK OF AN ADULT DIPLODOCUS' BODY DETERS MOST MEAT-EATING ATTACKERS.

SENSING THAT SOMETHING HAS DISTRACTED THE MOTHER DIPLODOCUS, TWO ALLOSAURUS SEIZE THEIR CHANCE AND RACE IN FOR THE KILL.

BUT A SMALL, YOUNG DIPLODOCUS HAS LITTLE DEFENCE AGAINST AN ATTACKER'S SLASHING CLAWS AND TERRIBLE TEETH.

THE ALLOSAURUS SPLASH ACROSS THE SODDEN GROUND FOR AN EASY KILL.

THE RAVENOUS KILLERS WATCH AS THE DIPLODOCUS TRUNDLE THROUGH THE LASHING RAIN TO FRESH FEEDING GROUNDS.

THEN SUDDENLY, THERE'S ANOTHER CHANCE...

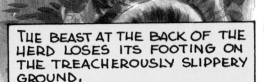

THE BEAST AT THE BACK OF THE HERD LOSES ITS FOOTING ON THE TREACHEROUSLY SLIPPERY GROUND.

ONCE THEY HAVE FILLED THEIR RUMBLING BELLIES, THE SNARLING BEASTS GO THEIR SEPARATE WAYS...

...LEAVING THE DEAD DIPLODOCUS IN A POOL OF BLOODSTAINED MUD, WHILE THE REST OF THE HERD CONTINUES ITS SEARCH FOR FOOD.

Improve and test your knowledge with...

FACT FILE

Fascinating facts
to read and
10 fun questions
to answer!

Fossils bombed

Many important fossils were destroyed when museums were bombed during air raids in World War II. These include the original specimens of Spinosaurus and Poekilopleuron.

1 What does *Secernosaurus* mean?
a) scissor teeth
b) separate reptile
c) swimming reptile

2 Which fossil-rich country was *Elaphrosaurus* found in?
a) Tanzania
b) Argentina
c) France

3 *Secernosaurus* was the first South American:
a) sauropod
b) stegosaur
c) hadrosaur

5 During the Permian Period, the world became:
a) wetter
b) colder
c) drier

6 When did the first dinosaurs appear?
a) during the Triassic
b) during the Permian
c) during the Jurassic

8 Prehistoric snails had eyes:
a) on either side of a nose
b) on horns
c) in the back of their heads

9 What killed Blue Babe?
a) lions
b) cold and hunger
c) bears

4 *Megaloceros* had big horns:
a) for fighting
b) for flying
c) for showing off

7 What was *Alamosaurus'* best weapon?
a) its fierce eyes
b) its massive tail
c) its giant horns

In the early 1700s, the true nature of fossils was only just being realised. Johann Beringer, a lecturer at Wurzburg University in Germany, spent much of his career studying a series of fossils that turned out to be hoaxes manufactured by his colleagues.

Slasher shrew

In Oligocene Nebraska, USA, there lived a kind of sabre-toothed shrew. It was called Sinclairella and was about the size of a squirrel. No one really knows what it ate with its sabre-like incisor teeth, but it must have been something pretty special!

Heavy croc

The most massive crocodile yet discovered is Purussaurus, which lived during the Miocene in Brazil. It was about 12m long and must have weighed about 8 tonnes.

The mane chance

Lions roamed across Europe, Asia and North America in Pleistocene times. These lions were maneless. Manes are only useful as symbols of recognition and leadership if lions live in large prides, as they do in Africa today. On the northern continents in the Ice Age, food would have been too scarce for lions to live in big groups.

10

Metamynodon looked like a:

a) hippo
b) crocodile
c) horse

ASK THE EXPERT

Dr David Norman of Cambridge University answers your dinosaur questions

Was T rex clever?

This dinosaur is unlikely to have been considered intelligent by human standards, but it would have been a natural hunter, and able to track and capture its prey by anticipating its movements, just like hunters today. If this is a measure of intelligence then, yes, it was bright. However, when people attach labels such a 'bright' or 'dim' to an animal, it is meaningless in the natural world. Animals use their intelligence to solve the problems they face in their daily lives.

Why did some dinosaurs walk on two legs?

Walking on two legs helps an animal to be more agile and run faster. This helps them to chase prey and run away from predators!

Did Triceratops charge and bellow like a modern-day bull?

Charging and bellowing? I have no idea, but being built the way it was, it may well have charged from time to time, just as a bull does today. Whether or not they could bellow would depend upon their lungs and voice box.

Since most reptiles make some noise, from hissing to bellowing, it's possible that *Triceratops* bellowed as well.

Did any dinosaurs eat grass?

No, dinosaurs did not eat grass. There is a simple reason for this, and that is that grass just did not exist during the Age of the Dinosaurs. Grasses appear to have evolved in the middle of the Tertiary Period, tens of millions of years after the dinosaurs had died out. Grasses went on to form the main diet of many mammals, such as horses.

DINOSAURS!
DISCOVER THE GIANTS OF THE PREHISTORIC WORLD

UINTATHERIUM

One of the first big mammals, rhinoceros-shaped *Uintatherium* had six bony knobs on its head.

After the dinosaurs died out there was a huge increase in the numbers and types of mammal that roamed the world. These new animals were small. The biggest were only the size of a large dog today. But by Early Eocene times, the first heavyweight mammals had arrived. *Uintatherium* was a rhinoceros-shaped animal with a body as long as a car. It was an extraordinary-looking creature with a distinctive, knobbly head and long fangs.

LEAFY LUNCH

As it lumbered across the plains of Utah and Colorado, USA, *Uintatherium* looked for the soft-leaved plants. Its massive body was supported by trunk-like legs as it stood munching a large, leafy lunch.

BETTER BALANCE

If you stand on tiptoe, it is difficult to keep your balance. When you stand with your feet flat, it is easier to balance because you have a broader base to support your weight. *Uintatherium*'s feet were very broad and tipped with five, stubby toes which spread apart, giving extra stability.

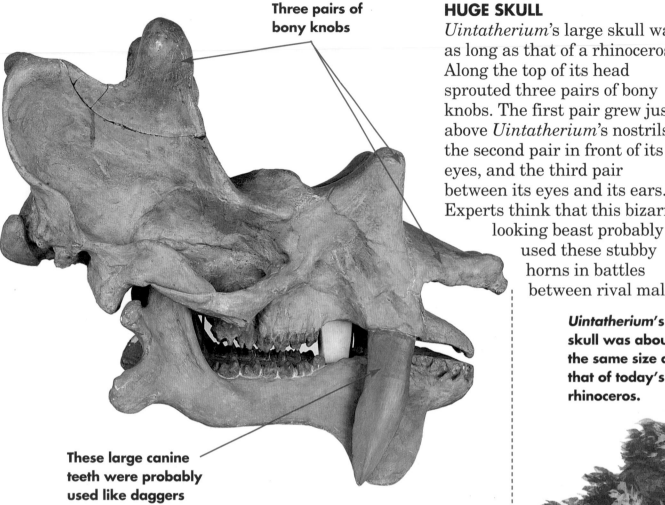

Three pairs of bony knobs

These large canine teeth were probably used like daggers

— 74cm —

HUGE SKULL

Uintatherium's large skull was as long as that of a rhinoceros. Along the top of its head sprouted three pairs of bony knobs. The first pair grew just above *Uintatherium*'s nostrils, the second pair in front of its eyes, and the third pair between its eyes and its ears. Experts think that this bizarre-looking beast probably used these stubby horns in battles between rival males.

Uintatherium's skull was about the same size as that of today's rhinoceros.

IT'S A FACT

FEUDING FOSSIL HUNTERS

Two 19th-century fossil hunters, Edward Drinker Cope and Othniel Marsh, were great rivals. They both collected fossils of *Uintatherium* but had very different ideas about what the animal actually looked like. Cope thought it was an elephant-like creature with a trunk and long antlers. Marsh's ideas were much closer to how today's experts draw this early mammal.

DAGGERS DRAWN

A male *Uintatherium* had large canine teeth, about as long as your hand, which hung from the top of its mouth like fangs. Today, a male hippopotamus uses its tusks to wound opponents in fierce battles. *Uintatherium* males probably used their strong teeth like daggers to make deep gashes in a rival's thick skin.

BROAD AND BLUNT

At the back of its jaw *Uintatherium*'s teeth were much less frightening. Broad, low molars provided a blunt surface for grinding soft leaves and shoots. The teeth in *Uintatherium*'s upper jaw had v-shaped crests.

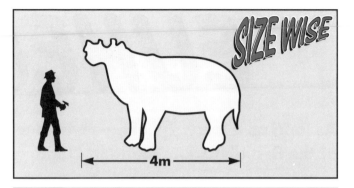

SIZE WISE

◀—— 4m ——▶

MONSTER FACTS

- **NAME:** *Uintatherium* (oo-win-tah-thee-ree-um) means 'beast from Uinta', after the Uinta Mountains in Colorado, USA
- **GROUP:** mammal
- **SIZE:** up to 4m long
- **FOOD:** plants
- **LIVED:** about 50 million years ago in Early Eocene times in North America and India

Uintatherium plodded along on its broad, flat feet, munching soft-leaved plants that grew at the forest's edge.

415

EUHELOPUS

As long as a lorry, *Euhelopus* was one of the first dinosaurs found in China.

 Swedish expedition discovered *Euhelopus* in the 1920s. It was a large sauropod, similar in shape to long-necked *Mamenchisaurus*. Chinese dinosaurs may have lived in harsher surroundings than those enjoyed by North American dinosaurs. Shallow, salty lakes and dry scrublands made life hard for plant-eaters in China. Long-necked *Euhelopus* may have fed on the tall conifers that grew on higher ground.

SLOPING BACK

Euhelopus walked on four pillar-like legs with its neck and tail balanced like a seesaw. Because its front legs were slightly longer than its hind limbs, *Euhelopus'* back sloped downwards. Its broad, flat feet worked like snow-shoes to stop this heavy dinosaur from sinking into soft ground.

SIZE WISE

15m

MONSTER FACTS

- **NAME:** *Euhelopus* (yoo-hel-oh-pus) means 'good marsh foot'
- **GROUP:** dinosaur
- **SIZE:** up to 15m long
- **FOOD:** plants
- **LIVED:** about 150 million years ago in the Late Jurassic Period in China

SAFETY IN NUMBERS

Euhelopus probably travelled in a group for safety. Young sauropods walked at the centre of the herd, protected by the big adults.

SHORT HEAD

Euhelopus' short, deep skull was well preserved, and experts saw that it was quite unusual. Unlike other sauropods, its nostrils were near the front of its head rather than at the top.

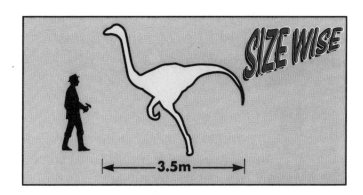

GARUDIMIMUS

Ostrich-like *Garudimimus* had a strange ridge above its eyes.

nly remains of *Garudimimus'* skull have been found but these were so unusual that scientists placed *Garudimimus* in a group of its own – the garudimimids. With a bony hornlet above its eyes, it looks very like today's emu, which is a flightless Australian bird.

MONSTER FACTS

- **NAME:** *Garudimimus* (ga-<u>rood</u>-ee-<u>mime</u>-us) means 'Garuda mimic' after Garuda, a mythical bird
- **GROUP:** dinosaur
- **SIZE:** up to 3.5m long
- **FOOD:** plants, possibly insects and mammals
- **LIVED:** about 80 million years ago in the Late Cretaceous Period in Mongolia

NIMBLE
Garudimimus was a nimble dinosaur that strode along on two, slender legs with its tapering tail held high and straight behind it.

LIGHT WEIGHT
Its legs were built for speed as they did not have to support a heavy body. Instead of wings, it had two arms which it held close to its chest as it ran.

LONG STRETCH
Garudimimus grew to be as long as a car. It was probably able to browse on branches high above the ground, clutching at twigs which it pulled into its rounded, toothless beak.

NOT JUST LEAVES
It is possible that speedy *Garudimimus* ate a variety of food besides leaves and plants.

FAST FEEDER
With its well-balanced, agile body and keen eyesight, it was probably able to spot and chase small creatures as they scuttled through the undergrowth. Or perhaps it was fast enough to capture flying insects by plucking them from the air.

SIZE WISE

3.5m

417

Tusks and trunks

There are only two kinds of elephants alive today but in prehistoric times there were many more.

Although today's elephants are the world's largest land animals, some prehistoric elephants were even bigger. But there were dozens of species, ranging from mini-elephants the size of small pigs, to mega-mammoths twice as big as today's elephants. They evolved many kinds of weird trunks and tusks.

FIRST OF THE DYNASTY

Pig-sized *Moeritherium* was the first-known elephant. It lived in Africa 40 million years ago. It had short legs, a stout body and a long head. Its eyes and ears were on the top of its head, like those of a hippo. It may have waded and wallowed in the water like a hippo too.

TINY TRUNK AND TUSKS

Moeritherium had the beginnings of a trunk and tusks. The trunk was a bendy snout, like that of today's tapir. The tusks were small, about the size of your little fingers.

ELEPHANTS EVERYWHERE

By the Miocene Epoch, 25 million years ago, elephants were becoming more numerous. They spread from Africa to every continent, except Antarctica and Australia.

Tusks were used to find food, impress mates and frighten enemies.

Deinotherium was one of the most successful of all elephants. It was huge – 4m tall – and survived for about 20 million years, spreading from Africa across Asia and Europe.

Elephants today probably descended from the great *Stegodons*.

UPSIDE-DOWN TUSKS

Elephants evolved bigger bodies and heads, longer trunks and tusks, and fewer teeth. *Deinotherium* had two large tusks that curved down from its lower jaw. This is the opposite of today's elephant, whose tusks curve up from its upper jaw. *Deinotherium* probably used its tusks for digging roots or stripping bark from trees.

Large body size meant that fewer predators were likely to attack. Big bodies lose heat more slowly in cold conditions

Head became very large to hold the teeth and tusks

Neck became shorter and thicker to carry heavy head, trunk, teeth and tusks

Trunk developed so the animal could reach food and water on the ground

Specialised teeth became bigger and harder for grinding tough plant food

Legs got more like pillars or tree-trunks to carry the increased weight

What is? A TUSK

It's a very long, large incisor tooth. Elephants, wild boars, walruses, narwhals and some deer have tusks. They are made of ivory, which is a hard, white substance, and they grow throughout an elephant's life.
Elephants use them to:
- pick food from the ground
- dig up roots and strip bark from trees
- gouge salts and minerals from rocks
- frighten and attack enemies
- battle with rival males
- impress females at breeding time

FOUR-TUSKERS

Phiomia was another early elephant. It lived in the forests that covered Egypt 35 million years ago. It was 2.5m tall and a member of the mastodont group of elephants. It had four small tusks – two short upper ones and two flat ones sticking out from its long, lower jaw. It also had a short trunk. *Gomphotherium* lived in Miocene times and was another four-tusked mastodont.

DIGGING FOR DINNER

Platybelodon, another large Miocene mastodont, had a mouth that looked like a shovel! The chisel-shaped tusks in its long lower jaw formed a spade, probably for digging up water plants. Its trunk was wide and flat to hold plants on the shovel. *Platybelodon* lived in Africa, Europe and Asia.

Here are the enormous skull and tusks of a mastodon. *Mastodons* became extinct about 10,000 years ago.

TOP TUSKS

Anancus looked much like today's elephant, but with incredibly long, straight upper-jaw tusks. At 4m in length, they were nearly as long as its body. *Anancus* roamed Europe and Asia six million years ago, browsing on forest leaves and rooting around in the leaf litter on the ground. It became extinct when the woodlands disappeared and grasslands developed.

Moeritherium

Phiomia

Gomphotherium

A

Platybelodons probably used their shovel-like tusks to scoop up plants from the water.

LAST OF THE LINE

Stegodon had long upper tusks and lived in Asia and Africa about two million years ago. It was probably the ancestor of the mammoths and today's elephants. The largest elephant ever was the steppe mammoth. It was 4.5m tall and weighed 12 tonnes. The smaller, woolly mammoth roamed Europe, Asia and North America.

ALONGSIDE PEOPLE

Some kinds of prehistoric elephants died out by the last great Ice Age, two million years ago. But others survived and lived alongside prehistoric people. One was *Mastodon*, or Mammut, in North America. It had two large tusks in its upper jaw, a long trunk, and long hair all over its body. It died out less than 10,000 years ago, when people spread across the continent.

IT'S A FACT

USEFUL TRUNK

A trunk is a very long nose and upper lip combined to form a tube. It is strong, flexible and sensitive. Elephants use them to:
- reach for leaves high in trees
- sniff the air for scents
- breathe when under water
- suck up water to squirt into their mouths as a drink
- spray water over their backs for a refreshing shower
- trumpet to friends and enemies
- touch and stroke mates, babies and friends

acus   Mastodon   Stegodon

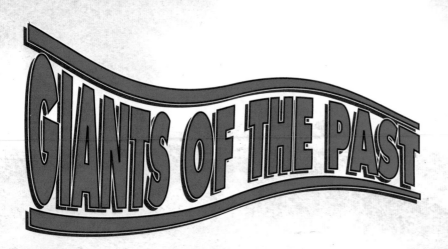

GIANTS OF THE PAST

In Early Eocene North America, a noisy battle is taking place between two heavyweights. These male *Uintatherium* are fighting for the leadership of the herd. The females look on from a safe distance. With a sickening thud the huge creatures crash into one another. Each lurches to the side, trying to avoid the bony knobs on the head of its opponent. But even more to be feared are the huge canine teeth which can slash through a rival's skin like a dagger.

3-D Gallery 79

DROMAEOSAURUS

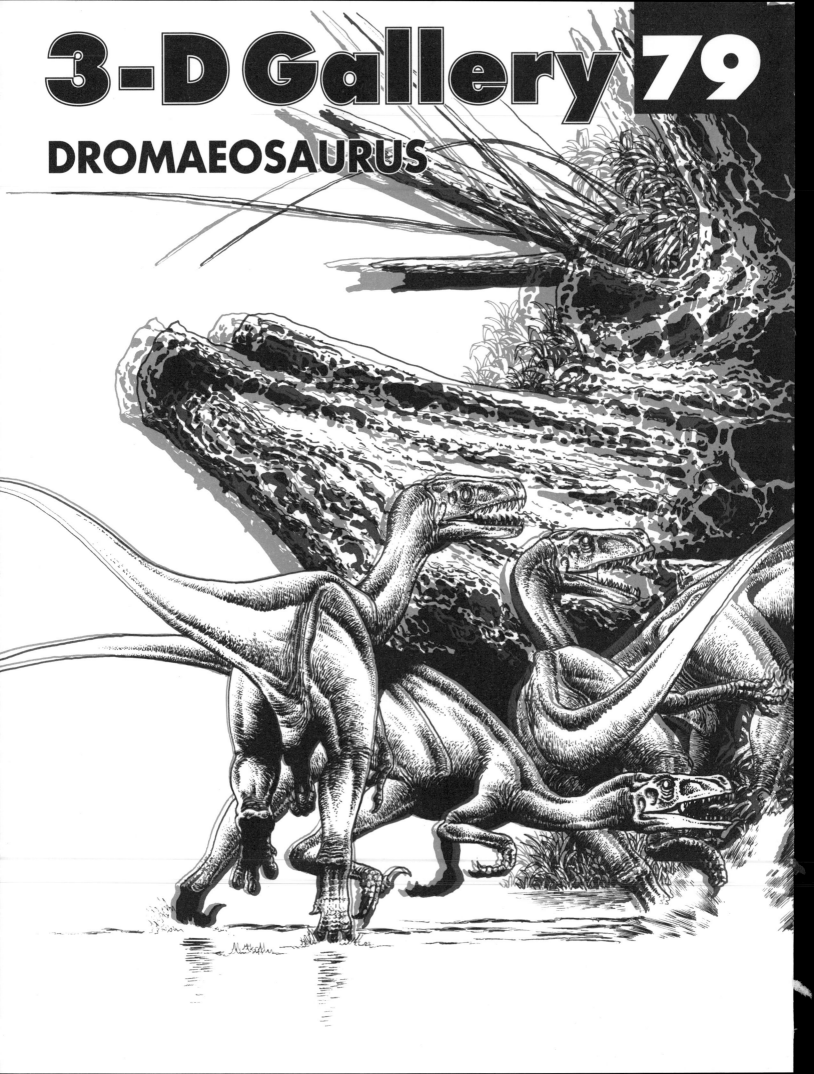

While peacefully searching for food in a dried-up streambed in Cretaceous North America, a *Leptoceratops* is surrounded by a hunting pack of hungry *Dromaeosaurus*. It stands little chance of escape from these killers with their sharp, curved teeth and sickle-shaped claws.

Dino film stars

Can we see dinosaurs alive today? Only in films and on television, often using amazing special effects.

Ray Harryhausen

Gertie (left) was a cartoon and *King Kong* (right) used stop-motion animation.

Many stories featuring dinosaurs have been filmed. Model-makers and special-effects experts create the dinosaurs for films. Their techniques have improved over the years, from gluing fins to live lizards and dressing actors in dinosaur costumes to the astonishing electronic effects used in *Jurassic Park*. A famous palaeontologist said that some of the dinosaurs in this film were so realistic they took his breath away.

DINOSAUR MOVIE STAR

Gertie was the first dinosaur ever to appear in a film. It was a cartoon made in about 1912.

KING OF THE APES

One of the most famous films to feature dinosaurs was *King Kong*, made in 1933. All the beasts in *King Kong* were brought to life using a technique called stop-motion animation. Small, jointed models were moved slightly and photographed each time. When the photos were run together it looked as if the animals were moving.

In *Gorgo*, filmed in 1959, the gigantic dinosaur was actually an actor wearing a costume.

DISNEY DINOS

The great film-maker Walt Disney used dinosaurs in some of his films. *One of Our Dinosaurs Is Missing* was made in 1976. *Fantasia*, one of Disney's classic animated films, includes a sequence on the death of the dinosaurs.

COMPUTER DINOSAURS

Undoubtedly, the most dazzling dinosaur special effects so far were in the 1993 film *Jurassic Park*. Many techniques were used to portray dinosaurs – stop-motion animation, actors in costume, full-scale models of dinosaurs and animation using computers.

MODEL MASTER

Ray Harryhausen created model dinosaurs for several classic films during the 1950s and 1960s. This great animator made jointed rubber models which he set in real backgrounds and filmed using stop-motion animation. In his films people fought dinosaurs such as *Allosaurus*, *Triceratops* and *Ceratosaurus*. Pure fantasy, of course, because humans and dinosaurs did not live at the same time. The tiny model dinosaurs were filmed separately from the people, then merged so that they looked as if they were monsters fighting the actors! Although the films were made many years ago, the action is still very exciting and the dinosaurs some of the best ever filmed.

In *The Land That Time Forgot*, filmed in 1974, the dinosaurs were puppets, worked by rods hidden from the cameras.

SCREEN SCARES

In *Jurassic Park*, the results of using these techniques are stunning, from huge sauropods rising through the mists, to a herd of ostrich-like dinosaurs fleeing through a group of humans. The cunning *Velociraptors* were bigger than they were in real life, but the film-makers created the most life-like dinosaurs to date.

Prehistoric babies

Prehistoric mammals spent a lot of time and effort raising their young.

Many animals hardly care for their babies at all. They lay eggs but do not wait to see them hatch. Mammals are quite different. They continue to care for their young for days, months, even years after they are born. Millions of years ago, their prehistoric ancestors behaved in the same way.

QUICK START

Newborn mammals have to grow up quickly in order to survive. Some grow faster than others. Baby deer are more like small adults. They can run with the herd hours after they are born. Today, the antelope-like pronghorn relies on speed to escape attackers. It can sprint at an incredible 80kph. Millions of years ago, a baby *Ilingoceros* pronghorn must have dashed away just as quickly when danger threatened.

LIFE SUPPORT

To protect their babies, some mammals give birth in nests or burrows that are hidden away. More than 30 million years ago, the prehistoric rabbit *Palaeolagus* probably burrowed in the ground to make soft, secret nests for her babies.

A mother *Palaeolagus* makes a safe burrow for her young.

To survive, a young *Ilingoceros* needed to grow up very quickly.

Left: a kangaroo is a marsupial. Its baby grows in a pouch.

Right: a baby rabbit grows inside its mother.

MY PAL JOEY

The kangaroo is the best known marsupial. A baby kangaroo, known as a 'joey', stays in its mother's pouch for several months. It is born blind and it has to find its way into the pouch by smell. Inside the pouch is a nipple to which the baby attaches itself and sucks to get its mother's milk. As it gets bigger, the joey leaves the pouch now and then to explore. *Procoptodon* was a giant kangaroo that lived two million years ago. A young *Procoptodon* would have been about the same size as today's adult kangaroo.

BABY BAG

The mothers of one group of mammals, known as marsupials, carry their babies in a pouch of skin underneath their bodies. This keeps the babies safe until they are strong enough to survive on their own. Some of the earliest mammals were marsupials. The opossums of America evolved between 100 and 75 million years ago. The kangaroos of Australia appeared much later in Miocene times.

BABY LOVE

It is usually the mother who feeds and cares for her young, and forms a strong bond with them. Deer, sheep and other hoofed animals are so close to their own babies they'll turn on any others that come near. The mothers know exactly how their newborn babies smell. If a baby smells different, they reject it. Prehistoric hoofed mammals behaved in the same way.

A joey will return to its mother's pouch to suckle until it is a year old.

IT'S A FACT

BIG AND SMALL
Marsupials can be as small as a mouse or as big as a kangaroo. As baby marsupials grow, their mothers' pouches stretch so that they are always big enough to hold them.

PLAYTIME

Young mammals have to learn how to survive on their own. Meat-eaters learn how to hunt by watching their parents. And they develop their hunting skills by playing with their brothers and sisters. Tiger cubs spend several hours a day chasing each other or having mock fights. While this might look like just fun and games, experts think this probably helps to make the cubs more alert and stronger so that they become better hunters. More than 30 million years ago, cubs of the sabre-tooth tiger *Eusmilus* must have learned through play, too.

GROWING UP

A baby mammal gets all its nourishment from its mother's milk. Providing enough milk is very hard work. Some mothers have to eat nearly twice as much as normal to make enough milk for their young. So mammal mothers are keen to wean their babies (move them on to solid food) as soon as possible. Once young mammals stop drinking their mothers' milk, they start to become much more grown up and independent. Many mammals leave their mothers when they are weaned, but some stay with them. Mother monkeys, for instance, carry on caring for their young long after they are weaned. They were probably doing the same in prehistoric times.

Many mammals, such as these baboons, stay with their family group for the whole of their lives.

Is it true

that some baby mammals stay with their mothers a long time?

Yes. A baby orang-utan is an ape that suckles its mother's milk for about 18 months. It spends the first year of its life clinging to its mother and stays very near her for several years after that.

430

ONE BIG FAMILY

When young mammals stay with their parents, they form big family groups. Many modern apes do this and so did their ancestors. The prehistoric baboon *Theropithecus* lived more than five million years ago. Young female baboons probably spent their whole lives with the same group. A mother *Theropithecus* might have sat with her daughters, granddaughters and even great grand-daughters.

CHECK IT OUT

Baby mammals in the wild have a lot of learning to do. They must learn who are their friends and enemies. They must also find out what food they can eat and what they can't. They must understand where their home territory begins and ends. And they can't afford to make a mistake – or it might be the last mistake they make! If they stray out of their home territory, they could get into a nasty fight with their next-door neighbours!

A baby *Theropithecus* might have lived in an enormous family group of up to 100 members. It would have had to learn where it fitted into the group and who to avoid.

The rough and tumble of family life 30 million years ago would have had a serious side for a group of *Eusmilus*. It helped the young to develop hunting skills.

DINOSAUR PARK

WHEN DAN CHURE WAS A BOY IN AMERICA, HE LOVED THE CINEMA. HIS FAVOURITE FILMS WERE KING KONG AND OTHER MONSTER MOVIES...

WOW! I LOVE MOVIES LIKE THIS!

SO DO I, BUT I WANT TO HEAR WHAT'S HAPPENING — SO SHUT UP!

WHEN HE LEFT HIGH SCHOOL, DAN WENT TO COLLEGE AND STUDIED GEOLOGY AND PALAEONTOLOGY.

I'D REALLY LIKE TO WORK IN UTAH SIR, AT THE DINOSAUR NATIONAL MONUMENT.

WHAT ARE YOU GOING TO DO WHEN YOU GRADUATE, DAN?

IN THE 1980s, PALAEONTOLOGISTS BEGAN TO DIG UP THE FOSSILS OF PREVIOUSLY UNKNOWN CREATURES AT THE MORRISON ROCK FOUNDATION.

WHAT DO YOU THINK THIS IS, YOU GUYS?

LOOKS LIKE A BONE FROM SOME KIND OF FROG!

THE FOSSILS TURNED OUT TO BE OF PREVIOUSLY UNKNOWN SPECIES OF SMALL VERTEBRATES, NOT UNLIKE MODERN SALAMANDERS, FROGS, CROCODILES AND LIZARDS. BUT, THERE WAS ALSO...

IT TOOK THREE YEARS TO COMPLETE THE EXCAVATION. THE BONES WERE CAREFULLY CRATED AND CARRIED BY HELICOPTER TO THE VISITORS' CENTRE AT THE NATIONAL MONUMENT AREA...

OOOPS! DON'T DROP IT, FOR GOODNESS SAKE!

IN A LECTURE HALL AT THE VISITORS' CENTRE.

WHERE'S ITS HEAD?

Improve and test your knowledge with... FACT FILE

Ichthyosaurus holds all the answers. See how you score in the quiz.

The good ship Dino
When the first big dinosaur discoveries were made in Canada in the early 1900s, the site in Alberta was very difficult to reach. So the palaeontologists' camp was built on a barge and sailed up the Red Deer River. It returned laden with fossils at the end of the season.

1 *Dromaeosaurus* had sickle-shaped:
a) teeth
b) claws
c) feet

2 How many head knobs did *Uintatherium* have?
a) twenty-six
b) six
c) two

3 The name *Tyrannosaurus rex* was first used by:
a) Charles Lutwidge Dodgson
b) Henry Fairfield Osborn
c) Edward Rinker Cope

4 The dinosaurs in *The Land That Time Forgot* were:
a) rubber models
b) puppets worked by rods
c) live lizards

5 The first-known owl was called:
a) *Oswald*
b) *Ornithomimus*
c) *Ogygoptynx*

6 Jurassic Park's *Velociraptors* were
a) smaller than real life
b) the right size
c) bigger than real life

7 *Palaeolagus* was a:
a) prehistoric rabbit
b) ancient crocodile
c) mammal-like reptile

8 *Moeritherium*, the first elephant, was:
a) hippo-sized
b) pig-sized
c) mouse-sized

Completely different
A big, 15-million-year-old snake from Australia was called Montypythonoides after the TV programme.

434

Spines or plates?

Dacentrurus, a stegosaur found in Britain, France and Portugal, had spiky spines down its back and tail rather than the plates displayed by most of its relatives. Over 4m long, Dacentrurus was a Jurassic plant-eater.

Eggs-tra large!

The biggest dinosaur eggs known, those of the sauropod Hypselosaurus, had a capacity of 3.3 litres. Each egg would have made an omelette for 40 people.

Fishes eat birds

We know that water birds were common in Miocene times because scientists keep finding feathers in coprolites (fossil dung) produced by Miocene fish.

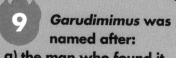

9 Garudimimus was named after:
a) the man who found it
b) a mythical bird
c) the place it was found

10 Which animal had a mouth like a shovel?
a) *Platybelodon*
b) *Mastodon*
c) *Smilodon*

Right name for the wrong reason

Many people think that Centrosaurus was so named because it had a single horn in the centre of its face. It is actually named after the hooks at the top of the frill that point towards the centre of the skull.

ASK THE EXPERT

Dr David Norman of Cambridge University answers your dinosaur questions

Who invented the name Tyrannosaurus rex?

The name was first used in 1905 by an American scientist called Dr Henry Fairfield Osborn. He was looking for a name for the partial skeleton of a large carnivorous dinosaur that he had found in northern Montana, USA. *Tyrannosaurus rex*, which means 'king of the tyrant reptiles', is an appropriate name for such a massive predator.

What did dinosaurs smell like?

We have no idea. Many dinosaurs may not have smelled at all in their natural habitat. Reptile houses in zoos tend to smell rather nasty. But this is an unnatural environment, and may be caused by poor ventilation or rotting food.

Could dinosaurs crack nuts?

Some dinosaurs, such as the oviraptorosaurs, had short, powerful toothless beaks which were very like the beaks of parrots today. Of all the known dinosaurs, the oviraptorosaurs definitely had the greatest nut-cracking potential!

How many bones are there in a dinosaur skeleton?

There are about 300 bones in most dinosaur skeletons. Some, however, have extra bones in the skin, which make up their defensive armour-plating, or spines or plates. The large armoured ankylosaurs probably had the most bones of all.

TALARURUS

Talarurus carried as much armour as a medieval knight.

Talarurus was an ankylosaur, like *Euplocephalus,* which lived in North America. It was found in Bayn Shireh in southern Mongolia in the early 1950s. Its well-preserved skull and skeleton show that *Talarurus* had an amazing set of armour to protect it from its enemies.

FLEXIBLE BANDS
Because it lived alongside fierce flesh-eaters such as *Tarbosaurus* and speedy *Velociraptor, Talarurus* needed to be very well-protected against predators. Like an armoured tank with legs, *Talarurus* was longer than two small cars. Slabs of bony armour covered its body in bands. These made it both strong and flexible, rather like an elasticated, metal watchstrap.

LOW DOWN
With its small head bent low, *Talarurus* nosed its way through the vegetation of Cretaceous Mongolia. It fed on low-growing plants and shrubs, and nipped off shoots with its broad, toothless beak. Inside its jaw, small, feeble teeth mashed the food, but all the heavy-duty, crushing work was done inside the dinosaur's muscular stomach.

MIGHTY MUSCLES
Talarurus' squat, heavy body was supported by four powerful legs. These were attached to the dinosaur's shoulders and hips by strong muscles, which helped *Talarurus* to move quite nimbly for a creature of its size.

437

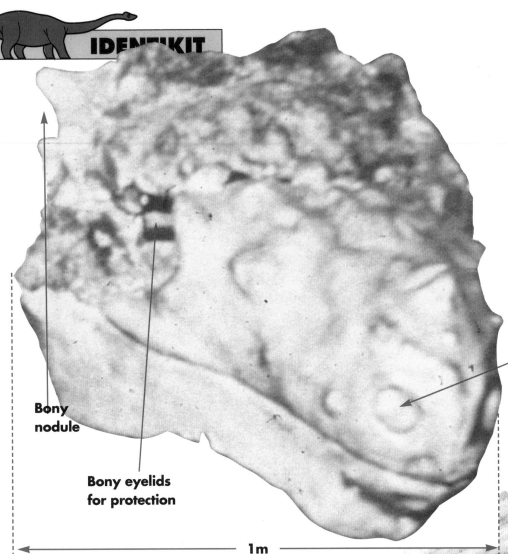

The skull of *Talarurus* was heavily armoured with bony nodules and plates. Its body was heavily armoured too.

Bony nodule

Bony eyelids for protection

Talarurus' nostril. This ankylosaur had a very good sense of smell.

1m

EARLY WARNING

As it stood feeding peacefully, a good sense of smell probably helped to give *Talarurus* early warning that a predator was on its way. From the top of its head to the tip of its tail, *Talarurus* had a covering of armour and hollow spikes. But it was possible for a determined hunter to find its weak spot.

WEAK SPOT

If a flesh-eater was able to get close enough to flip *Talarurus* on to its bony back, the ankylosaur was in big trouble. Its soft underbelly had no armour and was an easy target for sharp teeth and deadly claws. So it was very important that enemies were kept at bay.

Is it true

that *Talarurus* had a basket-shaped tail?

No. Although its name means 'basket-tail', it was actually the bones in *Talarurus'* hips that were shaped like a basket. On either side of its spine, the dinosaur's ribs were attached to shelf-like hip bones. Powerful muscles attached to the hips helped *Talarurus* to swing its tail and move its big hind legs.

LEG BREAKER

Talarurus had another, very effective weapon that it used to repel predators more than twice its size. At the end of its tail there was a bony club that could be swung from side to side with great force. Even an enemy as big as *Tarbosaurus* could be toppled by a mighty blow from this weapon. With its leg broken, a *Tarbosaurus* would lie helplessly at the mercy of other predators while *Talarurus* plodded off to safety.

SIZE WISE

5.7m

ON THE RUN

In spite of its heavy body, *Talarurus* was not the slowest member of the dinosaur world. Although it was not as nifty as *Protoceratops*, it could probably keep up with large sauropods such as *Nemegtosaurus*.

MONSTER FACTS

- **NAME:** *Talarurus* (tal-a-<u>roo</u>-rus) means 'basket-tail'
- **GROUP:** dinosaur
- **SIZE:** 5.7m long
- **FOOD:** plants
- **LIVED:** about 80 million years ago in the Late Cretaceous Period in Mongolia

439

YOUNGINA

Youngina could bite through hard skin with its wide, sharp teeth.

Youngina was a reptile about as long as a rabbit is today. It roamed the desert-like regions of Permian southern Africa with reptiles such as *Moschops* and *Coelurosauravus*.

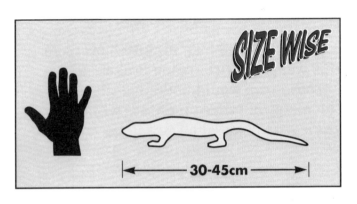

SIZE WISE

30-45cm

HAPPY ON LAND

Youngina's limbs sprawled outwards on either side of its low-slung body. Unlike its swimming relative, *Hovosaurus*, it was suited to life on land. It grasped rocks and could climb trees.

MASS EXTINCTION

At the end of the Permian, *Youngina* disappeared together with many other creatures in a mass extinction. The Permian extinction, 245 million years ago, was even greater than the one that removed dinosaurs from the face of the Earth nearly 200 million years later.

SNAIL CRUSHER

Youngina had a high, deep skull with strong jaws. It snapped at its prey with sharp, broad teeth. It probably ate insects with brittle skins or even snails, crushing them with ease.

Youngina's long fingers and toes helped it to grasp rocks and tree trunks.

MONSTER FACTS

- **NAME:** *Youngina* (young-guy-nah) was named after a fossil collector called Young
- **GROUP:** reptile
- **SIZE:** about 30-45cm long
- **FOOD:** insects, snails
- **LIVED:** about 260 million years ago in the Permian Period in southern Africa

GERANOSAURUS

All that remained of this unusual dinosaur were its jaws and a few teeth.

Geranosaurus was a close relative of *Heterodontosaurus*. It was as long as a large dog and knee-high to an adult human. When its jaws were found in South Africa, early this century, experts knew it was unusual.

DIFFERENT TEETH

Geranosaurus belonged to the group called the heterodontosaurids. It had three different kinds of teeth. At the front of its jaw, the teeth were small and sharp for nipping off leaves. At the back, they were ridged for grinding. Lastly, there were a pair of short fangs.

MONSTER FACTS

- **NAME:** *Geranosaurus* (jer-an-oh-saw-rus) means 'crane reptile'
- **GROUP:** dinosaur
- **SIZE:** up to 1.2m long
- **FOOD:** plants
- **LIVED:** about 200 million years ago in the Early Jurassic Period in Cape Province, South Africa

SIZE WISE

|← 1.2m →|

DIGGING AND DEFENCE

Flesh-eaters with fangs use them to stab and wound their prey. Plant-eaters have other uses for them. Like the wild pig of today, *Geranosaurus* probably used its tusks for digging up plants and for self-defence.

Geranosaurus **probably held out its tail for balance.**

LIGHT AND SPEEDY

Geranosaurus probably walked on two legs and used its arms to pull down branches or grasp tough shoots while it fed. It was an agile dinosaur and light enough to be a speedy runner.

441

Mammals, birds and flowers

When the dinosaurs died out, the mammals became the most important animals. This was the Tertiary Period and it lasted 64 million years.

If you could have flown around the world during the Tertiary Period it would have looked a lot like it does today. During the Tertiary the continents began to drift towards the positions they are in today. The landscape began to resemble the Earth we see today – flowering plants began to appear and mammals and birds moved to places once occupied by the dinosaurs.

POLAR JUNGLES

During the Tertiary the continents continued to move. This changed the climate. For the first 20 million years, the weather became warmer. There were even steamy jungles in the far north and south, near the poles. Early mammals and birds flourished in the damp, warm climate.

COOLING WATERS

The oceans cooled around the poles and ice sheets formed. The climate became more extreme. Many of the early mammals and birds disappeared, but ancestors of today's animals, such as the dog, were seen for the first time.

Moropus

What is? THE TERTIARY

Tertiary means 'third age'. It is the third of the three distinct ages: Primary (most ancient), Secondary (next most ancient), Tertiary (third age). The Tertiary began when the dinosaurs died out, 66 MYA. It ended 2 MYA. The Tertiary Period is divided into five main Epochs:

Palaeocene 66–56 MYA   Miocene 23–6 MYA
Eocene 56–35 MYA   Pliocene 6–2 MYA
Oligocene 35–23 MYA

MYA = Million years ago

IN NORTH AMERICA

North America was the birthplace of the pouched mammals, some very early plant-eaters, the multituberculates, such as *Ptilodus*, and the first rodents such as squirrel-shaped *Ischyromys*.

DOGS AND SEALS

The first dog, *Hesperocyon*, appeared in North America in the Oligocene Epoch. So did the first seal, *Enaliarctos*. There were giant, hoofed mammals such as *Brontotherium*.

MIOCENE ZOO

In the Miocene Epoch, the American prairies looked like today's African savannahs. There were elephants (*Gomphotherium*), pronghorns (*Merycodus*), deer-like *Syndyoceras*, giant pigs, the giant, clawed horse *Moropus*, camels (*Oxydactylus*), sabre-tooth ancestors (*Dinictis*), rhinoceroses (*Miotapirus*) and hyenas such as *Osteoborus*.

The first squirrels and dogs appeared in the Tertiary Period.

Oxydactylus

Gomphotherium

Syndyoceras

Osteoborus

Dinictis

443

Index

Page numbers in **bold** refer to Identikit descriptions.

Page numbers in *italics* refer to action pictures in Giants of the Past or 3–D Gallery.

Picture Credits

Dino Factfile Answers

Measurement Conversion Chart

Approximate conversions from customary to metric units and vice versa.

When you know:	You can find:	If you multiply by:
Length:		
millimeters	inches	0.04
centimeters	inches	0.4
meters	yards	1.1
kilometers	miles	0.62
inches	millimeters	25.4
feet	centimeters	30
yards	meters	0.9
miles	kilometers	1.6
Area:		
square centimeters	square inches	0.16
square meters	square yards	1.2
square kilometers	square miles	0.4
square hectometers (hectares)	acres	2.5
square inches	square centimeters	6.5
square feet	square meters	0.09
square yards	square meters	0.8
square miles	square kilometers	2.6
acres	square hectometers (hectares)	0.4
Mass and Weight:		
grams	fluid ounces	0.035
kilograms	pounds	2.2
megagrams (metric tons)	short tons	1.1
fluid ounces	grams	28
pounds	kilograms	0.45
short tons	megagrams (metric tons)	0.9
Liquid Volume:		
millimeters	ounces	0.034
liters	pints	2.1
liters	quarts	1.06
liters	gallons	0.26
ounces	milliliters	30
pints	liters	0.47
quarts	liters	0.95
gallons	liters	3.8